PRAISE FOR FALEEHA HASSAN

"Faleeha Hassan, 'the Maya Angelou of Iraq,' wields a mighty pen."

—Oprah.com

WAR
AND
ME

ALSO BY FALEEHA HASSAN

'Cause I'm a Girl (1991)

A Visit to the Museum of the Shadows (1998)

Five Addresses for My Friend the Sea (2000)

Even after a While (2008)

Splinters (2008)

Lack of the Happiness Cells (2008)

Mom's Poems (2010)

Water Freckles (2010)

A Dream Guard (2012)

I Hate My City (2013)

Let's Strongly Celebrate My Day (2015)

Swallow (2016)

We grow up at the speed of war (2016)

Lipstick (2016)

Mass Graves (2017)

Breakfast for Butterflies (2018)

A Butterfly's Voice (2020)

WAR AND ME

A MEMOIR

FALEEHA HASSAN
TRANSLATED BY WILLIAM HUTCHINS

Text copyright © 2022 by Faleeha Hassan
Translation copyright © 2022 by William Hutchins
All rights reserved.

Published by Amazon Crossing, Seattle

www.apub.com

Amazon, the Amazon logo, and Amazon Crossing are trademarks of Amazon.com, Inc., or its affiliates.

ISBN-13: 9781542036177 (hardcover)
ISBN-10: 1542036178 (hardcover)

ISBN-13: 9781542036184 (paperback)
ISBN-10: 1542036186 (paperback)

Cover design by Caroline Teagle Johnson

Cover image: *Spring in the City*, 2020, by Leila Kubba Kawash © Leila Kubba Kawash

Printed in the United States of America

First edition

WAR
AND
ME

Prologue

One night I dreamt I was searching a public library in my native city of Najaf for the poet Louis Aragon's book *Le fou d'Elsa* when the librarian informed me it did not circulate. I felt somewhat miffed, but when I started to leave, the librarian called after me: "Faleeha! Take this! It's Aragon's pen. Use it to write whatever history we have left!"

She handed me a rectangular glass box wrapped in red velvet. I opened it to find a gleaming gold pen inside. Then I took the pen and departed.

When I woke, I prayed that God would turn this dream into a reality and grant me an opportunity to write at least my story!

Chapter One

From the events I recount in this memoir, you will understand that next to my name in the Unknown World or beside it at the moment I was born, the only comment inscribed must have been: "Faleeha Hassan will coexist with war for most of the years of her life."

My mother told me that I was born early in the morning, at dawn, 6:00 a.m., on a steaming hot day in July 1967, a year during which many important events occurred in the world. I interrupted her and said, "The most important event that year was my birth."

When she laughed, I asked whether the birth of a child that year was anything to laugh about. She ignored my question and continued: "I had a small framed picture of three female angels and prayed to God that I would have three daughters exactly like those angels. Your father did not object to this idea when he heard me repeat my prayer—even though such a prayer would sound very strange to an Arab man like him, since a son was what an Arab man desired from his marriage. God answered my prayer, and my first pregnancy brought me twins: you and . . ." She fell silent.

I really wish I could remember the day I was born. Some scholars claim it is quite possible for a child to recall the day of her birth, but I say that's impossible. I have tried repeatedly but never succeeded. I have even wished to travel back through time to watch my mother give birth to me. What did I look like then? How did the midwife's hand grasp me? What was my mother's facial expression? I want to relive details I have heard concerning that day so I can compose a complete, "thick" image of it.

"Did I really have a twin sister? Or are you uncertain about the gender of the other fetus? That's what my grandmother told me once."

"It's hard for me to remember the details. You know how the war destroyed my memory."

Damn! Even this memory, which I have struggled hard to grasp with both hands and preserve as a gift from my mother's mouth, was crowded out by the war.

My mother closed her eyes, pressing her eyelids down as if squeezing her mind to furnish a snapshot of that day. After her expression softened a bit, she said, "You know even when I married, I did not leave my father's house for the conjugal house—as they refer to it here—because once I married your father, my father sold his house in the Abu Khalid District, which was a beautiful neighborhood where we had many rich neighbors, and invested all the proceeds of that sale in *anbar* rice—but lost money on that contract. Meanwhile, your father had left his hometown of Nasiriyah after his mother died of smallpox and his father was killed in a traffic accident. He came to live with his paternal aunt in the city of Najaf in al-Hawish District. After a large fire destroyed the restaurant he ran with his cousin and his financial circumstances deteriorated, he agreed with your maternal grandfather to share a house with him after our marriage. Then we rented a house in the district called al-Jadida, which is inhabited by people from different economic levels.

"When I became pregnant with twins, I did not go to the gynecologist's clinic until my belly swelled up more than usual in my fourth month and—as everyone who saw me told me—I seemed to be carrying something more than an ordinary child. That's why your grandmother, who was your grandfather's sixth and only surviving wife, said, since she was living with us in the same house, that she would take me to see the woman doctor. I agreed, and we went to her clinic one afternoon.

"The physician said as she placed her stethoscope on my belly: 'You are pregnant with twins. I hear the two different heartbeats.' I did not ask her for any details. I didn't want to. All that mattered to me was to know I was carrying twins.

"Throughout my pregnancy I lived on nutritional supplements the physician gave me and on my own traditional therapy, which I deliberately did not reveal to her. I did not feel especially tired during all the months of my pregnancy, because I didn't work outside the house and your grandmother helped me with the housework. In our free time, she and I, together with some close friends who visited us frequently, would sit together in the afternoon and drink tea and eat *kleicha* pastries while preparing the clothing, bedclothes, and various sizes and colors of covers that the two of you would need.

"Your grandmother surprised me one day when she brought two small down pillows from her room and asked me to embroider covers for them, each a different color. When I inquired where the feathers had come from, she asked me impatiently, 'Do you think the ducks we purchase, slaughter, and cook are only good for their meat?' Then I laughed as I realized why your grandmother had always objected whenever I asked to climb to the roof terrace: 'Pregnant women don't climb stairs. Do you want to have a miscarriage? So-and-so's mother told me that.' Then she would begin narrating a long tale she had heard from one of her friends. The fact was that she didn't want me to discover her secret: I mean the duck feathers she washed, cleaned, and placed on plastic trays to dry in the sun there.

"I did not choose your name myself. Your father did. Or let's say that in keeping with traditions and the custom here, your father's name—Hassan—chose it for us. When people called out to him, or anyone else named Hassan, they referred to him as either Abu Falah or Abu Faleeha—even before we were married.

"He whispered to me once, 'If we have a boy, we'll name him Falah. If we have a girl, we'll name her Faleeha.'

"'I expected that,' I told him, but whenever I tried to think of a name for your twin, I found that hard. Names all seemed to fade and flee. So I postponed the matter to the day you were born, a day that arrived after an entire sleepless week. Everything in my body weighed me down painfully. I would walk back and forth through the house, begging you twins to come out of me so I could sleep, if only for a few minutes.

"My labor pains grew more intense at dawn, and I felt certain that something other than childbirth would occur. I would die or lose both of you. What I felt then far surpassed what my girlfriends who had given birth repeatedly had described. All I remember of the day you were born was swimming in a sea of pain, into which I quickly sank and almost drowned, as a red wave covered me, choking me. When I woke, I found myself in the hospital: a half-dead, limp body."

I interrupted my mother's narration to ask, "Mother, didn't you say I was delivered by a midwife?"

"Yes, *you* were delivered at home by a certified midwife named Umm Amal al-'Alawiya, but she—as your grandmother told me in full detail that day—could not draw your sister from me. She said Umm Amal al-'Alawiya, when she was totally unable to extract the second child, started slapping her face and chest and shouting that if we didn't take both mother and child to the hospital, they would both die."

My grandmother completed the story for me: "We were a family that would *never* let a man we didn't know into our house, but that day, your father allowed the taxi driver to enter your mother's room to help him lift her body, which was stretched out on the bed, and to carry her, with Umm Amal's assistance, to the vehicle. The three of them placed her in the rear seat of the vehicle, while Umm Amal, sitting in the back with her, tried to calm her by saying encouraging words, which I think your mother definitely didn't hear.

"When they removed your mother from the bedroom, I was the only one who thought about the screaming baby girl swaddled in a piece of white cloth. The terror of the situation may have muffled your voice, leaving me the only one who heard you cry and paid attention to you. I gave thanks to God, both for you being alive and for me hearing you and attending to you and also because your father had asked me to stay in the house, arguing that an old woman like me who would need assistance would be of no use in such a situation and would definitely be a hindrance. You were screaming so loudly that I wasn't able to clean your mother's room of the mess and smell of a totally abnormal childbirth."

"Is that how I was born?" I asked myself.

"Your cries, which seemed to be growing even louder, made me race to you and lift you from the bed to my breast. But your screams did not diminish. Then I had to play the mother's role. I brushed aside the front edge of my long black scarf and, with my right hand, unbuttoned the top of my tunic. I drew out my left breast, which resembled a tree's withered leaf that the force of years had dried out, and placed its dry nipple to your hungry mouth. You didn't spit the nipple out but kept sucking on it vigorously, as if trying to extract something from that aged teat. Ever since that moment, I've felt that you are my daughter, even though my dry breast did not afford you the blessing of milk."

"And where was Grandpa, when I was born?" I asked my grandmother.

"As you know, he used to work as a night guard at the electricity station in the al-Sa'd District. That was the only job he could find after his enormous commercial loss, and he worked there till the day he died. He could not be present at the early hour you were born and came home as usual at ten that morning—after your mother had returned from the hospital. But he was happy with you. Indeed, I had never seen him so happy during all the years I spent with him.

"When your mother returned from the hospital, she was so exhausted that she could barely walk to the doorstep. Then she sat down and stretched her legs out a little on the ground in the courtyard to regain her energy. Eventually, assisted by your father and Umm Amal, she walked to her room, which I had cleaned and aired out quickly, after your sucking on my wooden nipple had worn you out and you had fallen asleep, though still hungry, in my room. I could not see your mother's face clearly when I entered her room, but it was almost blue, and her body, which was covered by her black abaya, was bent forward. Her hands were clenched together over her belly, which was as inflated as before she gave birth to you. That made me wonder whether your sister was still inside her womb. What knowledge did I have of pregnancy, childbirth, and nursing? I simply removed her abaya and brushed the sweaty strands of hair from her face. Then I helped her sit on her bed, the dirty sheets of which I had replaced with clean ones. Umm Amal praised God loudly for your mother's survival, and I did too. Then she went home, after your father gave her some money, which she refused to accept from him until he insisted.

"After he saw Umm Amal out, said goodbye to her, and locked the door, your father did not speak much. He merely told me: 'They could not save the other child.' He looked at your mother and said, 'Praise the Lord; it's enough for us that she survived safely.'

"Then I saw your father's eyes look all around the room for you, as if trying to ascertain whether you had been born. He was embarrassed to see I noticed—for how could he have forgotten to check on you when he first entered the house? I told him you were sleeping. Then I turned to your mother to tell her you were very hungry.

"Your mother summoned all her strength to say in a low voice that was hoarse from screaming: 'I feel thirsty!'

"I raced to the kitchen and opened the refrigerator, meaning to take out the plastic water bottle. But then I heard your father say: 'Auntie, she can't drink cold water. I'll give her water from the tap.'

"Just as soon as your mother drank the water your father brought her, she regained some semblance of consciousness and a few memories and screamed with alarm: 'Where are my daughters?'

"I could not answer her question and looked at your father, who at first seemed uncertain. Then he quickly gained control of himself and replied, 'You weren't pregnant with twins. The physician was mistaken. You had one girl, who is sleeping now in her grandmother's room.'

"I did not make a peep. I raced out of the room and returned with you, bringing you to your mother. The moment I held you before your mother, she sat up and prepared to take you from me. Then you woke, crying. She opened the zipper of her tunic, which still smelled of childbirth and the hospital's pungent Dettol disinfectant, and pulled out a breast that was full of milk. Your mouth swallowed its rosy nipple, and you began to nurse very hungrily. Your mother closed her eyes calmly, and tears flowed down her cheeks—I had no idea why.

"Your father quickly left the room and beckoned for me to follow. In a low voice he said, 'Listen, Auntie, I'm going to the Department of Education and will be right back. I'm going to request leave for a week.'

"I replied, 'God willing.'

"Then I went to the kitchen to prepare for your mother a serving of *baht*, the warm rice, milk, nigella seed, and sugar porridge offered to new mothers, which one of my friends had taught me to make.

"I knew that your father had left the house when I heard his departing footsteps and the sound of the door closing behind him. I knew he had changed into his uniform after I found on the edge of the bed the shirt and pants he had worn when he accompanied your mother to the hospital.

"I returned to your mother's room with the dish and a spoon. When I saw that the tears on your mother's cheeks had dried, I privately gave thanks to God, who had spared me the task of persuading her to stop weeping.

"She looked at the dish I held and said in a tired voice, 'I can't chew food. I feel my jaws aren't up to that.'

"'Don't worry. Just try to open your mouth a little and I'll ladle a bit in. This is easy to swallow and digest. Just open your mouth. Open your mouth!'

"Your mother yielded to my pressing desire to feed her and began to open her mouth for me as I fed her one spoonful after another. Meanwhile you were busy nursing and enjoying the flowing flavor of the milk. Your mother ate all the porridge, and that delighted me. Her face gradually began to regain the glow of health that the pain of pregnancy and delivery had stolen from it. She asked me when you might fall asleep, and I replied anxiously, 'By God, I don't know.'

"I returned to the kitchen with the bowl, which was empty except for a bit of rice swimming in a pool of milk at the bottom, and the spoon, which I had placed in it. Then I returned to your mother's room and gazed deeply at the miracle that had materialized this day in the form of a little girl, who was you. This is the miracle in which one spirit emanates from another. I have never experienced it, even though I asked God and then all the righteous saints to intercede for me with Him so I could become pregnant. Even so, fate has not afforded me this blessing. Then I smiled as I remembered the advice of one of my relatives in the village. She had visited us three years after I married your grandfather. That advice of hers cost me a visit to a dermatologist, two weeks of treatment to cure the itch on my thighs after ants bit them, and lots of censure from your grandfather, who, whenever he entered the room and found me moaning and putting ointment on those ulcerated scars, would explode with anger and scream at me: 'What were you thinking? How could you have done this to yourself? Why do you believe everything people tell you? Are you irrational? All power and might are God's alone!' He stormed out to keep his anger and ire from escalating beyond a few mere words.

"I laughed at myself and at that relative when I remembered how we had gone to a deserted house, where she made me sit on an anthill. As soon as a group of the large black ants we call here 'Persian ants' swarmed over both of my legs and began to bite me and I started to moan with pain, I remember her face beamed with happiness. The more I groaned, the more she encouraged me with words, which, at that time, I thought were a magical spell she was addressing to me: 'A month from today, the moment you and your husband meet in bed, you will become pregnant and forget this pain.'

"I laugh a lot—at myself and at her—whenever I remember how I was moved by her words without ever pausing to consider them, even for a moment, or to ask myself what relationship ants had to pregnancy.

"When I sat facing you, I praised God repeatedly that he had allowed me to live long enough to see a child born in our house. I saw you had grown tired of nursing and fallen asleep. Your mother placed you very gently beside her, stretched out calmly in the bed, and entrusted to me the task of looking after you—one that lasted for many years."

My father never told me when or how he informed my mother that my twin sister had died or how she handled that news, given that she had heart problems. Instead, he told me that, after he obtained leave from work for a week and my mother told him her breasts did not provide enough milk for me, he began—based on the advice of a neighbor who had given birth to a boy three months before I was born and who had visited to check on my mother—to wake at five each morning to ride his bicycle for approximately half an hour to buy a bottle of milk from a milk-processing plant in the Khan al-Makhdar region and then return with it in a metal basket that he had attached to the front of his bike specifically for this purpose.

He said, "I never complained about that at all. To the contrary, I was happy to have this task, even though the streets were occasionally dark at that hour and I, as you know, don't see well with one eye. What happened to me on the sixth day, though, was truly frightening. I had placed the bottle of fresh milk in the basket and was riding along calmly, returning the way I did every day on a road that was totally free of both pedestrian and vehicular traffic. I had no sooner crossed the main road than an automobile appeared from some side road, I don't know where, and almost slammed into me. I lost my balance and was barely able to cling to the handlebars of the bicycle, which landed hard on the concrete pavement. But the bottle of milk was thrown from the basket and broke. Then its milk created a large white splotch. My first reaction was astonishment that I had escaped from an accident that—save for God's mercy and grace—would have killed me. The second was a mighty fury at the reckless driver for wasting that milk.

"Then I sensed that in any event I needed to give thanks to God, praise Him for safeguarding me, and return to the processing facility again as quickly as possible to buy another bottle. There was no way I was going to hear you cry from hunger while I stood by silently—even if the trip cost me my life. I returned to the plant once more at top speed. This time I bought two bottles. I carried one in my left hand and placed the other in the basket, the way I had on previous occasions, while I steered the bike with my right hand, cycling slowly. The moment I reached the house, I heard you crying, even before I opened the door. I entered our house carrying one bottle in each hand after leaning my bike against the wall. Your grandmother sped to me to receive them and take them to the kitchen to fix a bottle for you.

"'What happened?' your mother asked when I entered her room. 'You seem shaken up.'

"'Don't worry about it. There was a small problem: your daughter's milk almost cost me my life today.'"

I understand now why my mother laughed the way she did when I asked her about the day she gave birth to me. That was an ironic laugh about a birth that had almost killed everyone.

Even as I grew older, my grandmother continued to treat me like a living doll and to wrap me in her extravagant care. For example, she would make sure I had nourishing and healthy types of food to eat, even if that meant expending all her monthly budget on supplies to prepare delicious dishes that would make me feel hungry the moment their aroma wafted from the kitchen. She changed my clothes three times a day and kept a wardrobe in her room for my clothes, which she arranged by the time of day I wore them. Tunics embroidered in various colors were for mornings; red and white ribbons to tie on the ends of my short braids went with skirts and long-sleeved blouses—or short-sleeved blouses with lace; and multicolored, striped socks were for afternoons. Stored in the bottom drawer of the wardrobe were many kinds of leather shoes without heels. When evening came, she would dress me in silky white satin pajamas that made me look like a pampered princess.

I loved being coddled this way by my grandmother. I don't know when she started, but it may have begun the moment I was born or when my younger sister was—a year after me—since she was delivered a month early and needed extra care from my mother.

My grandfather spoiled me too, and the moment I heard his footsteps as he entered, I would sense that the whole house had turned into a plate of delicious, tempting sweets. I would race to him and try to grab hold of his legs, because he was a large, tall man, whose chest I could not reach when he stood up straight, no matter how hard I tried. Even so, whenever I saw him, I rose on my toes and stood as tall as I could, trying to embrace him. Before I could feel discouraged by my failed attempts, he would lean down and open his arms to me. Then I would melt into his chest. When I walked beside him on the street, I felt like I was walking under the protection of one of God's special friends.

I had not turned six yet when my grandfather died in the Medical City Hospital in Baghdad, two days after he was admitted. I was not able to say goodbye to him and still don't know his cause of death. My grandfather's demise struck our family like a thunderbolt because he wasn't an old man and had never complained of any illness. Parting from him came as a blow to me, especially because I was a thin brown girl and did not inherit either his massive body or his light complexion. This meant that when we walked together, a passerby might look repeatedly at our faces and still fail to detect any resemblance between them. In my grandfather's presence I became a princess who could command and forbid.

I remember how the three of us—me, him, and my grandmother—would sit on the floor around the dinner mat. Even though he knew I had eaten before he arrived, he would always ask me the same question: "Are you hungry—or is it time for a sweet?"

I would reply as blissfully as ever: "It's time for sweets."

My grandmother would insist that he not give me all the candy he had brought at once and just offer me a single piece. Then he would ask me to close my eyes and open my hand, into which he would place a sweet. I would raise it to my nose, my eyes still closed, and sniff it while allowing my imagination to conjure up whatever images it wanted.

Once, my grandfather placed in my hand three different sweets wrapped in silver cellophane. I recognized the feel and the sound of cellophane around the candies, which we called *al-jalkit* in Iraq. I lifted them to my nose and began to discuss my joy.

I told my grandparents I was now a princess sitting in a garden, surrounded by flowers on every side. "Here comes the sparrow bringing me a nosegay of mint in its beak. A rabbit is rolling an orange toward me. Meanwhile, Granny's chicken has laid a caramel egg for me."

My grandfather laughed out loud and said, "As always, you've guessed right! Open your eyes." When I did, I found the three candies: one was mint-flavored, the second orange, and the third caramel. I placed all of them in my mouth at the same time (after removing their wrappers) and closed my eyes as I started to savor their flavors, which mixed together in my mouth.

After my grandfather died, he was referred to, simply, as al-Marhum—the man who had passed into God's care. My grandmother then became known as the spouse of al-Marhum, after previously being called Umm Ghayib for years—like other women whom fate had never granted offspring.

◆ ◆ ◆

Many things in our lives changed after my grandfather departed to another realm. My father had to work a second job to support his family, which increased in size almost every year. Now he was a cook in a restaurant that sold *pacha*, a mutton stew of trotters and heads, in the Khan al-Makhdar Market—a place that was jam-packed with different types of restaurants and that also served as a local market where individuals and merchants went to purchase retail or wholesale goods: fish, fruits, vegetables, rice, flour, oil, and the like.

My father's workday was divided into two parts. At seven in the morning he would go to the Education Bureau, where he was a clerk. That was in al-Amir District. He would return at three for lunch and a nap. Following the afternoon prayer, he would embrace his vocation as a father by showering us with educational advice and pointers on good conduct. At times he would tell us stories drawn from history, hoping that we would heed their lessons and benefit from them in the future. Those stories did not help me, since I was a teenager by then and because my experiences were far more challenging than any tale I heard my father recount.

If he could not find a story in his quiver, he would leave the house and sit in a men's coffee shop, a *kahwa*—even though he did not like to play dominoes, which was the game usually favored there. He did, though, like to watch young men compete at that game.

When my father told us that the owner of one of the big coffee shops had bought a color TV, I asked to accompany him there so

I could see what programs were being broadcast. At first, he refused because we had a black-and-white television at home, and he could not guarantee that what was shown on the coffee shop TV would be suitable for children. The men there typically watched sports—especially football—or shows like *Science for Everyone*, which was a weekly scientific digest of the latest technological advances and news of space exploration. I begged him to take me because I was curious to see whether the presenter's suit was nut-brown or even indigo, a color I didn't like.

So he took me there one day, and, on the television, I witnessed another world, unlike anything we possessed in our house. I was so astonished by this colorful world, which spread before my eyes as a different color flashed on the screen every second, that—without consulting my mother, which he typically did when purchasing a new appliance—my father decided to buy a color TV, but medium-sized, not a huge one. I don't know where my father found the money for a new color television, which replaced the black-and-white one in the parlor. The moment our neighbors heard about it, my father was besieged by many of their children, who asked to watch cartoons in color with us. When my father agreed, it became very normal for us to hear children knock on our door almost every day right before 6:30 p.m., when the children's programs came on. My parents' bedroom gained the black-and-white television, which now seemed old-fashioned.

My father resumed work for a final time each day after midnight, when he and a friend went to the restaurant to prepare and cook sheep heads for the *pacha*, which most men in Najaf liked to eat early in the morning for breakfast.

My mother gave birth to a third child—a boy this time—and named him Yas, for Iyas, after the famous Iraqi singer Yas Khidr. Then almost everything changed in my family, except for my grandmother's preferential treatment of me. That continued, and she still took me with her each month when she went to the pension bureau in the Wilaya District to collect her survivor benefits from my late grandfather's pension. We might also go to the pharmacy, where she purchased medicine for her gallbladder infection, which she had suffered since she lost my grandfather.

Naturally, as our economic situation fluctuated, we moved from one rental house to another, from al-Madina Street to Khan al-Makhdar to al-Jadida. These neighborhoods all had rather narrow streets with approximately the same type of houses, which were made of brick and white lime plaster. The exterior walls were coated with stucco. These houses, which were referred to as *hoosh* or *hawsh*, consisted of several rooms, a bath, and a water closet. There would be a small courtyard that was surrounded by these rooms, and it was typically circular and open to the sky. The walls of these houses adjoined each other with a beautiful familiarity, and whenever I looked at them, I felt that these houses were connected by a sense of kinship. All these neighborhoods were linked by side streets that teemed with young children leaving school.

Children of affluent families rode their bicycles in the street there, and other kids played simple games—boys played marbles, and girls enjoyed tug-of-war, hopscotch, and similar diversions. Meanwhile, some elderly women used the stoops of their houses as benches, where they gossiped with each other at this same time of day.

Our streets were bustling with life, and everyone looked forward to afternoon, when the onus of the sun's heat diminished. At this time, young girls would sweep the doorsteps of their houses with a palm-frond broom and sprinkle them with water before they started to play. Even women like my mother who were not old enough to sit on their doorsteps spent afternoons hosting girlfriends, who came to sew garments, embroider bedclothes, crochet, or knit. Almost all men headed to coffee shops at this hour. Everyone seemed to wait till this time of day to proclaim as one their hold on life.

Once the sun set, everyone went home, and stillness engulfed the streets, where almost nothing was audible save the voices of muezzins issuing the call to the sunset prayer. We heard these cries clearly, amplified by the loudspeakers that were attached to the minarets of mosques large and small.

The primary-education regulations of that era would not allow me to enter school until I turned seven, and that meant I began in the ninth month of 1974. A neighbor woman, who was a friend of my mother, took me one morning to register me and her daughter in a coed elementary school called Palestine. A few days after my enrollment, my father bought me one dark-blue piece of polyester fabric and a white piece of cotton. Then my mother carried both fabrics to the house of a seamstress who lived in our neighborhood, and she sewed me a uniform consisting of a smock and a blouse. On her way home, my mother purchased ribbons and white socks from a store called Luxuries, which had opened directly opposite the door of the school. It was run by an old woman whose husband had left her only a deranged son people called Crazy Nasir.

My grandmother bought me a leather backpack for school and a pair of cloth shoes from one of the shops in the Grand Souk in the Wilaya District after one of our monthly trips to collect her pension. This marketplace operated under a metal roof and was subdivided into sections called *kaysariyat*, or "Caesarean sections," that were owned by Najaf natives known as Almshahda. Each section was dedicated to one of many trades or crafts. We saw goldsmiths, textile merchants, tailors for cloaks, coppersmiths, oil and spice merchants, and pickle vendors, as well as merchants selling shoes, perfumes, leather, clocks, silver, mirrors, and so much more. Despite this great variety, each section adjoined the next one very harmoniously. At the entry to this market stood the mausoleum of Imam Ali, the son of Abu Talib (peace upon him), with its large dome and golden minarets.

My first day in school had a flavor I had never experienced before: the scent of the paper in the textbooks and the new notebooks mixed with the chalky smell of the finger paints, and with the fear pulsing through every part of me. My fear quickly became a tremor that spread through my body when I lined up with the other pupils in my class at the door of the room where we would receive the school supplies. That burgeoning fear increased and prevented me from setting foot in the room until one of the teachers handing out supplies noticed that my feet were planted at the door to the room. He then approached me calmly and said in a very relaxed voice, "Come in. Don't be afraid."

So I entered hesitantly. Then he began chatting with me, as if he had previously met me, while he lifted a pile of books and notebooks that were carefully bound together with a blue hemp cord.

"Here. Take this stack. It's for you. Where's your bag? Tell your mother to put covers on these books and notebooks this week. We want the books to stay clean. Don't forget!"

I held my empty bag out to him with trembling hands. He took it and filled it with all those school supplies. Then he asked me to press my right thumb gently on a wet sponge in a small, clear glass bowl placed on the large table near the bundles for the other students, lift it, place it extremely carefully this time on a dark-blue ink pad, and lift it again to press down on the school registration form for receipt of these materials beside my name, which was recorded there. My fear gradually began to fade once I left that room. By the time I entered the classroom, I had forgotten what had happened and was thinking about how I would carry my book bag, which was almost exploding with its heavy contents.

After a few days, though, I quickly fell in love with that school, which was only one side street away from our house. Its tall, faded red wall was totally different from those of the houses adjoining it, and the teachers devoted a lot of attention to us new pupils and treated us like pampered children. By the end of the first half of the school year, they had offered us tips on personal hygiene almost daily. They taught us how a pupil should sit in class, acquire good morals, and be respectful when speaking, especially to teachers. This was in addition to teaching us the Arabic alphabet and addition and subtraction.

The school day began at 8:00 a.m. and ended at 1:00 p.m. I would leave my house each morning and race down the street to enter the school just seconds before the morning bell rang for the taking of attendance. When I saw the school janitor close the school's metal gate right after I had entered it, I would feel a great satisfaction that lasted throughout the day. I imagined then that the entire school day hinged on my entry to the school and that everyone had been awaiting my awe-inspiring entrance.

My first three years of school passed like a breeze on a scorching day. I was never hesitant about going and never failed to understand any school subject, no matter how much difficulty other pupils had. I acquired an important status among them when one of the teachers named me class proctor whenever he stepped out of the room. I was so happy to bear this responsibility on my shoulders that I prayed God would prolong that instructor's absence or have him arrive as late as possible in the morning to provide me more time to exercise this responsibility, which built my self-confidence.

At home, I started reading to my grandmother the newspapers my father bought almost every day. On many occasions I would read aloud to her stories I didn't understand. I read the newspaper at that early age not to understand the stories but to show everyone who knew me that not only could I read—I could read proficiently.

My two siblings Iqbal and Ahmad were born during those three years. They were born only a year apart. Whenever my mother had another child, I felt anxious and wondered why someone who had suffered from asthma for years and who took heart medicine daily kept becoming pregnant and giving birth.

I did not grasp her reasons clearly until years later, when I married and had four children. Then I understood that my mother—exactly like me—had been fighting against her own mortality by attempting to create new life repeatedly by giving birth.

I did not feel at all jealous of my siblings, whose presence filled the walls and rooms of the house. Since I was the eldest, my siblings were just kids who always needed my affection. Being the eldest child means you are born mature—no matter how young you are.

The moment I saw my shadow spread out on the street next to my younger sister's as we returned from school early in the afternoon, I realized that I would need to forget about racing to school and begin walking there and back at a sedate pace with small steps, crossing the street only after looking to my right and left, watching carefully for cars with drivers who might not see us crossing—even if this meant eschewing the daily pleasure of running to school and arriving only seconds before the school gate closed. My joy in feeling someone needed me trumped that.

I escorted my sister to the door of her classroom every day, guarding her against any possible harm, no matter how trivial. During our short ten-minute breaks between classes, I made sure she ate the snack that we brought, which had been prepared by our mother or grandmother. Even when she was playing with friends in the school's courtyard, I kept an eye on her.

This mission, which I had assigned to myself, ended when we entered the house. The moment I took my pack off my back and placed it on the floor, I would forget about everything else and embrace my grandmother's world. She would be waiting eagerly for me to tell her everything that had happened during the day. I considered those events very commonplace, but she thought them extraordinary.

During the next years, most members of my family, including me, suffered many mishaps. My sister Iqbal, for example, drank some of the kerosene we used to fill the tanks of the heaters we lit in the winter. She easily found the kerosene storage containers no matter how hard my mother tried to hide them. Every time, she had to go to the hospital to have her stomach pumped or to stay in the emergency ward.

My brother Iyas fell down the steps that led to the roof terrace, and his hand was in a plaster cast for more than two months. A massive wooden wardrobe toppled onto me when I was trying to clean its interior, and I was unconscious for an entire day. None of those accidents was nearly as severe and brutal as what happened to my brother Ahmad in 1977.

Chapter Two

The climate of Najaf is almost desert-like, and its only two seasons are winter and summer, which from time immemorial have divided the months of the year between them. We hardly understood the meaning of the words "spring" and "autumn," which instructors taught us in school and spent a long time defining and explaining. When they discussed the four seasons, they used color photos from magazines or nature scenes visible locally only on the television screen. Streets decked in blossoms, butterflies flickering, brightly colored wings, and leaves changing from green to a gleaming gold and falling to the ground were sights that existed only in our imaginations, since they definitely did not exist in our reality, which was dominated by cumulative, intense heat waves accompanied by red dust storms, especially in July and August. Then, once September arrived, black clouds saturated with rain accumulated in our sky to warn us to prepare for cold weather.

Hawsh-style courtyard houses like our dwelling were especially exposed to these rude gifts from the sky. You would find us, when we sensed an approaching sandstorm, struggling to seal every crevice and pore of the house with old clothes my mother and grandmother saved for this very purpose—to spare my asthmatic mother from experiencing choking fits, which might afflict her if she inhaled the friable sand or dirt particles delivered by the storm. We would sit attentively in our rooms, and if that storm dispersed without infiltrating our house, we would immediately leap to our feet to clean it completely and use a number of hoses to wash down the walls in order to safeguard my mother from a feared asthma attack.

If we woke in the morning to find the sky enveloped in black clouds, we would hastily imprison ourselves in our rooms after sealing their doors—and the kitchen's as well—with pieces of old foam bedding. Through our windowpanes we would watch attentively as rainwater descended from the roof's downspouts in elegant, transparent cataracts. When the rain was especially intense, it fell straight into our courtyard, which was paved with medium-sized, orange tiles, and gradually formed a small square pond there, confined by the closed doors of the house's rooms. Then the water would slowly dissipate and pour down the mouth of the open drain, which we had uncovered for this reason.

On either side of our house's large gray door, next to its stoop, stood two benches made of polished marble. We had no idea how these benches found their way there, because neither their squared-off shape nor their polished marble, which had almost every color in it, matched the stones of the street or the color of the walls of our house or those of any others on our street. My grandmother and her friend frequently sat there to chat during the afternoon, and an onlooker might easily have thought the benches had been placed by the stoop of this house solely for this idiosyncratic purpose.

I don't know how early it was when my father woke me in the house of some relatives with whom we had spent the night during an especially heavy rainstorm. My family had sought refuge with them when we feared that our own house would be flooded and that its walls, which had begun to crumble, might collapse. My father wanted me to accompany him somewhere. As I woke, the sun's rays were beginning to light the clear sky, which was dotted with tufts of cottony clouds.

My father pushed open the door of our house, and as soon as my eyes caught sight of its interior, I felt sick to my stomach and started to throw up. My father pulled me away from the open door and sat me down on the sidewalk. He asked me to be calm and take a deep breath. As I did, he watched me anxiously. A short time later, my nausea ended.

Then he asked, "Will you be able to do this job?"

"Yes . . ."

"Do exactly what I do."

My father was holding two old aluminum bowls. He handed me one and entered the house. I followed him cautiously. The floor of the whole house, including the kitchen, where the door was open, was completely covered with water on which floated brown turds that had emerged from the broken toilet and mixed with the stinky water that had backed up from the house's drain because of the torrents of rain that had fallen since the previous day.

The putrid smell that rose everywhere almost suffocated me, but I pulled myself together and stopped breathing through my nose. I clenched my teeth in disgust when I saw my father scoop up a clump of turds with the basin and carry it outside, where he dumped it on a big sheet of aluminum beside the stoop. There were many such sheets, which had previously been used to store a kind of vegetable oil called "al-Raee," as their logo indicated.

I watched my father plow through the sea of shit, going and coming, as he collected what he could and then returned, seemingly oblivious to the stink that almost blocked my nostrils. Then I closed my eyes, pursed my lips, and reached out to a pile of turds beside my foot, lifted it, and rushed outside. For fear of slipping, though, I was forced to open my eyes and proceed cautiously. My catch helped cover that sheet of metal completely with shit and stinky water.

"Put it there," my father told me in a commanding but tired voice on my next trip as he pointed to another sheet of metal, not too far from the first.

I went and emptied the contents of my bowl on the other sheet, which I had previously seen on the flat roof of the house, without understanding its purpose. I made many such trips between the house and that sheet of metal while lifting my feet calmly and setting them down firmly on the tile.

After we covered six large metal sheets, the house was almost clean. Only three piles remained in the center of the house. When my father came inside to clean the kitchen floor, which we had not sealed off with foam covers as we had done for the other rooms, I removed my sandals and walked quickly to a pile to collect it with my basin. But the floor of the house was covered with stinky water, and the putrid smell overwhelmed me. I lost my balance and fell.

My father raced out of the kitchen, lifted me by my armpits, and carried me quickly to the bathroom. He opened its door, set me down inside, and said, "Take your clothes off and bathe. I'll bring you another tunic."

After turning on the bathroom light, he shut me in there and left. I could not bear to raise my head and look my father in the eye. Instead, I gazed at the soiled bottom of my tunic, which had little bits of wet brown shit clinging to it. My stink became more pronounced once the door was closed, and it penetrated every pore of my body. Then I felt disgusted with myself and despised this house, where we had experienced nothing but calamities. It really deserved to be covered with shit to its very foundations. I also hated the rain a lot.

Little by little, tears began to flow from my eyes and land hot on my cheeks. They mixed with the cold shower water, which struck my head as I shivered from the cold. I quickly forgot the cold, though, when the perfumed soap diffused its fragrance as I scrubbed my body with it forcefully, trying to clean away everything: the stench, the color of the excrement, and the taste of poverty.

I put on the clean, dry shift, which my father brought me, after I had thoroughly dried my body and hair with the towel hanging on the bathroom wall. Then I went outside and saw my father struggle to carry those sheets of shit, one at a time, to a location far from our house, among some rubble between two houses. He covered them with the wet foam sheets we had used to seal off the bottoms of the doors to the rooms in our house before we left the previous day. Then he immediately covered them with some of the broken bricks and pieces of wood that were scattered through the rubble. Before he left that site, he examined the spot carefully, more than once, to make sure the wind would not blow the sheets of metal away and disclose our secret, leaving us exposed in an unfortunate manner.

Then he entered the house quickly, fetched clean clothes for himself from his room, and headed to the bathroom. My father left the door of the house open, and I sat on the stoop, keeping an eye on those sheets of metal from a distance.

"I'll fetch someone with a wagon to haul them out of the city before too many flies start collecting there," my father said as he dried his short, fine black hair with the bathroom towel, which then he left on the wall of the house and departed.

I waited, seated on one of the two ill-omened benches in front of the house, keeping an eye on the flies that had begun to gather on the sheets of shit.

Next my memory brings me a scene I wish that I could forget or that it would forget me. This episode created a rift between me and my family in general and especially between me and my mother. I recall how my astonishment and confusion brought someone a calamity and how a fleeting moment of negligence led to the death of a member of my family. I bite my forefinger remorsefully when I remember I did not close the door properly that day, as I *always* did when my father entered the house, and the sight of those two huge kettles, each of which stood on a black metal tripod, beneath which burned pieces of wood and flaming embers. I was fascinated then by watching the two men who were busy cooking. One stirred the stew of meat and chickpeas with a large paddle called a *mass*. The other man was adding more wood to the fire beneath the second kettle, in which water was boiling more briskly than any I had ever seen. The red of the embers with their fingers of flame, the smell of the burning wood, and the fiery summer heat correlated perfectly with the image of hell I had tucked away in my memory, based on my grandmother's repeated description of it as a giant bubbling cauldron and an angel of retribution preparing to incinerate sinful human beings.

I remember how at that moment one of the men cast me a look as fiery as his flaming embers. It penetrated my spirit like burning arrows released by a Hazara hunter at a weak prey. I raced back inside and closed the door behind me with a trembling hand, but not hard enough to shut it properly. I quickly went to the bedroom and took the copy of the Qur'an down from its gilded wooden shelf, which was as high as the room's window. I hugged the holy book and sat down cross-legged in the corner, attempting to drive the image of that terrifying man and his demonic glare from my mind by relying on God. I began reciting to myself the short *surahs* I knew by heart. Just as I finished reciting the final *surah*, which is called al-Nas, or "The People," I heard my mother scream. I raced to her, my heart beating faster, clutching the Qur'an to my chest. I found her and my grandmother slapping their chests and screaming "Yabuuu!" as my father entered our house, accompanied by another man, carrying my little brother, whose flesh had melded with his white dishdasha as they both burned.

I was dumbfounded and raised a hand to block the scream that was trying to emerge from my mouth. Then the Qur'an slipped from my grasp and fell to the floor.

I don't remember what happened to me after that. The most I recall of that day, before I fled to hide on our flat roof, are glimpses of a door wide open; my father exiting through it quickly, wearing plastic sandals that did not match in size or color, carrying my burning little brother; one of the men standing by the door of our house mumbling words I couldn't hear; two women—my mother and my grandmother—beating their faces and chests and screaming bloody murder; and the Qur'an falling on the floor.

Even today, I don't know how I ended up on the roof! Did I climb the steps one at a time? Or did I leap up them in a bound? All I remember is how the fiery heat on the roof terrace that afternoon burned my feet as my eyes scanned the area for a place where I could escape from the horrific terror of that spectacle, from my family, from that man's eyes, which were spying on me, from myself—from everything.

I leaned against the wall, which transferred its intense heat to my body the moment I touched it. Then I collapsed and sat cross-legged, attempting as best I could to summon back my spirit, which had drifted away in its fright. But my heart pounded faster and faster, and I felt something almost strangle me from inside—I didn't know how. But this force quickly reached my heart and began to squeeze it hard. I screamed so loudly that my cry echoed everywhere till it reached the ears of my grandmother, whom I then saw standing bareheaded, without her long black scarf, at the door to the roof, with the pocket ripped from her blouse.

That moment lasted so long it seemed an eon as I attempted to say a word, to utter something, if only a single consonant. But I had lost any ability to speak, my lips had frozen, and I was overcome by exhaustion. My grandmother approached me, took my hand in hers, and helped me stand. I clutched her hand as I walked, afraid of falling into an abyss, without knowing how it might loom before me. I closed my eyes as I walked, wishing that everything that had occurred moments ago was merely a terrible nightmare that would vanish the moment I opened my eyes!

I don't know how long I slept, but when I woke, I found the man with those red eyes in front of me, and now his eyes were even redder than before. He stood the way I had seen him—beside a large kettle of boiling blood. When he stretched his hand toward me, I saw his long, hideous fingernails, which were soiled with soot. Slowly and gradually his hand elongated till it could almost seize the hem of my tunic as I sat cross-legged on the roof. I tried to move my body away from him, but his hand kept drawing closer and closer. I pressed my back against the wall time and again, trying to puncture it and hide from that frightening hand in some cleft there. But I failed and began to scream, "Granny! Daddy! Mommy! Save me! He's going to burn me! He's going to burn me! Help!"

"God, guide me; guide me, God. All power and might are God's alone. My Almighty and Exalted God, what has befallen us!"

I heard my grandmother whisper this as she placed a cool, damp cloth on my sweat-drenched forehead. Then I tried to pull myself together and force my eyes open. Perhaps everything I had seen and experienced that day was merely a nightmare. I tried my best to look at my father, who had also come when he heard me scream.

Standing by my head, he asked, "How is she today?"

"Not as well as we would hope. We need to take her to the doctor—her too," my grandmother replied.

"Her mother's no better either, despite all the medicine she's taken," my father remarked, in the mournful tone of my grandmother's voice.

My grandmother continued. "Don't be angry with her. It's not her fault she left the door open and your son crawled outside. What happened, happened. Everything is preordained, my son. Don't vent your anger on your daughter. That will only make matters worse."

I did not hear my father say anything more. Instead, I heard his heavy, troubled footsteps as he left the room. I buried my sorrow inside me and tried to fall asleep again. Then I found myself standing in the house's courtyard with my brother while the sun's rays scorched my head till I almost went up in steam, it was so hot. My brother stood in a heavy shadow, the source of which escaped my sight. I was curious to see what was casting this shadow, which also seemed chilly. But I was alarmed to see that the door was wide open and a tall man was quickly entering and heading toward my brother. The man picked him up and departed.

The door's two panels closed after them. Then I was alone and shouted after the man: "Thief! Thief, return my brother! Don't burn him!"

A cold cloud appeared, showering its rain over my forehead. Then the precipitation covered my face, and I woke up, frightened, to find that my grandmother had washed my face with cold water. I attempted to look carefully at my grandmother but could only see a foggy image cloaked by black. I opened my mouth slowly as drops of water entered it. The water tasted different. I wanted to tell her I had not killed my brother. I mumbled some words, which I doubt she heard. She promptly seized a glass of water and brought it to my mouth. I began to sip from it while my eyes were still half-closed.

I don't know how many days I slept. All I heard from my family was that my mother had been in the hospital for a week. My father stayed with her while my grandmother stayed home, caring for me while I lay feverish in bed.

My family summarized my brother's death, saying he had seized the opportunity created when I left the door open and quickly crawled outside. Then he tripped on his dishdasha and fell off one of the benches into the flaming embers beneath a kettle. He died from his burns without anyone noticing.

My father did not hold a wake for my brother. Instead, he recited the Qur'an's 36th *surah*, Ya Sin, for Ahmad's spirit each time he completed his prayer ritual. He continued that practice till the day he died in 2007.

My mother gathered all my brother's clothes and placed them in a cloth case, creating a pillow she used even for naps. I would frequently find her embracing that pillow and weeping.

I had suddenly become a harbinger of misfortune for my entire family—except for my grandmother, of course—even though they never said so openly. Anyone who knew the story of my brother Ahmad's death, however, could plainly see that in their eyes. Back then, for approximately a year, I played the role of a silent, kindly ghost with them. I would only leave my room to help with the housework or to care for my siblings, whose repeated mistreatment of me I decided to ignore, even when it was intentional and premeditated. Once I had completed the work expected of me, I would disappear inconspicuously into my grandmother's room, which I now shared with her. I began to split my time between studying and trying to sleep. My attempts to fall asleep were the most difficult moments for me; it isn't easy to entice sleep to approach your eyes when you are suspended inside a space where you don't know who you are or when you will leave your body. In the moment when you dangle between drowning in some gelatinous entity, which correlates with nothing in physical reality, and the fear of a sudden awakening caused by some sound penetrating your hearing, which is both alert and tired at the same time, you cannot sleep comfortably, given all this frightful vigilance. No wakefulness can raise your body, which is exhausted by fatigue. In such circumstances, this space seems to squeeze you—or perhaps you are compressing space as you sit stuffed inside your body, unable to move.

No matter how hard I tried to demonstrate to my family that—for the ghosts of my tribe—eating and breathing were not nearly as essential as love, I unfortunately never succeeded, and all my days were marked by a dreary sameness as I discovered that the people closest to me had become unknowable and that, no matter how hard I tried, they would expect me to do better than I could.

Events a year later, though, forced everyone to discontinue my punishment and drove my mother to reach out for my help again.

"Salutations for Muhammad and Muhammad's family! God has recompensed you with two sons! Didn't I tell you, Son, that God's mercy is limitless!"

My grandmother declared this in a loud, jubilant voice as she ran to my father the moment my mother was brought out of the delivery room. My father had been waiting for her in the corridor leading to the maternity ward. Now, because my father did not believe my mother had already delivered a baby safely, he asked my grandmother, "Are you sure she's still alive?"

My mother gave birth to twin boys this time, and my father named them Falah and Sabah. They were also born in the morning—at dawn to be exact—like most of my siblings. My brother Sabah was born healthy and fit, in every way like other babies, and my mother entrusted his care and custody entirely to me. The moment he was placed in my arms, I became his little mother, even though I was only eleven. I was a mother who had just graduated from the Palestine Coed Elementary School, enrolled at the Algeria Middle School for Girls, and still needed many more days of practice wearing a black abaya when I left the house—like any other girl who had completed elementary school—without tripping over my abaya's hem and falling to the ground.

The physician, however, needed to prick my brother Falah all over his body to find a suitable vein into which they could insert a feeding tube. When he did not find one, he was obliged to place it on the right side of Falah's head; it stayed there for an entire year because my brother was very weak when he was born. His body showed few signs of movement, he breathed with great difficulty, and his skin was rippled like a newborn kitten's. He did not open his eyes for the first forty days after he was born. During the first two months, my mother wrapped him in pieces of white gauze and cotton till he looked like a little pharaonic mummy.

The weird thing is that when my mother was wheeled out of the delivery room and saw the two babies near her for the first time, she contemplated their faces for a while and then said in a tired voice: "I know, only too well, that I will die on account of them!"

My father and grandmother disapproved of this bizarre statement and attributed it to the effects of their delivery. But that prophecy of hers was eventually fulfilled when my mother died on account of Falah and Sabah in 2005.

Falah and Sabah looked so much alike that the resemblance was frightening. A person seeing them separately would be certain they were the same child, since they shared the same facial features and were the same height. Once Falah recovered fully, thanks to my mother's unprecedented care for him, he looked exactly like his brother Sabah. Even we family members who lived with them could only tell them apart by the color of their clothes, which my mother strove to keep different. If one of them suffered some accident, the other boy would suffer something similar that same day.

Meanwhile, our neighborhood of interconnecting streets underwent a great transformation: the majority of our neighbors and acquaintances left for other parts, most of which were beyond our ken. Almost everyone lost longtime friends.

Many of the residents on our street were students and families of students enrolled in the Shi'i Seminary of Najaf. Many of these were either Arabs from other countries (especially Lebanon), Hazara from Afghanistan, or Iranians. Others studied at the Religious University of Najaf in the Sa'd District, the Lebanese school in the new district, or other religious schools affiliated with Najaf's Hawza al-Ilmiyya. These scholars studied Arabic grammar, Arabic morphology, logic, homiletics, scholastic theology, the science of the Hadith of the Prophet, philosophy, and Qur'anic exegesis in preparation for becoming a mujtahid in the religious sciences. But our neighborhood was emptied out overnight when these students were exiled from Iraq by a Republican decree.

The Khan al-Makhdar Market overflowed then with used household items because peddlers of secondhand goods purchased from the residents of these houses their personal effects at the lowest possible prices and then rushed to sell them in that market, touting them with different cries and rhythms. Even though we badly needed some of these items—like an electric washing machine, an iron, or a floor fan—which were all being sold at extraordinarily low prices, my father refused point-blank to purchase any. His argument for this position was that the rightful owner had been forced to sell the item because of the banishment decree.

When the district's *mukhtar* suggested to my father to unlock our next-door neighbor Abu Alaa's house, because he had been exiled, and live there rent-free, my father shouted at him: "Have you no shame? Do you think I don't fear God? Would I live in an arrogated house?"

"Arrogated" quickly entered our daily vocabulary, and the word had a frightening ring to our ears. Anyone guilty of arrogation or who was too casual about the concept fell subject to the word's curse, which would be realized through frightening events that culminated in certain death. The children of people who lived in arrogated houses fell from the roofs of those structures, the men of those families were electrocuted by touching a live wire, or the women died suddenly and unexpectedly. The curse on those houses might even end the new residents' lives in some conflagration. It became common for us to hear that a fire had engulfed one of those houses, and we would ignore that news.

One fire that did leave a painful mark on the memories of people on our street—indeed of the entire district—was the fire that broke out in the room of Crazy Nasir the morning after he uttered "Down with the president!" when some unidentified person trained him to say that. He had begun repeating it loudly, giggling, without understanding what it meant or what awful consequences would ensue. He ran from one house to the next as his mother chased after him, trying unsuccessfully to catch and silence him. We woke to find this fire blazing one morning in September 1980, and it served as a prophecy for what happened to us subsequently. The ashes of that poor fellow's remains seem to have been scattered over all our lives, smudging them with gloom.

For me, two important types of events served as landmarks for those years: my mother having another child and my promotion from one grade to the next in school. Anything else that happened in a year did not concern me in the least, because neither my chronological nor my mental age was capable of processing political or economic events, no matter how serious their impacts were on society as a whole. Thus, when President Ahmed Hassan al-Bakr resigned from office after he fell ill with Parkinson's disease and was unable to fulfill his duties as head of state and his vice president, Saddam Hussein, became president of the Republic of Iraq, nothing whatsoever changed in my life. The true turning point that year was my successful completion of the first year of middle school and promotion to the second year. This meant that I was faced with much more difficult school subjects than ever before: chemistry, physics, biology, algebra, and geometry. At a time when everyone else, including my father, was fixated on the changes affecting Iraqi society, after the new president assumed control of the country, my mind was infested with a series of logarithms and exponents in the decimal system—all requiring precise mathematical calculations. I frequently felt uncertain and anxious as I searched for a correct solution for equations for chemical reactions. I would get migraines from memorizing and discussing Newton's laws of motion, because even if my success would not directly influence society in any way, my failure naturally would disgrace my family, whom people on our street would then refer to as the "household with the lazy girl," as they typically dubbed homes of female students who failed academically and were obliged to quit school and marry extremely young. That was why, when I received my results at the end of the school year, our neighbor Umm Nayran was incredulous. Looking at the 89 percent average of all my grades, she asked: "If the curriculum was that easy, why did my daughter Nayran fail?"

Fear of being embarrassed by failure drove me to succeed and excel that year. Fear of failure, though, played no role in my continued success throughout my subsequent years in school to 1988 and thereafter. Another crueler and more bitter fear imposed itself on all Iraqis, not just on me.

Although 1980 was not an auspicious year for a birth, in its third month my sister Hala was born—the final grape in our bunch. That was exactly six months before the disaster. This year and the following ones tattooed all Iraqis with loss and death.

From the start of this year, we had witnessed and heard about unfamiliar events, ones that our ears and eyes found off-putting. We anxiously attributed them to random opinions, but a saying that was often on the tongues of people was: "Where there's smoke, there's fire." Everyone expected a fierce, blazing conflagration to erupt after smoky rumors circulated with the speed of lightning from one person to the next. These suggested that clashes and serious military attacks had occurred between the Iraqi and Iranian armies. And then there was the September 17 televised appearance of President Saddam Hussein, dressed in a military uniform, during which he declared null and void the Algiers Accord reached on March 6, 1975, ending the struggle between Iraq and Iran. On that fateful day in 1980, the president had that era put to rest. It was the end to the secrecy around events occurring beyond the Iraqi public's eyes and ears. Suddenly, overnight, all the information that had leaked out on the street from soldiers returning from the borders became a bloody reality that spread across all the following days. Even my subsequent academic success was deprived of its joy, and I received my marks as suspect gifts that brought me no delight.

From the opening day of that school semester, which began as usual at the end of June, before the events of the catastrophe floated to the surface, where their brutality could be seen by the naked eye, I sensed that something I could not fathom or describe would definitely occur. It would be more brutal than my mother's illness and more profound than her deep-rooted grief at the loss of my brother Ahmad. I could almost feel the delicacy of its frightening, smooth, effortless advance as it drew closer till it besieged all of us like some giant serpent, depriving us of our vivacity. Teachers—who were at the time an excellent source of news we were not yet allowed to know—whispered to us anxiously:

"The Iranian Army launched an attack yesterday on our borders!"

"The Iranian Army bombarded the cities of Khanaqin, Zurbatiyah, Mandali, and al-Muntheriya."

"They occupied the district of Zain al-Qaws."

"Our government hanged the prominent religious authority Muhammad Baqir al-Sadr!"

"Sitt Najat's son died as a martyr at the borders last night!"

"Iran has closed the air space between it and the Gulf states!"

"Iran will inevitably occupy Iraq in a few days!"

I couldn't share any of this with my family, because any leak that found its way to the ears of government spies—who had sprung up suddenly everywhere, like weeds—no matter how innocent the words were, would wreak havoc on my family. I did not want them to be branded a "fifth column," since that label would easily and quickly send all of them to the gallows, together with all our cousins, even those four times removed, or to life imprisonment without parole. Each whispered comment dug the trench between me and any peace of mind that much deeper. This gap rapidly increased in size till it became a deep ravine, and I could no longer pretend that my day at school had been a regular school day filled only with lessons and learning. No matter how hard I tried to divert my gaze from those whispering mouths, the news issuing from them drew my ears to them. All I could do when I returned home was to climb to my house's roof and begin to whisper to myself what I had heard, trying to liberate myself from those suppurating secrets. Then I would climb back down to pursue my day's chores, while remaining hypervigilant.

President Saddam appeared on the official state television channel, Channel One, with a stern expression, wearing his khaki uniform, in which he always appeared from that day till the end of the war, and in a serious, stentorian voice, commanded the Iraqi Army, almost all of whose legions were stationed on Iraq's borders with Iran: "Combat them, fearless stalwarts!" Everyone took to the streets—not to support the decision to go to war, which had been announced September 22, nor to protest against it. We as a people had no right to reject or accept. We were simply puppets swayed by decisions issuing from the mouth of the government and its president. I, however, attributed the enormous turnout in the streets to the burden that all those secrets had imposed on our breasts, which exploded with a single shout: "With our spirit and blood, we will sacrifice ourselves for you, Saddam!"

At least now, everyone shared the war's news, no matter how brutal it was. Such information was no longer considered the monopoly of one group, and everyone, both men and women, became political analysts. Their commentaries, which were not informed by military expertise but by their imaginations and which totally contradicted views expressed on television, quickly became a way for people to escape the terrifying question that troubled all of us and limited our ability to make predictions. It was what we asked everyone around us once, and ourselves, repeatedly: "What do you suppose will become of us?"

From the beginning of that ninth month of 1980, I was obsessed by a feeling of revulsion—as if a large snake had swallowed me. At every moment of the day, I felt I was nearing its gastric juices, even though I frequently struggled to ignore the viscous sensation. The announcement of this war made me feel disgusted by everything—even myself—but I did not encounter those gelatinous gastric juices of the serpent's digestion until a few days later, in the courtyard of our school.

That day, when the sun should have been shyly sending kisses to our cheeks after suddenly emerging from behind the clouds and leaving us surprised by its beautiful and warm September glow, I woke to find nothing overhead but a thick layer of stale yellowish air. Perhaps the angels had inhaled the kisses before us, leaving behind only exhaust to stifle us. This layer of stale air weighed so heavily on our house that it formed a roof over it. I felt no desire to eat breakfast when I saw it. So, after washing my face with soap and water and brushing my teeth with the banana-flavored toothpaste my father had given me, I put on my school clothes. Then I put my bag on my back; hid it beneath my abaya, which made my bag look like a hump that had suddenly fallen asleep on my back; opened the door gently; and left before my siblings began to wake. (My mother and grandmother had started to take turns walking my siblings to school and bringing them home when I started middle school.)

I walked quickly, attempting to flee from that thick layer of suffocating air, but it soon covered the entire street, and I sensed that it was spying on me, intent on suffocating me. I met several girls who looked just like me in their black abayas, which also hid the humped protrusions on their backs. I felt unable to smile at them as I typically did each morning. I rushed into the school and, as soon as I traversed the corridor from the courtyard to the classrooms, began to tremble, the palms of my hands starting to perspire.

A student approached me when she saw me trembling and asked, "What's wrong with you? Do you have a fever?"

Even my voice shook when I replied, "I don't know. I don't feel right."

"Perhaps you're hungry. I'll buy you a sandwich from the school store," another girl offered.

"No, thanks. I don't feel hungry," I told her in the same quavering voice. I took my seat in the classroom and tried to pull myself together, but my physical tremor affected my spirit. I sorely missed my grandmother, because she alone would have been able to explain what was happening to me.

"Line up!" shouted the class proctor in an unexpectedly loud voice after the bell rang in the courtyard. I filed out with the other students, dragging my body forward as best I could.

A clamor erupted as one student after another asked versions of these vexing questions: "What's happening?" and "Why this sudden roll call?"

Typically, courtyard assemblies occurred only at the end of the week; Thursday morning, to be precise. All the same, every girl took her place in the orderly ranks facing the Iraqi flag on its pole. Our teachers rushed to join us from numerous administrative offices and line up between us and the flag, facing it. When everyone had found her place and silence prevailed, the school principal, Madam Nazanin, who was dressed in a black suit, a white blouse, and a gray jacket, took her place before us.

Then she said, "*As-Salam 'alaykum wa-rahmat Allah wa-barakatahu.* Greetings, my excellent teachers and dear students. I am honored to bring you our sage government's decision, which was announced last night, to close schools for ten days, until our certain victory over the infidel Persians is announced.

"Long live the army! Long live Iraq! Long live the president! Long live the Arab people!

"Now I ask you to go back to your classrooms and prepare immediately to return home. Stay safe."

Even though our Kurdish principal's speech was concise, hearing each word drew me closer to the gastric moment I had imagined. My body started shaking violently, and I fainted and collapsed to the ground. No one around me paid any attention, because everyone was deeply stricken by astonishment, terror, and incredulity.

This was what my antennae had been sensing since I woke that day: ten additional days of home confinement, even though I had repeatedly prayed that God would end summer break quickly so I could return to school. Perhaps some spark was setting fire to my foggy life. I slowly raised my body from the ground once the courtyard had emptied almost completely. Supporting myself with the walls, I entered my classroom.

I sat surveying the other students, many of whom were incredulous about what was happening. How could a war waged on distant borders force the closure of all our schools? One girl, though, was hoping this closure would last for the entire school year. Some other students supported this hope. Then a discussion broke out between those who embraced the closure and those who rejected it. I gained control of myself and pulled my abaya on. I carried my backpack in my hand and departed, walking slowly back to my house, trailed by my disappointment. I wondered: What if the war didn't end in ten days? What would become of me without school?

My return at that hour to our house was anticipated, because my siblings had already arrived there. They looked happy to have ten days added to their summer vacation, which had lasted three whole months. My mother and grandmother, though, did not approve of this idea of closing the schools. They had been counting the days till schools opened and they could get some daily rest while we were at school.

As soon as my father sat down to eat lunch with us, my mother asked, "How far is it from Najaf to Basra?"

"About 440 kilometers," my father replied, swallowing. "Why do you ask?"

She raised another question. "Has the Iranian Army entered Iraq?"

"No. Definitely not. To the contrary, our armed forces will occupy Tehran very soon! Haven't you heard the news? They say the Iranian Army is weak."

My father's voice was filled with pride, and he placed his spoon beside the plate on the mat. I don't know why my father's face at that moment reminded me of the presenter who was on the TV screen so often, so many times every day that we had learned the location of all the blemishes on his face.

"In that case, why are they closing the schools?" she asked him.

"I believe it's a precautionary measure," my father replied. "Nothing more."

Not everyone—including my father—was satisfied with this reply, because we had no way to second-guess the government's decisions, even if they seemed illogical to us. All the same we left the meal, each of us thinking about what might happen during these next ten strange days.

I spent a long time in my grandmother's room with the large wooden box of my grandfather's old books in hopes of finding one that might offer me a prescription, plan, or suggestion to help me survive the days of this war. But I failed. Instead, my search led me to a thick book without a cover. It had crumbling yellowed pages, which had to be turned very carefully. Its title was *The Thousand and One Nights*. At first glance it did not look appealing to me, especially since it was unrelated to our current reality. Once I discovered the tale about Sinbad the Sailor, though, a tale I had almost been raised on, watching the cartoon on television, I felt I was one of the book's characters and fell so madly in love with it that I spent almost all my days reading it. Although its formal literary Arabic proved challenging for me, what mattered was the gist of the story, not its details.

During these ten days, a large change occurred in the tastes of my family—both the adults and the children. My father was only interested now in following on the TV screen news of the movements of the Iraqi troops on the battlefront. If the television presented, instead of war news, a romantic song or an Arab film, no matter how well plotted, instead of watching, my father would search for news on his small battery-powered radio, which he brought with him wherever he sat. *Little House on the Prairie*, a translated foreign serial that my mother and grandmother had watched since the television set entered our house because its family-oriented topics and varied social subplots appealed to them, was replaced by an extremely long Japanese serial subtitled in Arabic called *The Water Margin*. It had so many episodes that it ran almost to the end of the Iran-Iraq War—with its unusual music and the opening phrase, which almost every Iraqi memorized, about a hornless serpent that will grow up to become a dragon. Its hero, Lin Chong, who represented all weak people who struggle for their plundered personal freedom, immediately became a symbol for Iraq as it fought to recover its standing among the peoples of the world. My siblings lost all interest in watching the famous cartoon *Tales of Sinbad the Sailor* and his legendary adventures in famous spots in the dazzling city of Baghdad. Instead, they gathered right at 6:00 p.m. to watch *Manga Sarutobi Sasuke*, the dubbed Japanese anime serial that was nonstop combat and mayhem. Kids in the street, including my siblings, were quick to adopt the clothes and martial arts moves of its young ninja hero, Sasuke.

Ten days sufficed for us to adapt to what had happened, no matter how weighty the change was. We also grew accustomed to the war, which we had been promised would end in ten days, but which didn't. We learned its details, which were televised blow-by-blow during programs like *Pictures from the Battle*. We started to fall asleep to the sound of artillery fire. We woke to the pallid faces of prisoners and to piles of Iranian corpses, which were difficult to distinguish from the bodies of our fighters.

We returned to our classrooms after the school closure, during which almost everything had changed. Instead of our Thursday morning assembly, which we had attended with our teachers and our principal to pledge allegiance to the Iraqi flag, the roll call now began with excerpts from speeches by the president. These were read to us by one of the students, using a microphone. Then the school guard, who now wore a military uniform, would fire foul-smelling rubber bullets ten times into the air. Next a select group of five students, each clad in a khaki blouse and khaki skirt, would salute the flag. Then the middle student would raise that flag carefully while we started to sing the new national anthem, which we had been required to learn by heart. The physical education instructor had given us written and oral exams to help us learn its forty stanzas. Since I knew someone like me would never be chosen to sing this anthem, I only learned the first stanza:

> A fatherland has extended its wings over the
>   horizon,
> And worn the glory of civilizations as its
>   garment;
> Blessed be the land of the Euphrates and Ti-
>   gris Rivers.
> A homeland of glorious determination and
>   tolerance.

While the other students sang its other stanzas, I merely opened and closed my mouth to make the instructor charged with watching our mouths think I had memorized all of it.

Changes at the school were not limited to our salute to the flag. They also applied to the subjects we studied. Some were replaced by others; for example, social studies was replaced with national studies, a course that focused on teaching us the goals of the ruling party. A first-aid section was added to science, and certain topics were deleted from our history books. Maps of Iraq were changed to show new boundaries with Iran, and these changed after almost every battle—especially once President Saddam Hussein announced that our boundaries with Iran were wherever our army was stationed. Even the geography teacher commented on all those different maps on the classroom wall every time she came to teach us.

Once our principal and her assistant began to wear a khaki blouse and a khaki skirt every school day and our teachers stopped using cosmetics on their faces, which grew paler day by day, both my school and our house turned into battlefields I was forced to endure daily. The school was no longer a haven where I could escape from my fear of the unknown. Instead, school became a heavy duty that I forced myself, with difficulty, to fulfill. Bit by bit, the war infiltrated even my dreams.

I raced fearfully through the wasteland alone, with no abaya, wearing my school uniform and well-worn black leather shoes. I stopped suddenly to find everything around me swimming in a sea of red sand. I pirouetted, trying to return to my point of origin—a place vaguely visible on the horizon—a wooden door resembling that of my grandmother's room. But my feet sank into the sand, and I couldn't move. Then I screamed: "Granny, Granny! Save me!"

Suddenly that door opened to reveal a black phantom that heard my voice, raced back inside, and then threw me a long rope, which wound itself around my legs. The phantom began dragging me toward him. Then I started to moan with pain and turned back to see the track I left as he dragged me. The groove almost resembled a furrow in the sand. When I stared ahead again, I saw the rope's end tied to an artillery cannon mounted on a tank. My body was about to crash brutally into that tank.

Then I screamed and found my grandmother waking me. "You're having nightmares again! I seek refuge with God!"

This nightmare recurred throughout the eight years of the war. Each time, at least one small detail would differ. Once, I found myself in the sea. Another time, the phantom pulling me toward him was a bird, which dropped me in a pit with no visible bottom. The one motif that was repeated in all these nightmares was that I was totally alone, without an abaya, wearing black shoes without any heels. I never expected that this nightmare would later actually happen to me—not just once but twice.

Chapter Three

Over time the flame of our enthusiasm died down, and we became preoccupied by winter's cold and our inescapable anxiety and fear. In the afternoon we sat near the tall gray-green neck of our Aladdin kerosene heater—which most Iraqi homes used during the war and the subsequent economic blockade—to seek a little warmth and calm around the afternoon tea tray, a tray that my sisters and I took turns preparing. This stainless-steel tray, however, by then lacked any of its typical *kleicha* pastries and contained only the teapot and glasses with a sprinkling of sugar at the bottom.

The moment the face of the military news presenter appeared on the television screen, we all placed our palms on our cheeks and focused our eyes on him till they were hardly more than pupils, devoid of any gleam. We would cautiously and carefully await the moment his tongue moved to spray our ears with a drizzle of news about our armed forces. He began his broadcast in this manner: "Allahu Akbar and glory to mighty Iraq. God is Almighty and glory to the Arab community. Allahu Akbar and death to the enemies of the people and of the community."

We would listen attentively to every syllable of his report, even though we realized full well that no glory could be hoped for from a war that was waged for dubious reasons, lacked any clear achievements, and had no end in sight. Moreover, we realized that Arab people beyond

Iraq were not involved in this war to any real degree. Instead, in a matter of years, the rulers of the Arab people would consider the Iraqi people to be vicious aggressors who had destroyed their safety valve and torched the gardens of their peace. They would prevent an Iraqi, who had defended the eastern portal of the Arab world with his blood, from setting foot in their countries, if only for a visit. Once this broadcast ended, we would leave the tea circle to perform our various tasks like robots, with zero enthusiasm.

To a frightening degree, as the days of the war passed and became months, home, street, and school became communicating vessels in which the war assumed a uniform level. In each venue, there were the same conversations, news reports, pictures of the president wearing a military uniform, frightened faces, circumspection, and anxiety.

Adnan Shannan was a handsome boy who lived in our district, and his muscular build made him the dream of every girl. His sole ambition in life was to travel and see the world, but this goal quickly evaporated with the advent of the war. Surrounded by his friends, he liked to stand with his foot resting against the wall of the school. Someone seeing him from a distance would think he was engaged in a somber conversation with his buddies. On drawing closer, though, this person would observe that, although Adnan was busy talking, he was intently observing the parade of girls entering our girls-only school. Even though he did not address any of us, he attracted our attention with his very fashionable clothes and the distinctive aroma of his Marlboro cigarette, which never left his mouth while he stood there.

He spoke to almost every girl with his eyes, commenting on her in a way that pleased her. After Adnan shaved off his black hair, which had hung over his broad brow, he looked even more handsome. All the same, we sensed there was some secret reason for this haircut. Some girls suggested that his new look stemmed from Adnan's desire to attract the attention of even more girls. His subsequent, unexpected disappearance easily could have been attributed to any number of reasons had it not been for the raging furnace of the war.

One day, I left school as usual at one, feeling stifled by the tedious repetition of my days, which were all the same drab color. Despite the cold weather, I walked slowly down streets devoid of passersby. The moment I entered our street, I was shocked to see a huge sign attached to a wall. Made of black cloth, it bore an inscription from the Qur'an in large white calligraphy:

> In the name of God, the Compassionate, the Merciful:
> Think not of those slain in God's way as dead. They are alive, finding sustenance in the presence of God Almighty.

It continued:

> The Fatiha will be recited in the Rahbawi Mosque on al-Madina Street at 3:00 p.m. today and the next three days for the spirit of Adnan Shannan, who was martyred in the city of al-Muhammara on the southern front January 11, 1981, defending the nation and the honor of Iraq's three Majidat: chastity, chivalry, and collective action.

My jaw dropped as I tasted again the bitter, disgusting flavor I had experienced when my brother Ahmad died. Death was one reason that had not crossed any girl's mind as an explanation for the absence of a young man whose presence had brightened our gloomy days, which were advancing toward an unknown destiny. I felt the burden of the moment—how could I share this news with my mother or grandmother?

How would I find the courage to tell them that this young man had offered a spark of hope to girls to continue attending school when heavy khaki-colored boots smashed our heads at every moment?

I cloaked myself in silence and exorcised my pain by drawing in one of my old notebooks. I dearly wished that the next day was Friday so I would not need to go to school and see the girls' eyes filled with tears. I wondered secretly if there was some way I might erect a fortress where I could shelter from their infectious weeping. When my father returned from the mosque, my mother and grandmother conducted a small wake. They slapped their chests fiercely, and their tears flowed hot for the loss of this boy my father described as having "seen nothing of life yet."

I wished then that I could ask my father: "Does dying hurt?" No matter how hard I tried, I wasn't able to imagine Adnan's radiant, smiling face contorted in pain by the fingers of death.

After a dark night of pain, morning dawned without a glint of light for me, bringing only a leaden sky and cold weather. Feeling no interest in life, I made my way to school. When I reached the place where Adnan had usually stood, I examined that section of wall carefully. The only difference I noticed was how ordinary it looked—exactly like the rest of the wall. There was nothing at all radiant about it. I realized then that places retain no magic once they're stripped of the people associated with them.

Even though girls entering the school, dressed in the same uniform, did not demonstrate any overt signs of grief, all their smiles had disappeared, and their whispers to each other had vanished into thin air from shock at what had happened.

They, like me, had not become accustomed to this new form of death that had begun to afflict children and young people. Old-fashioned death, as we had known it, was only associated with old or sick people. We could not imagine that the war was tailor-made to achieve this result—to grind up young men and transform memories of them into words on black posters.

Shortly before the school bell rang to announce the beginning of the day, Salima arrived. She was a student known for pestering teachers and other students. She was dressed in black from head to toe. When our teacher entered the classroom and asked why, Salima responded in a low, mournful voice: "My fiancé was martyred yesterday!"

We were all surprised by that. How could she have failed to tell us about her engagement—we shared all our secrets! Once the class ended and our teacher left the room, Salima quickly took her place at the front of the class and chastised us: "I didn't know you were all such cowards. I thought everyone in class would wear black today!" She slammed the classroom door behind her as she left in a rage.

So Salima wasn't actually engaged but had summoned the daring and courage the rest of us lacked to show her sorrow at the loss of someone she loved, even if that meant lying. We had grown accustomed to keeping our emotions, no matter how powerful, secret from other people. Who could pay attention to us when everyone was inevitably confined inside a circle that squeezed us tighter at each moment?

During the war, days passed quickly, and death notices on walls multiplied. We grew accustomed to guessing the name of the deceased martyr even before it was inscribed there. The moment the small white pickup truck entered a street bearing a corpse wrapped in the Iraqi flag and stopped at the door of some house and an officer got out of the cab to knock on the door, one or more of the children would hastily abandon the games they had been playing and scream: "They brought so-and-so home a martyr!"

As days passed, we came to associate death with the pickup truck, the Iraqi flag, and the hoarse voice of a screaming child, as, like poisonous mushrooms and without warning, the names of places we had never heard of before sprouted on those banners: al-Muhammara (Khorramshahr), Azerbaijan, Isfahan, Kirman, Hamadan, Ardabil,

Khorramabad, Saveh, and Qasr-e Shirin. These names became associated with those of our departed young men. When two or more martyrs shared the same name, someone discussing one of them would distinguish him by the place he was martyred, saying, "Sa'd Dezful was one of the bravest soldiers, and Sa'd Khorramshahr was a fine fellow with no moral defects!"

Each of these posters acquired a sacred status with people the moment it was pasted to a wall. No one would take it down till time's hands had damaged it, the changing weather had turned it into a worn-out scrap with an illegible message, and its black color had faded to a pale lavender.

Martyrs' mothers were regarded differently by different people. Some considered a martyr's mother a patient woman who deserved respect for bearing a courageous hero whose intercession would certainly benefit her on Resurrection Day, when she would doubtless enter paradise. Others saw her as a woman whose child had been stolen from her and needed to be consoled, no matter what.

That continued to be true until avarice afflicted hearts when a law was enacted to compensate a martyr's family with a two-hundred-square-meter tract of land, an automobile, and a sum of money. At that time, families of martyrs lost their distinguished status in society and were viewed as people who had traded the blood of their son for a vehicle!

A martyr's wife then became the most sought-after wife—no matter how many children she had from her deceased husband or how old she was—because of the material goods awarded to her by this same decree.

Overnight, mosques large and small in our district became crowded with mourners because funerals were conducted twice a day, in the same place. These ceremonies, which were attended only by men, involved escorting the body to the mosque, where a funeral prayer was performed. The first funeral service was at 3:00 p.m., and the second came directly after the sunset prayer service.

Women's mourning rituals were conducted in the martyr's home, where women beat their chests and wailed nonstop till nightfall. Within a year of the start of the war, we became used to seeing funeral processions for martyrs either on the television or in real life. Not a day of the week passed without our waking to the scream of a woman. That would be followed by a wake that might last more than three days. Eventually black became the color of our school uniform and was worn by teachers and students who had lost one male relative, if not more.

My mother's female relatives, who had previously faulted her for repeatedly bearing daughters, now began to envy her, believing, incorrectly, that she would never see a son participate in this war and that no male child of hers would experience fear in the trenches, no matter how long the war lasted. Whenever my paternal aunt, who had six sons, visited my mother, she would express her envy with no embarrassment: "You are really lucky! No son of yours will set foot on a battlefield!"

My mother always ignored her and smiled, which infuriated my aunt. But one day, my aunt addressed her remarks to my grandmother: "Umm Ghayib, you are the luckiest woman of all. You have never had to worry about a *ghayib*, an unborn son, or weep sorrowfully for his loss."

My grandmother was angered by this woman's impertinent remarks and immediately decided to restrict her circle of grief and anxiety to current events, especially since each of the men in her immediate life had long rested his head on a mound of moist earth and his body was now concealed by some cemetery. So she rose at once and left the group to seclude herself in her own room, which she left only to bathe, to perform her ablutions before she prayed, or to answer the call of nature. Even at mealtimes, she no longer joined us around the mat. Instead, she ate alone while listening to radio broadcasts of Shaykh Abd al-Basit Abd al-Samad reciting *surahs* of the Holy Qur'an. She soon delegated to my father the task of picking up her monthly pension and purchasing her medicine and other daily necessities. If my mother wanted her to watch my younger siblings or to care for them while she did housework, she would need to bring those children to my grandmother's room.

My siblings—no matter how they surpassed their fellow pupils at school—never earned the awards that were presented to pupils like me before the war. Those awards had been braided by hand from three thin strands, each different color representing a different quality. The school principal or head teacher would pin these cords to the chest of the pupil during the flag-raising ceremony on Thursdays as a recognition of distinction: the red cord for scholastic achievement, the green cord for exemplary comportment, and the white cord for personal hygiene. But these were replaced by a single cord that was attached to the chests of pupils and students of different grade levels to honor Martyrs Day, which became an official commemoration that was celebrated the first of December every year.

It was not long before the chests of most Iraqi civilians were also adorned, especially those of civil servants in government offices, in recognition of their sad ties to death and to hostile treachery. They received the martyrs badge: a round medal depicting the two greenish-turquoise half domes of al-Shaheed Monument, which was designed by the Iraqi sculptor and painter Ismail Fatah al-Turk, executed by the architect Saman Kamal, and erected in al-Rusafa in Baghdad. Written in black beneath the domes, between which a rose appears, is the phrase: "Martyrs are the most noble of us all." Attribution of this phrase is uncertain, although throughout the war it was credited to the president.

This martyr's medallion commemorated the battle of Bisaitin (also known as Bostan, Khuzestan), which happened near the southern Iraqi city of Basra in 1981, after the Iraqi Army invaded Iran. A friend who fought in this battle, who had forgotten the meaning of "sleep," and who never knew what any day's ration would be, told me about it through a haze of cigarette smoke. This was true, even though "luck had favored" him—as he remarked sarcastically.

He said: "Our armored brigade—number twenty-six of the Fifth Mechanized Division—clashed with the Iranians in a ferocious battle October 28 and 29. At first, the Iranian Army suffered large losses of men and material. But some of their brigades quickly turned back to encircle and besiege us. Despite our fierce opposition, we were eventually taken captive: both our soldiers and officers. The Iranian Army did not merely torture us after our capture; they killed three thousand of our soldiers and deliberately released some of us to carry to the rest of the Iraqi Army news that the city of Bisaitin had fallen into the hands of the Iranian Army. Those of us who escaped, thanks to this treachery, were burdened, through no will of our own, with conveying this barbaric message, and we became known as 'crows,' because we had returned with such an ominous message."

To encourage his troops to continue fighting battles when soldiers slept in trenches or military barracks before becoming corpses shredded by artillery fire or crushed under the wheels of tanks, President Saddam devised for them what were called "badges" and "decorations." With lightning speed, there appeared a Badge of Honor, a Badge for the Mother of All Battles, a Badge for High Merit, as well as the Decoration of al-Qadisiyah, the Martyr's Decoration, the Party's Insignia, and the Mother of All Battles Insignia, together with other decorations and badges that adorned the chests of soldiers before they were punctured by bullets. Those decorations and badges were once distributed in the trenches of death, amid the rattle of artillery shelling and incoming live fire. On one occasion, during a semi-official celebration, in closed chambers, after troops returned on leave from the battles in which they had fought and came back whole or missing a limb, their lost limbs were replaced with artificial ones.

My father never dreamt of receiving a decoration or one of those badges. Instead, his dream was to obtain his own house, because he had become exhausted by his hard work at night, toiling almost till morning, only to leave our house again shortly thereafter for his day job, which lasted till three in the afternoon, if not longer. I don't know which job exhausted my father more and aged him prematurely, but his hair turned snow white and all his teeth fell out before he turned fifty. Or was it the war, which they had misrepresented to us, saying in September 1980 it would end in no more than ten days, when we were now almost at the end of its second year?

Perhaps he was overwhelmed by the responsibility of supporting his family, which, including my grandmother, now consisted of ten individuals. Was it, perhaps, my mother's health, which we celebrated when it stabilized for a day only to be surprised the next day to find that it had deteriorated at an amazing speed? She suffered from asthma attacks and had difficulty breathing without the presence of a nebulizer—the misting device that rarely left her hand. Her weak heart had required her to take medicine for rheumatism since she was a girl. We praised God whenever we woke and found her still alive and breathing.

I felt sad when I looked at my father's hair, which had turned white so quickly, as if every crisis or problem he experienced had left a trace there. If I asked him to dye his hair, he would refuse, laughing as he said, "Your mother loves to see I'm clearly older than she is!"

If my mother heard us, she would say, "You always were older."

Their conversation would then lead them to specify the day, month, and year when each was born. Their discussion might also drift to events that had occurred the day of their wedding; then I would feel embarrassed and leave them alone to enjoy the pleasure of recalling that day.

So I was astonished when my father returned from his day job carrying a white bag that contained a bottle of black hair dye. I thought, at first, he had purchased it for my mother but immediately saw that his short hair was dark again. Once he finished shaving, he stood before me and said, "You've been waiting for this day impatiently for years. I owe my more youthful appearance to you!"

Then he dressed and left the house looking both delighted and apprehensive.

My father returned at eight that evening with a cylindrical container wrapped with colored paper. The moment he opened the door with his key, all my siblings ran to find out what he had in that package.

My father handed it to my sister, who started to open it. Then he protested and asked her to take it to our mother's room and wait till everyone assembled there, including my grandmother. Clearly my father was about to tell us something important.

When my sister went to invite my grandmother, she initially refused to come to my mother's room. So my father went and persuaded her, almost whispering. Then we all clustered around my father, who summarized the situation in the following way.

He said he was one of the employees of state agencies whom the government had chosen to receive a housing unit in a group of apartment blocks three stories high. These had been constructed by foreign companies in the region between al-Amir District and al-'Adala District. The rolled-up document was the deed to the unit to which we would move in a month's time.

Everyone shouted with joy at hearing this news. We would finally have our own house, and no one would force us to leave it. That was even true after he told us that our apartment was on the second floor and had only three bedrooms. That news did not diminish our delight, because ever since we were kids, we had shared a room.

I postponed my celebration, did not allow my imagination to become too involved in picturing this apartment, the buildings, or neighborhoods around it, or even ask the name of the place where that apartment was located, because I was trying to concentrate on diploma exams for the third year of middle school, and they were set to begin in a few days. I had never confronted examinations like these before; this time I had to cope with six difficult tests separated by only two days.

The first examination covered Arabic grammar and the principles of Islam. The second was in English. The third test was in social sciences, including geography, history, and Iraqi nationalism. The fourth was in math and covered both algebra and geometry. The fifth exam was in life sciences—in other words, biology. The sixth and final examination covered both physics and chemistry. These exams were considered major challenges for middle school students and forced us to study diligently, concentrate, and memorize. This set of exams usually began the first day of the seventh month of the calendar year.

Even though the weather was hot, I did not leave the large examination hall, which had only a few air conditioners that failed to cool the room, because I wanted to make sure I answered all the questions!

The days of this examination period were filled with moments of fear, anxiety, tears, and occasionally regret and ended with a deep sleep that lasted from the moment I returned from school each noon until the next afternoon.

A week after the examinations concluded, my father asked me to start packing our stuff into cardboard boxes he had purchased from a grocer. Next, I was to clean our current house thoroughly. Finally, he asked me and my sister Layla to accompany him to our new apartment to clean it.

After he returned from his morning job, my father hailed a taxi to take us through streets I had never seen before: clean streets with large houses that had low walls, most of which enclosed one or more palm trees. There were many modern-style government buildings, most of them painted beige or white, and large stores with their names illuminated with lights that burned even during the day.

When I saw these streets and houses, I sensed that we had not been living in houses, as I had imagined, but had been buried inside ruins we cavalierly referred to as homes. When the taxi stopped, my father handed the driver the fare accompanied by a smile, and we climbed out. Then my father pointed to the other side of the street, planted entirely with eucalyptus trees, which remained green all year long. He told us: "Our apartment is number nine in building thirteen. It's the first building in these housing estates."

We quickly made our way through that nearly vacant neighborhood in the center of which was a brick column with a sign that read: **Neighborhood of Residential Apartments**. I was enchanted by the quiet of the place and the similarity of its buildings, which were all painted light orange and beige. As soon as we reached building number 13, we found in its lobby six mailboxes that bore the number of each apartment. My father gave me the key for box 9, and I opened it. Even though my hand discovered only air inside, I felt that this mailbox would soon become my means of contacting a broader world than my eyes had ever seen.

My father calmly started up the building's marble staircase while grasping its polished wooden railing. My sister and I followed him. After climbing twelve steps, we found a small metal window on our left. My father pulled it open to show us how to drop bags of trash through it, down to a trash collection room on the ground floor. On our right stood a thick wooden door, which my father opened with a golden key that looked larger to me than ordinary ones. We entered a space that reminded me, through its design, of ones we saw on TV—even though the apartment consisted of only three bedrooms and one living room, which we referred to as a salon or parlor.

All the same, the apartment's five wide windows and the large balcony overlooking the street made it seem much bigger than the house we were living in. It did not take us long to clean that apartment. We merely had to wipe the windowpanes with damp wads of the newspapers with which my father had covered the floor to protect it from splatters of paint and white putty.

My father entrusted the windows to me and my sister while he washed down the tile floors of the bedrooms and the parlor with liquid soap, with which he had filled a new bucket he had bought for this purpose. The bathroom and the WC, which were covered with white ceramic tile, merely needed a wipe-down, which my sister and I performed as well.

After we finished cleaning the apartment and returned to our old house, I raced—without even changing out of my dirty work clothes—to tell my grandmother everything I had seen. My sister rushed to inform our mother about that too. My father, for his part, changed and quickly plopped in bed, where he fell fast asleep.

In not too many days, we left our old house by night, without telling our neighbors we were moving, because most of them didn't understand living in apartments, especially not in this type of residential community, which wasn't common in Najaf. Our new community was the first of its kind to be built there. Our neighbors would have thought apartment residents lacked privacy. Some of our neighbors even believed that the very design of these three-story apartments risked the reputation of all residents of the building.

Three days later, my father returned one morning at ten with a telecommunications worker to install a telephone in our apartment. The minute my father left with that worker, my siblings immediately started trying out the gray phone and playing with its round dial with black numbers. They all burst into laughter whenever they heard the dial tone and took turns lifting the receiver to listen to it. This game continued almost every day until my father found out about it and installed a wooden shelf his own height on the wall. He placed the phone there so my young siblings could not reach it.

That phone rang for the first time a month after it was installed, surprising my siblings while I raced to lift the receiver. I heard my father's voice tell me to put on my best clothes and prepare to head with him to my school for something important. I quickly replaced the receiver and told my mother what my father had said. Only ten minutes after I changed my clothes, my father returned, and we went together to the school in a taxi.

I entered the principal's office, which was crowded with students from the third year, waiting anxiously and fearfully for the results of the baccalaureate examinations. My father stood calmly outside. When I entered the office, I greeted all the students I knew in a low voice, and in only moments they transmitted to me their infectious anxiety and fear.

When my father noticed that, he came and drew me outside gently by my arm and reassured me about my results, which the principal had shared with him that morning, when she herself submitted the results for her school to the education office, where he worked.

The principal called out my name while I was conversing with my father. He smiled encouragingly at me and said, "Go! Good news, God willing!"

I made my way between the other students who were waiting in the office. I stood before the principal, her assistant, and the school janitor, who held a plastic sack almost full of paper currency in different denominations.

Looking at me and addressing me in a loud voice, the principal said, "Congratulations, Faleeha. You are in the top ten." Smiling, she added, "You need to buy yourself a nice treat." Then she nodded to Umm Muhammad, who immediately opened the bag of money and said, "May you enjoy goodness and blessings!"

I felt nervous as I held out my hand to the principal to receive my results, which were on a glossy sheet of white pasteboard slightly larger than the report cards we received in earlier grades. The marks were recorded in boxes, each of which contained the name of the subject matter and the result of the exam, followed by our principal's large and distinctive signature.

I could barely force myself to utter, "Thank you, Madam Nazanin."

Then I headed to Umm Muhammad, saying, "I'll get your present from my father." I raced to find my father standing right outside the door and told him what had happened. He reached into his pocket, brought out his wallet, and gave me some money—I did not check how much. Then I ran back to Umm Muhammad and handed her this tip as she was telling another student: "May you enjoy goodness and blessings!"

My father's happiness was visible on his face, and he spoke proudly when he discussed me with some other fathers who had accompanied their daughters. He said that I hadn't slept during the exam week and would be the first woman from our entire tribe to enter the Teacher Training Institute. I felt glum, though, when I heard my father mention the Teacher Training Institute.

As we left the school, walking side by side, I said to my father, "I don't want to attend the Teacher Training Institute. I want to enroll in preparatory school and the university after that."

He replied calmly, "Nothing can be guaranteed during this war, and I want to take credit for the results of my effort and exertion. My dream is for you to become a teacher!"

We returned home in another taxi, and my younger sister met us at the door. When my father informed her that I had passed with honors, she raced inside to tell my mother, who brought out a bag of *jalkeet* sweets wrapped in cellophane, opened it, and poured them over my head. My siblings were delighted and jostled each other as they picked candies off the floor. Everyone seemed happy then, even my grandmother, who joined us and embraced me, saying, "You deserve to have *gold* scattered over your head!"

I freed myself from her hands, raced to our room, and closed the door behind me nervously. My mother and grandmother were astonished, but before they could wonder aloud to each other about my strange behavior, my father told them I didn't want to enter the Teacher Training Institute.

I said nothing about this topic for many days, but my father was forced to raise it again when he brought home the continuation-of-studies form, on which I was asked to fill in all the blank spaces, starting with my first choice, which was the most important, down to my last choice. Based on this form, I would be assigned to an institute or a preparatory school, although my adjusted average would also be considered.

I listened carefully to my father's lofty words, which he had repeated time and again to me. He wished, for example, to boast to his cousins that I was the first of all the female members of our tribe to become a teacher. Had his circumstances permitted, he would have liked to be a teacher. Since I wasn't convinced by anything he said, I held my tongue.

Shortly before the appointed day for the form to be submitted to the school system, my mother came to me, sat down beside me, and asked me, "If you don't want to enter the institute, what do you want to become once you complete preparatory school?"

"I don't know!" I said. My confusion was obvious. Despite my rebellion and my rejection of my father's decision for me to enter the institute, I did not have any real or pressing desire to enter preparatory school. I was rejecting the fact that my father had made this decision.

"Where is the form?" I asked my mother, who had risen to head to the kitchen after growing tired of my silence. I followed her there calmly.

"In our room, in the top drawer of the . . ."

I raced to my parents' room before I heard all of the sentence. I removed the form from its place and picked up a blue ballpoint pen from the same drawer. Then I began to fill it out. I wrote "Teacher Training Institute" in large clear letters and left "preparatory school" for the last slot, where I inscribed it in small indistinct letters.

My father took charge of submitting this form to the principal, who had also objected to my enrolling in the Teacher Training Institute. My father, though, had ignored her objection. Instead, he gathered all the information he could about the institute: its address, the uniform students were required to wear, the names of its principal and of the teachers who would instruct me, the amount of money I would be obliged to pay the driver of the bus that I would take to and from the institute, and the time I was to wait for this bus every day, and where it would stop.

My father accompanied me to the institute on my first day. While we waited for the public bus at seven in the morning, a girl approximately my age was waiting for that same bus. She was slightly taller than me, wore her abaya exactly the way I did mine, and had light skin. My father sat in the row right behind us, so we two girls could sit together. He was just as happy as I was when he saw this girl get off at the same place we did and head to the entrance of the institute.

When I returned home at three that afternoon, I informed everyone how proud I had been when I entered the institute; how beautiful the Hanana District, where the institute was located, was; and how grand its old-style buildings were. I also told them about the color and cut of our uniforms, which we had been told would be delivered to us in a few weeks.

The enthusiasm with which I recounted all this information made it difficult for anyone who heard me now to believe how vehemently I had rejected and rebelled against my father for suggesting I should enter that institute.

My father was content to ask me just one question: "Did you learn the name of that girl who rode the bus with us in the morning?"

"Yes, her name is Maysun Hasan Kamouneh," I told him.

"Try to make friends with her," my mother suggested.

Maysun made a forceful entrance into my life. She differed from all the girls I had known before. Her smile never left her face, not even in the darkest moments, even as she scoffed at news of the war. It had never occurred to her that the war would ever affect a member of her family, since she was the pampered middle child of a wealthy, aristocratic family who lived in the very large house with a wall that ran the length of the street opposite the apartment complex. Her father sold watches and antiquities, her mother was a housewife of Aryan heritage, and her older sister was a teacher in a preparatory technical school for boys.

Our friendship took root quickly and evolved to link our respective families. It became routine for our conversations on the telephone to last for hours and hours—even about trivial things we had seen at the institute. Maysun frequently asked my mother to provide recipes for dishes she had eaten with us. Then she would surprise her mother by preparing those same dishes for her.

My mother was happy to oblige and would stand for long periods holding the receiver while dictating to Maysun a recipe. If Maysun's parents were going away for a night or longer, she would sleep over with us on one of the black leather sofas my father had bought for the living room on an installment plan and that we all went to pains to keep clean, reserving them for guests.

My favorite moment was leaving home in the morning and standing at the stop early, waiting for the bus, while watching for Maysun. Once we wished each other a good morning, she would begin relating the latest incident that had happened to her with her paternal cousin, who was a wealthy merchant and never stopped asking to marry her. She, for her part, took great pleasure in rejecting his repeated requests, even though each rejection stirred up a storm of familial anger that lasted for days and at times for months. I was dumbfounded by these accounts, which were beyond my wildest dreams.

"Would you like to accompany me to Baghdad next Friday?" Maysun asked me one day after we wished each other good morning.

"What? Me go to Baghdad with you? I don't know. I've only traveled on school trips with other girls to rural regions of Meshkhab in Najaf Governorate. I doubt my family will agree."

I did not sleep that night. Instead, I experienced daydreams of adventures that left traces of fatigue on my face the next morning. Maysun said, as soon as she saw me, "You must take a long nap when you return from school. I don't want to hear you snore on the bus!"

I retorted angrily, "First of all, I don't snore when I sleep. Secondly, what bus are you talking about? My family will never agree to my going to Baghdad—especially not my father!"

"We shall see!" Maysun exclaimed as we climbed onto the city bus. That was all she said till we returned home from the institute.

At five that evening, I was sitting glumly with my grandmother and siblings, listening to news about the war on its various fronts, which had increased in number till they included almost all the borders of Iraq. Then I heard knocking on the door and assumed it was Maysun, since she was the only person I knew who did not use the doorbell when she came to visit us.

When I opened the door and inquired why she had come so late, she smiled and asked, "Is Uncle Abu Falah here?"

"Yes," I told her.

"Then call him," she replied swiftly.

I went to tell my father in his room while I prayed to God that the evening would end well. My father liked Maysun and trusted her but would definitely not allow me to travel with her to Baghdad.

Maysun greeted my father very calmly and then approached to whisper a few words to him. He left our apartment swiftly after slipping on his leather sandals. Maysun entered the living room, sat down with me on the sofa, and began gazing at me provocatively without uttering a word—thus forcing me to guess what was happening. When one of my siblings came out to ask for my father, Maysun quickly told him, "He'll be right back!"

I disapproved of her abrupt reply to my younger brother, her avoidance of speaking to me, and the way she was letting me experience this troubling silence. My anxiety increased when my father's absence lasted for more than fifteen minutes. I rose then, opened the apartment door, and looked down the staircase for him. Once I heard his footsteps begin ascending, I quickly retreated inside, closing the door after me, and sat down beside Maysun, who had begun to laugh out loud.

I opened the door for my father when I heard the doorbell. He immediately began to address Maysun: "If Faleeha goes with you to the beauty parlor, don't try to convince her to dye her hair. Her black hair is very pretty with its brown sheen."

"No. Of course not. Thank you, Uncle!" Maysun replied, smiling broadly.

"What's happening? What beauty parlor are you talking about?" I asked.

"You mean she doesn't know about your plan? What a cunning girl you are!" my father said, looking at Maysun and laughing.

She stopped smiling and asked me to change my clothes quickly, since her father was waiting for us in his car down on the street. I hastily did. Before we departed, my father told us, "Don't be late. You need to go to bed soon so you can wake up early for the trip."

My tongue was tied at that moment, and I could not say even one word to him. I simply looked him straight in the eye so he could see how indescribably happy I felt.

We raced down the stairs, holding back our laughter until we reached Maysun's father's automobile. He was a short, thin man with a fair face, which I had never seen frown—not even on the day that he and some companions had been miraculously liberated by the police from captivity by a gang that had attempted to burglarize his house, tying up everyone and gagging their mouths, after killing the guard dog with poisoned meat.

When we reached the car, we burst out in giggles that infected Maysun's father too. He began to laugh, even without asking us what we were laughing about. Once Maysun calmed down, she began telling me how she'd told her father to convince mine to allow me to travel with them to Baghdad the next day.

◆ ◆ ◆

In the beauty parlor, Maysun sat in the beautician's large chair while her hair was washed and dyed. Approximately half an hour later it had turned as blond as rays of sunshine. Unlike her, I was entranced by the look of the place and the seductive yet solid appearance of its feminine products and appliances.

That was the only time in my entire life I entered a beauty parlor, with one exception: when I lost, by theft, the only memento that linked me to a boyfriend who was killed on borders we mistakenly assumed were ours. It was a wristwatch he had given me as a present for the holy Eid al-Fitr holiday.

Baghdad, where even Sinbad the Sailor could not describe the scent of its streets and the essence of what he found there, surprised me as soon as we entered its city limits. A billboard read: **BAGHDAD WELCOMES YOU**. I removed my abaya and felt, as I walked bareheaded along its streets, like a bird—with giant, invisible wings—that had just stepped out of the shadows.

Even though we seemed to be walking aimlessly down the war's dark, apparently endless tunnel, my friendship with Maysun afforded me a glimmer of light that allowed me to imagine myself as a girl whose dreams deserved to be realized.

That academic year saw me, Maysun, and almost all of my siblings succeed. No one was held back, except my sister Layla, to whom luck did not award success on the physics exam for the second year of middle school the first time she took it. She then refused categorically to retake the exam in that subject in the second round, as was required!

When my relatives heard she had quit school, they visited us more frequently and expressed their affection for her and for our family, out of a desire to marry her. The relative who came most frequently was a paternal aunt who kept visiting us over a period of three months, dragging with her one of her sons, on some excuse or other. Once she had exhausted all her excuses, she surprised my father one evening by saying, "I have come today to ask your consent for your daughter Layla to marry my son Hamid!"

Before leaving his seat, my father replied nervously, "Does this mean that all your visits to us were on account of Layla? She is merely a child. Don't fill her head with such ideas."

Even my mother vehemently rejected the idea of my sister marrying. My grandmother remained silent, but my aunt didn't let up until my father had turned down her request dozens of times.

One afternoon my father returned with a cloth backpack. When he saw us looking at this pack, he quickly hid it behind his bed. That evening he brought it out and began to try on the military garments inside it.

My mother collapsed when she saw my father nonchalantly try on the army belt, boots, and beret. She started throwing up right where she was sitting. My father and I rushed to her, picked her up from under her arms, and quickly carried her to the bathroom. My father washed her face with tap water. I returned to where she had been sitting on the floor and began to clean it with a damp cloth soaked with detergent. After my father brought her back to the bedroom, I helped her change out of her dirty clothes and then brought her a mug of hot lemonade.

My mother drank it in little sips as she gazed at that pack disgustedly and spitefully. So my father was obliged to take off his uniform, which had some of my mother's vomit on it, and put it back—ignoring the vomit—inside the pack, which he set aside. Only then did I realize how much my father and mother hated this damn war, which wasn't even worth cleaning off vomit from a uniform.

Once my mother had calmed down, my father contacted my aunt and asked her to visit us to discuss something important. She came with winged heels. Then he broached with my mother and my aunt the details of my sister's marriage, which was conditional on her consent.

At first, I was surprised by my father's retraction of his prior adamant refusal. When I thought longer about it, I realized that he was trying to reassure himself about the fate of at least one of his daughters before he went off to fight in the war as a member of the People's Army and get killed on one of the war's fronts.

Their engagement lasted a month while my mother and aunt prepared the bride. When my sister descended the staircase of our apartment building, swaying in a wedding dress with a long train, she resembled a plump white dove.

We all tried hard to appear happy that day, after convincing ourselves that the war was not going to end, that its furnace was inescapable, and that eventually it would destroy us all. What was strange, then, about us claiming a little break from it for our festivities? That happiness was expressed in trilling, singing, and dancing that lasted all night long.

The next morning the bridegroom asked me to come to their room and sit with them by the breakfast mat and encourage my sister to eat, since she was too embarrassed to eat in his presence. I did; they seemed to me, when I saw them both eat shyly, to be two children playing at being happy, oblivious to the times.

Layla had just turned fifteen, and Hamid was only three years older. They were kids, and the war had forced them to abandon their dreams and suffocate themselves in a matrimonial cage.

My father did not attend my sister's marriage ceremonies because he was scheduled for military training. My grandmother refused to attend simply because she did not care to see my aunt. She merely blessed the marriage by sending some presents. My mother and I returned from my aunt's house with my other siblings four days later to find Maysun waiting for me—eager to hear all about this unexpected marriage.

My sister's new husband was off to fight on Iraq's northern border. At the end of the ten-day leave granted to him, he returned to his unit, even while hoping to obtain a longer matrimonial leave. He departed in the morning, accompanied by his younger brother, after saying goodbye to his family and wife. When the two brothers passed the door of the district's blacksmith, Hamid noticed a metal grill designed to be placed over the grave of a martyr and advised his brother: "Tell Mom I want a lattice like this placed over my grave. Don't let them put anything else there."

After he said this, he left his brother, who was astonished by the unusual nature of this request, and boarded a bus that would take him to Najaf's northern bus terminal. From there he would take another bus to al-Nahda terminal in Baghdad and then board a third bus that would take him to Sulaymaniyah. A month later, nothing remained of him but burnt fragments after some Kurd, or what were called insurgents, blew up the truck he was driving and caused it to fall, engulfed in flames, down one of the valleys there.

The evening my father returned from his training exercises with the People's Army, he was too exhausted to eat dinner. He simply changed out of his uniform and bathed. Then my mother, my siblings, and I sat on the floor around his feet, which he had stretched out on the floor, and listened to his tales of the training camp. He did not begin, the way he had always done, with a comical story that would make us laugh or smile. Instead, uncharacteristically, he said, "I have a bitter taste in my throat and don't know why!"

My mother quickly asked him, "Have you been taking your medicine for diabetes?"

"Yes. The bitterness I've been tasting since this morning isn't related to any physical ailment. I have a premonition that something is about to happen!"

"Won't you stop scaring us?" my mother asked angrily. "Since you put on that khaki uniform, you have only talked about death!"

My father replied, almost shouting rather than in a normal tone of voice, "You speak to me as though I had donned this khaki uniform willingly instead of being forced to. Now you see how—when my vision in one eye has weakened and I've lost all my teeth because of diabetes—they have compelled me to enlist in the People's Army."

We children were all surprised by what was happening and looked at each other in amazement. We had never seen our parents quarrel before.

My father had never been able to fall asleep without first placing his head on my mother's bosom for her to caress his hair gently until he fell asleep. He would also never feel satiated unless my mother offered him a dish that she had made herself. Then he would tell her, "Your cooking makes me feel fine."

We thought it odd that they would continue to quarrel about a matter that was clearly beyond their control, because the war and his enlistment in the People's Army were decisions neither of them had made and that neither of them could change or protest.

Before their discussion grew more heated, the telephone in the parlor rang, and my father nodded for me to answer it. When I picked up the receiver, I heard a familiar voice—which was so hoarse from screaming and crying that I had difficulty identifying it: "Is Hassan there? Tell him they've brought back Hamid's body!"

The line immediately went dead. I was terrified and spent a few moments trying to identify the caller. Once I realized it had been my aunt, I returned to the room where everyone was sitting and stopped at the door, trying to collect my wits. I don't know why I chose the words I did to tell my father then, "My aunt wants you to come to her now."

"Why? Good news, God willing. Is your sister okay?" my mother asked.

"Yes. She's fine."

"What does she want from me at this hour?" my father said as he attempted to retract his legs. Then he stood up with difficulty. "One of her children has definitely caused a problem with the neighbors."

I went to my grandmother's room to fetch my abaya. Then I returned to tell my father, "I'll go with you." My mother did not object, so I descended to the building's lobby to wait for my father, who joined me there after donning a dishdasha, a white headcloth, and black leather sandals.

Once we were a short distance from our building, I looked back to make sure my mother wasn't watching us from a window. When I was certain of that, I drew a little closer to my father and told him in a low voice—as if I were afraid, even though we were some distance from my family, they would hear this horrible news: "Hamid has died a martyr!"

"Hamid?" My father stopped. "Which Hamid?" he asked me anxiously.

"Hamid, the husband of my . . ."

I had not finished my sentence before my father sat down on the sidewalk. He was too shocked for his feet to support him. Then he stood up slowly, pushing himself up with his arms. He flagged down a taxi and climbed in the front seat while I sat in back, directly behind my father.

"Police District!" my father told the driver and handed him the fare, even before the driver had restarted the engine. It shot off down streets covered in darkness, because even the streetlights had been painted black and were not powerful enough to light the massed darkness.

We drove along streets that were empty except for a few cats and the stray dogs we saw in packs rummaging through mounds of garbage. Some of these dogs tried to hide quickly from the taxi's high beams, which had accidentally discovered them.

Once we reached my aunt's street, we saw a pickup truck, with two military officers in the cab, parked directly in front of her house. The coffin, which was covered with the Iraqi flag, was in the bed of the pickup. Two women were hugging the coffin—one silently and the other wailing fiercely and audibly. Some neighbors stood beside the truck as if examining its contents cautiously.

My father opened the door of the taxi before it came to a complete stop and raced off. He had barely put his foot on the ground when he fell, stumbling over a large stone that had been placed on the sidewalk.

The silent woman broke free of the coffin and ran toward my father, bawling at the top of her lungs. Then she fell, motionless, at my father's feet. When one of the officers noticed my father's plight, confusion, and inability to carry my sister, who had fainted on the pavement, he quickly left the truck to help my father lift her from the ground. He took one of her arms, and my father lifted her by the other. I raced to pull her abaya over her head and helped walk her into the house, where she sat down in a bedroom, oblivious to everything around her.

My father and the officer then hurried out of the house and stopped near my aunt, who was still wailing ferociously. I followed the two men outside, unconsciously, like a sleepwalker, trying to comprehend what was happening, since all these events far exceeded my powers of imagination.

I never could have imagined, even for an instant, that a child as young as my sister would become a martyr's widow only a month after her marriage. I asked myself whether we had been predestined to confront this tragedy so brutal that it would never be erased—but had no answer.

The officer quickly told my father in a professional voice devoid of emotion: "My condolences, Uncle. Hamid was a true hero. I observed his chivalry and courage. We became friends the day I transferred to his brigade. May God help you bear his loss!"

My father had difficulty holding back his tears, and the only response I heard him make to the officer was: "What God wills is inescapable!"

"Yes, by God," the officer replied in the same tone. Then he proffered some official documents to my father, asking him to sign them, after designating my father as the deceased's next of kin and thus responsible for receiving the remains of his sister's martyred son. My aunt had been a widow for many years, and neither of her older sons was present to sign those papers. In fact, they were also fighting, just on other fronts.

My father helped the two officers unload the coffin from the truck and place it on the ground. One of them suggested to my father to make haste to wash the corpse, shroud it, and bury it, since it was entirely charred.

My aunt, though, insisted on bringing the coffin into her house and continued to hug it, keening till dawn. Once the sun rose, my father took charge of the corpse together with some local men. They took it to a corpse-washing station, which is known in Iraq as a *mgheesil*, the one located at the entrance to the Wadi al-Salam Cemetery. After the corpse had been washed and shrouded, a large number of men joined the funeral procession behind them and took turns as pallbearers, resting the body on a shoulder and chanting loudly: "I testify that there is no god but God" and "Allahu Akbar!"

After he was buried in Wadi al-Salam Cemetery beside his father's grave, those men headed to the grand mosque of Najaf to conduct the rites of the Fatiha for the martyr.

Following the afternoon prayer, my mother, who was dressed entirely in black, accompanied by my father, entered my aunt's room, which was filled with women who joined her in beating their chests and weeping for her little boy. When those women noticed my father, they left, one by one, to allow other rites of mourning that were even more fiery and bitter to occur. I watched my sick mother, my father, and my aunt beat their heads ferociously for the sake of a youth who had spent only ten days of his honeymoon with his bride.

My sister Layla was not capable of joining these obsequies. She woke the day after the funeral with hemiplegia.

Chapter Four

The morning my sister returned to our residence, she looked nothing like she had when she left home less than two months earlier. The bride, who had sashayed in a long white dress like a legendary princess who had just stepped out of some children's story, was now totally broken, clad all in black, with eyes that had lost their luster from many showers of tears and a mouth that was partially paralyzed. I don't know how she managed to climb the stairs of our apartment building, but I feel sure someone must have helped her, because her partially paralyzed body would not have been able to climb to the second story unassisted.

I, for my part, returned to the institute after an absence that lasted for the period when prayers were being said for the spirit of my sister's martyred husband. Once the other students saw me clad in black, they raced first to console me and then to learn how I was related to the martyr. Some wept ardently with me on learning he was the husband of my sister.

I wasn't the only student in my class whom the war forced to replace her uniform with the all-black uniform of a mourner. There was a direct correlation between the increase in the number of students wearing black and every battle we heard reported on television.

Our official uniform consisted of a gray smock cut from a single piece of cheap, tough polyester fabric that was produced from various petrochemical byproducts and did not need to be ironed after it was washed. Falling slightly below the knee, this smock had a small breast pocket on the left side, designed to display a laminated, black-and-white picture of President Saddam Hussein in his military uniform.

This uniform's rough fabric gave many students a rash. The only solution the headmistress had for this problem was for any student who suffered from such rashes to wear a cotton blouse beneath the smock as well as cotton tights.

After complaints multiplied among the students and the number of those with rashes increased, especially during the months of May and June, the headmistress stressed in one of her morning advisory addresses that her position obliged her to inform us of the necessity of wearing the institute's uniform and that she wanted to see all students wear the identical uniform even more than she wished them to attend regularly or succeed academically. Moreover, this uniform signified many things, most importantly love for our country and our leader. Therefore, teachers would be duty bound to report any student who came to the institute not wearing this state-sanctioned smock.

When the teacher of the national pedagogy course entered our classroom, her eyes fell on me and my black garb. She asked me to leave the classroom and report at once to the school office—even after asking me about the martyr and learning of my close relationship to him.

I went there, indifferent to what might happen to me, because I had committed no error and was merely trying to console my younger sister by sharing her grief for her husband.

I knocked politely on the headmistress's door, and she invited me to enter her large sparkling-clean office fragrant with damask rose perfume. From the moment I set foot there, I fell prisoner to the sweet-smelling fragrance. It was so extraordinarily beautiful that my eyes would have transformed everything in the room into delightful roses, had the hoarse voice of the headmistress not struck my ears roughly and brought me brutally back to reality.

"How are you related to the martyr?"

"He was my younger sister's husband and also my paternal aunt's son, Madam."

"That means he wasn't your father or your brother! Does your sister live with you now?"

"Yes, Madam."

"You said your younger sister, didn't you?"

"Yes, Madam."

"Come closer! If your sister did not live with you now, I would not have allowed you to deviate from the school uniform. Return to class and hand this paper to the teacher."

I accepted the form and left, almost running. I did not try to read what was written on the paper; I simply handed it to the teacher who had ordered me to report to the headmistress. For many days, I was haunted by the image of that beguiling place, where an intruder might easily find herself trapped in its snares, which were spun from its attractive perfume that seemed oddly incongruous with the large picture of the president in its carved and gilded wood frame—occupying approximately half of the wall on which it hung—and the Kalashnikov rifle that stretched across the desk of the headmistress.

After that day I shied away from getting into trouble, if only to prevent myself from falling into the clutches of that room again. I believed for years, especially since I only met with her face-to-face that one time, that the ever increasing number of students, year after year, had erased me from the memory of that massive headmistress, who had a stern, arrogant face and who was always shouting, for some reason or for none at all, right into students' faces. The only name we knew for her was her *kunya*, her sobriquet: Umm Shayma—"mother of Shayma."

In 2006, though, after I obtained a master's degree in Arabic and was transferred to work as a teacher in a secondary school in Najaf, I did see her again. She was enveloped in black, had gained a lot of weight, and appeared visibly older and broken. She was absorbed in a conversation with other teachers, describing to them details of what was being accomplished in a mosque she was building in Najaf in al-Askari District. I averted my gaze so she would not reawaken in my memory the image of the automatic rifle that used to lie across her desk. It was loaded and ready to fire the moment the finger of the headmistress touched the trigger. All the same I did see her one more time as I entered a classroom where she had been teaching physics. Still seated in the instructor's chair, she said, "Welcome, Ms. Faleeha. Those days in the institute were beautiful, weren't they!" I merely looked at her condescending smile and did not bother to respond with even one word, because I try hard to avoid lying, even in a pleasantry!

My sister could not eat, drink, or bathe without assistance from my mother or grandmother. Even though house calls were expensive, my father brought her a specialist in nervous ailments, and this physician prescribed tranquilizers. He also asked us to maintain a restful and calm atmosphere for her and to shield her as best we could from any news that might cause her health to further deteriorate.

One evening my grandmother approached me after she noticed the tears in my eyes while I watched my sister's attempts to move her hand. She told me, "Listen, darling, there's a medicine you can try on your sister. If it succeeds, then God will have placed in your hand the secret of her cure. If it doesn't, God will reward you for trying!"

"A medical prescription?" I blurted out.

"I don't know how to express this, but I mean healing with the preamble of the Qur'an, the Fatiha. Just apply a few drops of olive oil to the fingers of your right hand and massage your sister's arm and foot gently while you recite, repeatedly, al-Fatiha one hundred and twenty times, once every day for forty days."

My sister began to feel more relaxed and calm and fell into a sound sleep merely on hearing my voice whisper repeatedly the words of the Fatiha while I massaged the paralyzed side of her body, starting from the top of her head and ending with the arch of her foot. I repeated this massage every day, right after the sunset prayer, so she would start sleeping, reasonably comfortably, all night long. Little by little, her pain and bouts of weeping diminished as did the cramps that had afflicted her without any warning, like electric shocks.

The day before the conclusion of the specified forty days, we were all surprised to see my sister attempt to stand up, bracing herself against the wall. My siblings and I rushed to assist her, but she declined our help and walked with slow, timorous steps to the bathroom.

My father was beside himself with joy when he returned home to find Layla waiting for him at the open door, healed of her hemiplegia. He quickly embraced her, and they both began sobbing. On the evening of the next day, my sister asked my father's permission to visit, on foot, the sepulcher of Imam Ali (peace upon him) to fulfill a vow she had made to him for her cure.

My father agreed but wasn't able to accompany her then, because he was worn out from moving between trenches. So it fell on me. That Friday afternoon, after two hours of walking slowly, we reached this holy sepulcher, which we circumambulated, performing our "visit" and prayer ritual. We took the bus home and were back before seven that evening.

Despite my sister's sorrow and repressed pain over her shocking situation, she started to regain her health gradually, day by day, and did not experience another comparable health relapse until 2018, when she suffered a stroke that left her blind in the right eye after her only son was brought back from Mosul with life-threatening shrapnel wounds. One fragment was lodged behind his eye while another required him to undergo knee-replacement surgery on his right leg.

A day came when we heard a genuine warning siren for the first time, although we had heard members of the civil defense force on television issue advisories about it and there had been lessons concerning it in our first-aid course. We had learned that there were three types of warning sirens. These differed in length. To detect the level of danger, we had to listen very carefully to the siren. If it sounded intermittently for sixty seconds, that meant danger was imminent and we had to take the necessary precautions—like hiding in air-raid shelters if any were available, staying away from windows to avoid being hit by shards of glass, darkening rooms by turning off all the lights, and keeping a safe distance from places where containers of butane or kerosene were stored.

If the siren came in louder and softer waves for sixty seconds, that indicated danger was actual. Then all we could do was remain silently, wherever we were, until this warning was lifted and the danger had passed. All clear, the end of the danger, was also announced by a continuous siren blast of thirty seconds.

Quite frankly, these precautionary procedures—including the siren and how long it sounded—were very easy, at least theoretically, for anyone to remember. The real difficulty was in applying this knowledge, especially given the fear and nervousness that afflict a person who hears airplanes approach on a bombing run and the difficulty of seeing anything during a raid at night, while you brood about the fate of individuals who need special care at such times, especially invalids like my mother, old people like my grandmother, or youngsters like my siblings. What made all this more difficult was my aversion to wearing a wristwatch. How could I tell the length of the siren without a watch?

The inhabitants of Baghdad had grown accustomed to hearing warning sirens since the first year of the war—to be precise, from dawn on September 23, when sirens throughout Baghdad sounded after the Iranian Air Force launched a major air raid targeting several residential districts in the city and its surroundings. The Iraqi military command announced that sixty-eight Iranian military planes were shot down that day. Even if that number was inflated, the appearance of a single war plane in the sky of a populous city was more than enough to alarm its residents.

For us, though, the first time our ears heard a real alarm-siren scream from loudspeakers, some of which were placed on the roofs of apartment buildings like ours, all the details of daily life changed, especially since my father had completed his military training by then and gone to join forces on undisclosed fronts.

We took some security precautions in the apartment, ones my father had cautioned us to adopt before he departed—like placing Xs with thick strips of sticky paper over all the windows to prevent shards of glass from injuring us. Whenever my mother or grandmother finished cooking dinner, we would detach the Butagaz canisters from the stove because if one of those canisters exploded, we would then be able to carry it and throw it out the kitchen window, which we left open a little for just this reason, even when it was bitterly cold. Once night fell, we would all congregate in the living room, provisioned with all the food, bottles of water, flashlights, covers, and pallets we could carry. Night after night, this room became a little shelter to which we retired, for fear of an unexpected attack.

Even though the Iranian aircraft never directly targeted Najaf, the shape of Iraq, the location of its cities, and its intersecting physical features forced those fighter jets, on almost any attack, whether they were targeting the country's central, western, or eastern regions, to pass over almost all the country's skies, terrorizing its inhabitants.

The roughest moments of a war occur when you aren't brooding about it. One night when we were all sound asleep, a siren deafened our ears, causing us to dash here and there aimlessly, screaming and bumping into one another, not fully awake. My younger siblings clambered, weeping, over my mother, clinging to her body, fore and aft, till she was almost smothered. My grandmother sat up, wrapping her light blanket around her, as she recited *surahs*. I raced to extinguish all the lights in the room but then froze in place while I tried to see the hands of the clock on the wall, hoping the siren would only sound for thirty seconds, even though the darkness had overwhelmed the entire room so I wasn't able to tell which alarm siren this was and what warning it conveyed. Then, I heard the noise of aircraft flying very fast across our pitch-black sky. An hour later, we heard another siren, which was continuous this time.

My fear did not allow me to think about anything then but my fear itself. My mother almost fell victim to our communal fear when she attempted to protect her young children, forgetting that she was not holding her nebulizer, which she needed to breathe. Even so, we did not hear any explosions nearby and could no longer hear the sound of the military aircraft, which had caused apartment buildings like ours to shake so violently that third-floor residents were forced to leave their flats and spend the rest of the night squatting beneath the building's staircase. Once the raid was over, we calmed down. We returned to our pallets on the floor, trying to expel the sound of the siren from our thoughts, but now heard a loud knocking from inside our large wardrobe, which had four doors. None of us was courageous enough to check on the source of this knocking until my mother finally caught her breath and said with a smile, "Go open the armoire for your sister, before she suffocates in there!"

We all raced to open the wardrobe. There we found Layla sitting cross-legged and covered with random pieces of clothing, sweating pro-fusely and red-faced. We all laughed for hours—not because of the way Layla looked but at our imaginations, which had caused us to think there was a prisoner in our wardrobe: an Iranian pilot who had parachuted to the ground, entered the open kitchen window, and taken shelter from us in the wardrobe.

As the warning sirens became more frequent, my siblings took turns hiding inside that wardrobe, believing that it was sturdy enough to save their lives. With the passing days, apartments like ours became exemplary self-sufficient societies, even a family like mine, which was temporarily bereft of a father. My siblings—male and female—took turns shopping for our household's daily necessities from the local market; if we needed some medicine, the district's pharmacy, which was stocked with medicines and beauty products for women, provided it. If we had a wound to be bandaged or needed an injection, we visited the shop of Abu Safa'a, the district nurse practitioner, who soon learned the names of all the residents of these apartments because he visited them so often.

Although these apartments were close to each other, this proximity did not create the real sense of neighborliness we had felt when we lived in houses in various other districts. My interaction with our new neighbors was limited to greeting women who were my senior when we passed or intervening occasionally as a mediator to resolve the simple disputes my younger siblings had when playing with kids their age in the street. Not even my mother had any true friends among our neighbors. She was satisfied with a weekly phone call to reassure herself about her relatives and acquaintances, all of whom had at least one man from their family participating in the war.

My father's unit kept moving from one front to another, and he would return from each of these with amazing tales, a military canteen covered with coarse khaki-colored fabric, and a sack of bread so we would know what soldiers were eating there. These military loaves consisted of a hunk of brown dough—not divided into flat loaves but lumps the size of a man's hand or slightly larger—baked until they were very hard, hard enough to wound a man and draw blood if you hit him over the head with one. This kind of bread, which was called *sammun*, had a peculiar smell that would deter anyone from eating it unless he was extremely hungry. The taste was also totally unlike that of ordinary bread.

Any time my father returned on leave was a festival for all of us, starting the moment he appeared. It did not end until he set off for the front again. He was quite nearsighted, used a complete set of dentures he removed every night, looked much older than his actual age, and had a limited range of motion. But none of this diminished the way we viewed him: he was the central pole that held up the tent beneath which we sheltered. We never detected even a fleeting glimmer of fear in my father's eyes.

If he was home with us during an air raid that rocked the entire building hard enough to shake free anything attached to the walls of our apartment or to shatter the windows, we didn't bother to extinguish the lights or avoid the windows at night. Instead, we continued with whatever we had been doing before we heard the siren. On many occasions we gathered to tell my father what had happened to us during previous air raids. Then we would fall over backward from laughing so hard about all the harrowing events we had experienced. Who's the idiot who gets scared with their father around? When our father was with us during the air raid, his presence provided us with strength and courage. Then the bombardment never frightened us no matter how violent it was.

My father's return from the trenches was always a surprise. There was only one time when he informed us in advance, calling to say he would return on leave on Friday. Then we launched a major effort to clean the apartment before he arrived. We even dusted the blades of the ceiling fan and the colorful bouquets of plastic flowers around the lamps.

My mother, who hated the idea of placing strips of tape on the windows, since in her opinion that tape destroyed their clean look and made them look dirty, even when the glass was clean, rolled up her sleeves and summoned all her strength to wash those windows right after she took her morning bath. She did not even wait for her long hair to dry. Instead, she simply threw a light cotton scarf over her head, removed the curtains from those windows, and rushed to complete the chore before noon.

A light breeze entered the apartment through those open windows, accompanied by a beautiful sense of anticipation of the moment my father would arrive. We all felt revitalized, except my mother, who, by the time she finished cleaning, started to feel a pain centered in front of her right ear. Then she slept longer than her normal two-hour nap. When my sister went to wake her to start fixing lunch, my mother told her to ask my grandmother to help because she felt a little under the weather.

My grandmother did fix us two dishes: okra stew and rice. When we finished our meal, I washed the dishes, and my sister prepared the tea while my grandmother checked on my sleeping mother. Then she returned to her room to recite passages from the Qur'an while we children did our homework.

Later that afternoon, we heard motion in my mother's room and thought she was heading to the kitchen or the bathroom. So we did not pay any attention. My mother actually did leave her room, but before she closed the door of the bathroom behind her, we heard a terrifying scream—as if she had seen something frightening there. We all dropped what we were doing, raced to her, and started scanning the floor, walls, and ceiling of the bathroom for the animal or bug that had scared her. When we did not see anything, we looked at her, standing before us, wailing fiercely, with both hands over her face.

We had no idea why my mother then raced from the bathroom back to her room. So we all followed her to find out what had happened. But she closed the door in our faces and would not let us in. My grandmother, who had been watching the commotion from the door of her room, asked us to return to whatever we had been doing and let her tend to our mother, believing that whatever had happened was some feminine matter.

Once we stepped away from the bedroom door, my grandmother knocked on it and asked my mother to let her in. My mother did open the door, and my grandmother entered the room. She did not emerge again for approximately an hour. Since the sound of my mother's weeping diminished when my grandmother joined her, I also expected that what had recently happened to my mother was some feminine complaint.

But when my grandmother finally left my mother's room, she was frowning, and there were tears in her eyes. She stood before us indecisively, speechless, unwilling to reply to our questions. Fear quickly overwhelmed us. We just wanted Mother to enjoy the moments of comfort that our spirits would feel the next day when Father returned home.

I examined my grandmother's eyes as she stood there silently. Perhaps some expression in them would reassure us about my mother's condition after my grandmother's lips had proved incapable of calming our breasts with even one word. When I could no longer endure her silence, I asked my grandmother, "Is Mom okay?"

"God willing, she will be fine," she replied in the voice of someone who did not believe what she was saying. My siblings did not wait for my grandmother's hesitant reply. Seeing the door to my mother's room ajar, they rushed inside and immediately began to weep loudly.

This loud weeping, which almost deafened me and pierced my eardrum, belied my grandmother's latest sentence. I imagined that my mother was a corpse stretched across the bed, surrounded by my siblings, who had burst out weeping after trying to revive her.

I have no idea how long it took me to rise to my feet and proceed to that room, which was only a few steps away. I did not dare enter before I determined what had happened. Everyone was weeping, and their contagious tears almost infected me as well. But my eyes were searching for my mother. Where was she?

Was she strewn across the bed as I had imagined? No, I found her seated on her bed, wailing calmly with my weeping siblings around her feet. Seeing her like this calmed me a little, and I skipped the apparently mandatory tears. Instead, I prepared to deal with whatever the difficulty was, so long as my mother wasn't dying.

When I entered the room, I was even more puzzled. I tried to extract some actual words from any of these crying mouths. But they ignored me. After calmly making my way between my siblings' bodies, which surrounded my mother, I approached her and started to examine her body, which was bent forward. I discovered that she was breathing normally. I lowered my eyes to examine the veins of her hands, with which she had covered her face. When she sensed me near her, she shoved me away, and I almost fell over my siblings, who were seated behind me now.

My mother said, "You're so hard-hearted!"

She did not realize that what had kept me from weeping like her other children wasn't my "hard-heartedness" but the thread of reassurance that had reached my heart when I saw her breathing naturally. I was ready to accept anything except losing her. All I wanted was for my father's eyes to rejoice on seeing her alive.

I did not feel angry at her and instead bore her hostility silently. Then I started to examine the lineaments of her face to discover whether she was all right. Once she revealed her face to me, I saw that her mouth had slipped completely to the right and that one of her eyes looked smaller than the other; it would continue tearing up for the next six months.

The moment he entered the house, my father sensed that something significant had happened, because this time he did not see our eyes sparkle with delight at his arrival—unlike all the other times. We had simply opened the door for him silently.

Even before he stepped inside, he asked, "Is your mother all right?"

"Yes, she's in the kitchen," my sister replied plaintively.

The moment my mother heard my father arrive, she hastily entered the bedroom. My father followed her rather precipitously, dropping his military bag at the doorstep.

My mother succumbed to a severe bout of depression and was unable to smile. Whenever she heard a loud sound, she became furious. She had also lost her sense of taste. She started to wear a hijab with a face mask, which she only removed when she entered her room. The various medicines she swallowed every day—after she was examined by several specialists to whom my father took her—did her no good.

One of our female relations suggested that my father should take her for treatment to a spiritual healer in one of the suburbs of Diwaniya because she might have been "touched" by one of the jinn. My mother refused that suggestion categorically.

My grandmother proposed to my mother a visit to the mausoleum of Imam Husayn and his brother al-'Abbas (peace upon him) in Karbala to ask them to intercede with God on her behalf and speed her cure, but my mother did not accept that idea either.

My mother's depression spread to almost all the members of our family, and even my father's visits no longer buoyed us the way they always had. Although he would shower us with a stream of kisses and a warm hug the moment he entered the house, he—like the rest of us—was no longer able to laugh or be merry around my mother when her face was veiled. To protect ourselves from discomfort, we focused on greeting my father when he arrived and then would leave him alone with my mother. We would not join them for meals—how could my mother eat with a veil across her face, since she would not raise that cloth and let us see it disfigured?

This kind of facial paralysis, which is called Bell's palsy, did not gradually leave her face, even though most of the doctors on whom my father spent his money and leave time claimed that it would.

For the next six months, my mother harbored only one wish. It was not to be cured of her chronic heart disease, her repeated asthma attacks, or the rheumatism that afflicted her bones and joints. It was to wake one morning and find that her mouth looked normal again—centered directly beneath her nose—and that when she drank water, it would not slide to the side.

I don't know how I happened to hear my mother's words, because I make a point of not listening to conversations when speakers do not include me. In any case, I was having trouble falling asleep and had dragged myself from our bedroom with my history textbook under my arm. I was heading to the living room to try to review the sections assigned for the exam the next day.

My mother was saying, "Do you know, Hassan, that whenever I look in the mirror, I ask from God nothing more than to have my face look the way it did before. Being ill isn't what matters—it's having your illness exhibited on your face!"

The philosophical depth of my mother's remark surprised me, since she wasn't an educated woman. I tried to find some way to fulfill that wish of hers but could not think of anything. So I started turning the pages of the history book.

> *"Wake up! Why do you think ill of me? I*
> *heard your prayer the moment you whispered it.*
> *It's just that someone else was already waiting*
> *for a response!"*

I sat up and saw three luminous faces radiating light, looking at me. I tried to move my right arm but couldn't. It seemed bound to my back by an invisible rope. Then, trembling, I started to repeat short *surahs* I had memorized but heard another voice say:

> *"Leave her, my boy. Faleeha is still young.*
> *Life's trials haven't affected her yet!"*
> *"Go to the bathroom now, girl, and take*
> *down from the wall the round mirror with the*
> *brass frame. Carry it to your mother's room and*
> *ask her to look at her face in it. I'm not Abbas,*
> *Zaynab's brother, if your mother isn't instantly*
> *healed!"*

The three faces faded, and their light gradually dissipated. I sat there, overwhelmed by tears, stammering as I repeated the *surahs*.

"Who were you talking to at this hour of the night?" my father asked. He stood beside me but did not wait for me to answer. Instead, he was enchanted by the aroma left in the room by the three visitors. With his eyes closed, he inhaled deeply and asked, "What is this aromatic fragrance that fills the room?"

I summoned all my energy and rose, leaning first against the wall, and then raced to the bathroom. I took the mirror off the wall, went to my mother's room, and woke her. Gazing at the ground, afraid to look at her face, I told her, "Please look at your face in it."

My mother condemned my request and seemed angered by it. She asked, "Have you gone mad?"

"This is what Imam Abbas instructed me to do," I replied in a voice muffled by the tears pouring down my face—without looking up from the ground.

So she took the mirror from me and looked at her reflection. Then, racing around, with the mirror still in her hand, she started shouting, "Hassan! Hassan!"

My father came, as if sleepwalking. When he saw that her face looked normal again, the way it had before, he prostrated himself to thank God while my mother sat on the couch and wept. Meanwhile I raced to my grandmother's room—where I found her awake and saying her prayers—to tell her what had happened. When she finished her prayer ritual, she had me sit down with her on her prayer mat. She started to caress my arm and praise God for my mother's recovery from Bell's palsy.

The next day my father purchased another mirror for the bathroom, and the brass mirror became a fixture of my mother's room. It was not smashed to smithereens till the day Iraqi forces struck Najaf with rockets and heavy artillery in 1991 in retaliation for participation by the local men in a popular insurrection.

News of my successful promotion to the second level of the Teacher Training Institute was well received by everyone, including me, but I did not savor the taste of this success enough to celebrate—not even with my classmates or my friend Maysun. All I remember of that day are the jealous eyes of the assistant headmistress and the frown on her face when we received those results.

My father had promised to buy me a present when he returned from the front. He normally did not tell us which front he was being deployed to whenever he left us, but this time it slipped out accidentally when he said, "I'll buy you a present when I return from Amara, God willing!"

My mother had heard him. Some days later we were all gathered around the television trying anxiously to understand what was happening on our borders, especially to our household's safety valve—I mean my father—who had left us for the trenches. Before we were seated properly, the earnest face of the presenter appeared, and he said in his stentorian, frightening voice: "My fellow countrymen, here is a statement released by the Regional Command: 'In the name of God, the Compassionate, the Merciful, you the mighty Iraqi people, sons of our majestic Arab fatherland, you volunteers in our fearless armed forces: On the sixth night of February, our heroic armed forces fought back against the treacherous military attacks that the hostile Iranian forces launched with the goal of penetrating our fortified fronts in the heroic city of Amara, after those hostile forces had slipped forward under the cover of darkness, using human waves as shields to cross the minefields. With the help of God, our forces were able to halt these attacks in the first hours of the following day. Now the mighty Iraqi people repeat, with the sons of its heroic army: 'By God, the Ultimate Force, praise to God for the mighty victory He has wrought.'"

We all acted out our anxiety and fright in different ways. Some of my siblings headed to bed. Others went to the kitchen to eat leftovers. My grandmother calmly retired to her room and sought refuge with her prayer beads, glorifying God and praying that He would end this war quickly with few additional casualties. I retired to our room to busy myself with writing about fantastic topics totally alien to reality.

Before I could find my personal notebook, which I hid somewhere different almost every day to protect it from my younger siblings' mischief, I heard my sister scream, "Mom's dying! Mom is dying!"

I found my mother stretched out on the floor, gasping for breath as her face turned a frightening shade of pink. We all surrounded her, not knowing what to do. My sister quickly placed the nebulizer in my mother's mouth and pressed on it, but my mother could not inhale anything; she wasn't able to breathe.

My young siblings' voices soared with alarm while my sister and I rushed to my mother's room to take her abaya down from where it was hanging. We draped it around her, after my grandmother gave us some money we did not have time to count. We lifted our mother and tried to carry her downstairs from the apartment but didn't succeed.

The clamor we made in that attempt, however, prompted a middle-aged woman to emerge from the apartment opposite ours. She offered to help us, and we did not object. With the assistance of that woman, we succeeded in carrying my mother down the staircase of the building while that woman's son, who had come out with her, raced down to the street to hail a taxi.

My sister sat with my mother in the vehicle's back seat while I sat in front, even though the driver was offended by my temerity. In Najaf, it was unusual for a woman to sit in the front seat of a taxi. Given my mother's critical condition and the difficulty she was having breathing, however, I felt justified in sitting in the front seat to allow her more room to be slightly more comfortable, however briefly.

When the driver asked us which hospital we were going to, I looked back at my sister to see what she would say because I didn't have an answer. She simply gestured with her head that she, too, did not know which hospital would be best for my mother's critical condition. So the driver chose to take us to the emergency room of the Saddam Teaching Hospital, which was only fifteen minutes from our neighborhood. The driver shot off at top speed when he witnessed the increasing difficulty my mother was having in breathing. The air rushing in through the open windows, however, made matters worse, and caused my mother to say in a choking voice, "Stop and let me die. Then I'll rest!"

My sister, with some difficulty, rolled up the window beside her but failed to close the window next to my mother. Then she attempted to turn my mother's face in the other direction, after apologizing to her. She eventually turned my mother's entire body toward the closed window.

The guard at the hospital's gate did not stop us; he allowed us to proceed straight to the hospital itself. As soon as he stopped the car, the driver rushed to get a wheelchair and helped us get my mother out of the vehicle and settle her into that chair. Then we raced her into the emergency room. I don't remember how much money I gave the driver but clearly recall him saying before he drove off, "May God aid us in recompense for what He has caused us to suffer!"

The foreign nurse, once she observed my mother's serious condition, quickly dropped the papers she was holding onto the reception desk while gesturing to an Iraqi nurse who was standing at the door of one of the rooms to wait a moment, and then they both rolled my mother into the emergency ward.

In only a few minutes, the Iraqi nurse in her white smock and rubber shoes came to us with a pile of forms and a ballpoint pen to ask us what chronic illnesses my mother had, the medicines she took every day and to which she might have developed a sensitivity, and the number of times my mother had suffered an asthma attack like this. My sister and I took turns answering these questions while we glanced nervously at the nurses entering and leaving the room where they were trying to help my mother.

My mother's condition stabilized a little after they placed her on a ventilator in the room to which they moved her the next morning. My sister and I had stayed up with her all night, watching her breathe, in and out, with difficulty. Whenever my mother needed to use the toilet, especially after they began treating her intravenously, we accompanied her and entered the bathroom with her.

My task was to move the pole to which a sack of solution was attached and connected to long thin tubes that carried nutrients to my mother's body through a vial implanted in her arm.

At first my mother was too embarrassed to urinate in my presence, but she eventually yielded to the demands of her bladder, which was filled with liquids. She sat on the toilet seat quietly while I watched the level of the saline solution decrease in the clear sack. I wished dearly then that I had continued my studies in a preparatory school and entered medical school. Then I would have known at least what medical solutions were in that sack.

By midday my mother was feeling a little better, and we were allowed to leave with her after a physician provided us with a simple treatment and advised her to avoid, as best she could, situations that might trigger recurrences of such attacks.

All three of us—me, my mother, and my sister—crowded into the rear seat of a taxi and returned home, where we found that all my siblings had cut school and that looking after them had exhausted my grandmother. But the moment my grandmother saw my mother enter the apartment with halting steps, followed by me and my sister, she forgot her fatigue and quickly helped my mother into bed and stayed with her until they both fell fast asleep.

Even though I was exhausted from staying up all night, it was hard for me to surrender to the pleasure of sleep or to rid myself of the feeling of revulsion that had seized hold of me the moment my eyes had fallen on a medium-sized notice placed on the glass door of the emergency room that read "Requirements for a Death Certificate." Such a notice would not under any circumstances encourage an invalid to endeavor to obtain one. Instead, it would propel him down the valley of despair and spur him to lose any hope of survival.

In view of my mother's suffering the previous day and her difficulty drawing air into her lungs, my siblings and I, without saying so out loud, agreed to stop watching children's programming on television for fear those shows would be interrupted by more news about Amara, especially since Iraqi TV broadcast all its programs on only one channel. The news might end my mother's life the next time. Then we abandoned the TV and no longer watched the cartoons we all loved.

As for news of the actual battles that occurred near Amara—penetration of that city by the Iranian Army, the severing of the Baghdad to Basra highway, and the Iraqi Army's Fourth Corps' pulverizing battles that allowed the Iraqi Army to regain control of the areas Iranian forces had penetrated—none of this news came to us from the mouths of television presenters. Instead, we heard these details from my father when he returned, two months later, from the city of Amara, with injuries to his left foot.

All my father's relatives and friends who visited him deplored the bad state of his injured foot, feeling certain that, since he was diabetic, his wound would never heal. Some even mentioned that wounds like this could quickly become worse and turn into gangrene, which would lead to the amputation of the affected limb. My father, however, ignored all these ill-omened prognostications that emerged unsolicited from his guests' mouths. He not only took the free hospital medicine he was given but consulted a specialist, whose skill allowed my father to regain his ability to walk gradually, without a cane, within a few months.

My father's visitors, though, were destined for terrible ends. My paternal uncle and his wife died of sorrow while awaiting the return of their son who was taken prisoner in Iran in 1986 and only returned to Iraq in 2003, when he redid their graves in the Wadi al-Salam Cemetery. Of my paternal aunt's remaining two sons, who visited my father in lieu of their mother because she was too devastated by the loss of her child, the martyred bridegroom, the elder disappeared without any trace until 2003, when, in a mass grave in Basra, they found his bones, some identifying documents, and his ID disc, a metal tag on which were etched his name, address, and blood type. These were all wrapped in scraps of his uniform. The other brother, after losing his leg in a landmine explosion in a battle in 1985 and becoming disabled, suffered from severe depression at the loss of his brothers, one after the other, and became a recluse. In the middle of the night in 2004, he heard knocking on the door of his house and opened it. The next morning the neighbors found his corpse on the stoop of the house beside a revolver fitted with a silencer.

My mother's paternal aunt had waited impatiently for the return of her son, who had been held prisoner since 1981, and could not comprehend when members of Iraqi Security Forces led him away immediately after his return from Iranian prisons in 1991. She had a schizophrenic episode and died a few months later. Her son's life could be summarized in these few words: once a prisoner of war, now missing.

The stories of the neighbors who visited my father also stretched the imagination. One smashed all his back and hip muscles and lived the remainder of his life severely disabled after he fell from his third-floor balcony while attempting to flee from policemen who had come to arrest him for trying to avoid mandatory military service. His brother, who was a year younger, pretended to be mute and insane for eight years, dressing in tattered garments and letting his hair grow long and disheveled. We did not see him with his head shaven, wearing clean clothes, and speaking fluently until 2003, when he was accepted as a student in the Teacher Training Institute.

Amid all these frightening events, I forgot about the present my father had promised me for my academic success. He, though, was determined to reward me with something beautiful. Thus, days after my father recovered from his injuries and could walk without a cane again, he woke me one Friday morning and asked me to come with him to see my present. When I asked whether we could go in the afternoon, he told me the place we were heading to would be swarming with men and boys by then and would not be an appropriate place for me.

We took a taxi to al-Madina Street. Then we walked toward Suq al-Manakhkha, which was a market located at the end of al-Madina Street in al-Nazla—or "the Descent"—District, which was named as a result of the land there sinking and leading to the district of Bahr al-Najaf. Suq al-Manakhkha took its name from all the camels to be found there, because when a Bedouin came to Najaf to visit religious sites or to trade, he would leave his camel tied up in this place and then carry out whatever task had brought him. This place had gradually become a market that specialized in buying and selling domestic animals of various kinds and all sorts of birds.

I walked between cages of doves, enjoyed the trills of colorful nightingales, and was astonished to see a white camel surrounded by a number of men examining the beauty of her build and her grace while negotiating with the broker over the price.

My father, though, was not astonished by what he saw—unlike me. Instead, he was searching for what he wanted to buy. When he found what he was looking for, he approached a tall young man who stood surrounded by several other men. The youth held a large net, which hung from his shoulder. This net contained dozens of starlings of medium size. They had been trapped near Bahr al-Najaf during their migration from other lands as they searched for warmer weather.

My father asked that young man to sell him the entire net full, and he agreed quickly, without asking my father why he wanted all these birds. As soon as the vendor received the money, he removed the net from his shoulder, and my father took it from him carefully with both hands and gently placed it on the ground.

Once the agitation of the imprisoned birds had decreased a little, my father opened the net. Then all the birds rapidly emerged and filled the sky overhead. I ignored all those who were observing with us what was happening and paid no attention to what passersby had to say about us. Instead, I followed the fluttering of those many wings, which flapped against each other while those birds tried to flee as quickly as possible. I was nonplussed by the calls of those birds that seemed to be praying for my father's welfare and congratulating me on my academic success. At that moment, I felt liberated too from that trapper's net.

I thanked my father profusely for this unique present, and we returned together to the house with my imagination nourished by the taste of freedom granted to these birds. After that, I never enjoyed seeing birds imprisoned in a cage—not even a cage made of diamonds.

For this reason, many years later, when one of my fellow teachers invited me to her home in al-Ghadir District, I could not bear the sight of the colorful little lovebirds with their plump bodies and wide tails, sheltering beside one another, confined in so many large cages that they filled almost an entire room. I categorically refused to visit that house again because I considered the members of that household murderous hunters who cared only for the personal enjoyment they derived from watching the birds, which were dying in their cages from a desire to recapture their lost liberty.

I don't know why it occurred to me to reassure myself about the destiny of those delicate birds when we returned to our normal life and went back to teaching in our schools after the events of the popular rebellion in Najaf had died down.

Then my colleague told me nonchalantly, "We left our house and went to the countryside, fearful that the fires of the bloody events taking place in the city streets would reach us. Then a bunch of hungry stray cats from the street scaled the walls of our house and entered it in search of food. When all they found were the birds cowering in their cages, those cats attacked the cages and devoured the birds."

After a brief silence, she added, "You cannot image what all those colorful feathers looked like! They were mixed with dried blood, as if a decisive battle had erupted in those demolished cages. We lost a lot of money feeding those birds."

I felt sick to my stomach while I listened to her and imagined the ravenous cats ferociously attacking those peaceable birds. I excused myself and headed to the restroom. I felt lucky when that teacher was reassigned, a few days later, to teach the afternoon shift while I continued to teach students in the morning shift. Otherwise, whenever I met her at the school, I would have imagined her covered from head to foot with feathers and blood.

Chapter Five

At the academic level that I had risen to, instruction was not character-
ized by its difficulty so much as by prolonged examination and attention
to details. Our indoctrination in the goals of the ruling Baath Party was
no longer limited to selected topics in the patriotic pedagogy course;
these were the subject of an entire book—more than a hundred pages
long—where they were elucidated in formal, recondite language.

The history text focused on topics that clarified the nefarious goals
of the West in our country and the victories of our heroic army down
through the ages. It explained the most important talking points of
some nationalist figures who had played an important role in revolts
against colonial powers—men like Omar al-Mukhtar.

Totally absent now were the still-life paintings we had imitated in
our arts education classes. They were replaced by subjects related to
the war. A feature of every exam—whether for a month, a semester,
as a midterm, or the end-of-year examination for arts education or
drawing—was a demand that we draw some scene from one of the
battles raging on our eastern borders. Our drawings needed to provide
victorious depictions of our heroic army. To pass this subject, we had
to mine all the materials we had stored in our head after gleaning them
from television or newspaper images. Our emphasis needed to be on
depicting the courage of our army and its victories, with our Iraqi flag

flying high, fluttering over battlefields. Even so, no matter how hard we worked to include a lot of details in those paintings to make them look like real miniature battles, we never received high marks for them.

The art teacher, simply put, gave high marks only to students who drew pictures of the president, based on photographs of him, even if these were merely pencil sketches that included numerous obvious errors.

When we protested this tendency, which had turned an enjoyable subject like drawing into a hurdle that was difficult to clear, and presented a petition signed by all the students from each of the different years, our goal was to obtain a review of those paintings and the grades awarded for them on exams. Our request was rejected by the school's entire administration—not just by the headmistress—on the pretext that it was necessary for us, as students preparing to teach and train the next generation, to acquire skill in drawing the features of our warrior president (may God preserve and watch over him). In reaction to the failure of our petition, we no longer bothered to color the images we were asked to draw on an exam. We would merely hand the instructor some pencil drawings at the end of the examination period because we were certain we would only receive marks of fifty out of a hundred, no matter how hard we tried.

Our physical fitness exercises, which we had performed almost every morning, were replaced with military drills like the ones practiced by soldiers. These consisted of standing at attention (with intervals of being "at ease"), walking in time to a beat, and jogging—all to the athletics instructor's whistle.

This gym teacher was also stingy with her grades. In this instance, high grades were awarded to students who participated in student parades and reviews presented in Najaf's stadium or who were selected to perform selections from operettas in the guildhall. Those young women were expected to wear special costumes, obviously without an abaya. This final condition was clearly difficult for most families to accept.

After the midterm break, as we returned to the institute to complete the second semester, we were surprised by the presence there of members of the People's Army—men slightly older than my father. They had selected a spot by the institute's gate to sit in rickety chairs. With their serious demeanor, weapons, and army uniforms, they looked ready to defend the institute against an imminent attack. At first, we believed their presence suggested that a street battle was probable.

We only learned the real reason for their presence at the beginning of the next academic year, in 1984. Members of our Iraqi Army were engaged then in decisive and continuous battles to ward off Iranian infiltration into our lands through al-Ahwar, the marshes. They were considered a natural boundary between the two countries and lay adjacent to the cities of Amara, Basra, Nasiriyah, and the governorates of Dhi Qar and Maysan. These marshes covered approximately twenty thousand square kilometers. Since water in them could be three meters deep in the winter, and thick clumps of reeds grew two meters high there, it was an easy place for a person to hide. In anticipation of a sudden military penetration of Iraqi cities, members of the People's Army were posted then to government schools and state institutions of various kinds to guard them, after most members of this army were withdrawn from the front ranks.

My father was also transferred to Najaf, and we saw him during the day when he returned from work to eat lunch with us. He spent nights guarding the Education Department, where he worked.

My siblings laughed a lot when they saw me enter our house with a cloth bag filled with an army uniform; they had never thought I would have the courage to wear such a uniform, if only temporarily, or to carry a rifle, even if it was loaded with rubber bullets.

I ignored their mockery and placed the bag in the bedroom, in the top drawer of the wardrobe, which I shut carefully to try to keep my siblings from trifling with those garments, which had been loaned to us on the understanding that we would need to return them to the institute at the end of the current school year and that any failure to bring them back would result in a fine. When my father returned from work at noon, I informed him that the leadership team at the institute, pursuant to orders they had received from on high, would begin having students perform military drills, under the guidance of members of the People's Army, for the next forty-five days in the courtyard behind the institute. That would be followed by marksmanship training in a place yet to be announced. I parroted this information to my father exactly as I had heard it from the megaphone the headmistress held in her hand when she addressed us as the garments were distributed.

My father could not control himself; he laughed uproariously when he saw me in this khaki uniform, because these rough clothes were not designed to clothe a short, slender body like mine. They had been designed for men to wear. My father quickly added extra holes to the wide military belt, called a *nitaq*, so I could fasten it around my waist. He drilled those new holes with a large nail he heated in the gas flame of our range.

My mother and grandmother cooperated to rip out the seams of the shirt and trousers and sew them back together by hand. I took charge of ironing them after that. I was troubled by the problematic military boots for as long as this military training lasted, because neither their size nor weight was appropriate for a female foot.

Courses were scheduled in a different way in the institute than they had been in primary or middle school, where every period of instruction was followed by a short break announced by a buzzer that one of the teachers or the assistant principal held. Those minutes were like a recess when a student could go to the restroom, drink some water, or eat a snack she had brought from home. At these two levels of instruction, there were never more than five subjects.

At the institute, on the other hand, a class was called a *hissa*, or period, and they were grouped together in pairs. As soon as the instructor for the first period left the classroom, after teaching us for forty-five minutes, the instructor for the second period would immediately enter and teach her subject for another forty-five minutes. Then we had a ten-minute break to prepare for the subsequent periods, although we didn't need the sound of a bell to inform us when those next periods began or when the breaks came. There were six of those instructional periods every day.

Once we began our military training, though, matters changed dramatically. The moment the sixth period ended, loudspeakers placed in the institute's corridors and in the front and rear courtyards began to blast out patriotic anthems and military songs at full volume. Then we students would rush to change out of the school uniform and into military attire, leaving our classrooms in waves to stand facing the flagpole, where the Iraqi flag was flying, and to salute it along with the trainers charged with drilling every class.

We would then form several circles, each around a different trainer. All of us women—with our military uniforms and serious expressions as we followed the trainers' directions—really looked like true combatants ready to launch and repel any sudden military attack. Everyone wore military trousers except for plump girls and teachers, who had special skirts that covered their lower extremities to their feet.

The forty-five days of military instruction were divided up in this way: the first ten days were reserved for an explanation of the parts of a rifle. We learned about the fixed parts of a rifle—like the barrel, the sight block, butt, grip, gas tube, pistol grip, receiver cover, the magazine, the body of the weapon, and the receiver—plus the moving parts of the rifle: the gas piston, bolt carrier, carrier spring, ramrod, and the release.

During the subsequent ten-day period, we learned how to break down and reassemble the weapon by pressing the palm of our right hand on the release that holds the magazine while holding the magazine with a finger of that hand. Once we freed the magazine, we raised it to a right angle until its cavity was parallel to its grip. Then we withdrew the magazine slowly till it was clear of the weapon. Next we opened the security lock and drew out the pieces after pointing the barrel of the weapon upward. Finally, we pressed on the button, lifted the cover, and drew the group of pieces back, lifting them entirely free of the body.

During the third ten-day period, we were fed salient information about hand grenades, including how to pull the pin and how long, after contact, a grenade takes to explode.

During the fourth ten-day period, we obtained important insight into proper ways to shoot when lying prone—which is considered the easiest of the shooting positions. Your feet are spread, and you brace yourself on the ground with your wrists. When shooting from this position, the shooter must be precise, steady, and self-controlled. When shooting from a standing position, which is considered the most difficult posture for shooting, you need to stand straight but lean forward slightly with your feet apart and your arms braced. You need to be in total control of yourself. We also learned helpful tips on shooting and taking aim—like the shooter's observance of the rules of timing, pointing, goal, pressing the trigger, breathing while shooting, and the best areas to strike on the target.

During the final five days, we reviewed all the materials presented to make sure we had understood and memorized them.

Each day, on my return from military training, my father would test me to see what I had learned. If I got something wrong, he would take it upon himself to review all the details of that military science lesson, allowing me to disassemble and reassemble his rifle while my mother and siblings looked on with amazement and my grandmother's pride showed in her eyes.

The day after our military training sessions ended, I went to the institute in the morning with Maysun, carrying my schoolbag, which contained my military uniform instead of my books. Large buses that normally transported passengers between different Iraqi cities were parked in a way that blocked the whole street in front of the institute. In each bus sat two men; the first wore a military uniform, and the second was dressed in civilian attire. With some difficulty, we squeezed between those buses and entered the institute. The gate was wide open and welcomed us with the military anthem "We Are Marching to War," played so loudly it was deafening.

In compliance with orders from the headmistress and our teachers, we almost raced to the classrooms, where we immediately changed clothes. Then we boarded those buses, leaving our abayas stuffed into our backpacks in the classrooms. Once I was seated on the bus, I felt uncomfortable for two different reasons. This was the first time I wore trousers in public and the first time I appeared without a head-covering in Najaf. I felt embarrassed that entire bus ride. The other young women also looked anxious, frightened, and upset by what was happening.

In less than an hour we reached the military garrison located on Abu Sukhayr Street near al-Ansar traffic circle. The buses stopped at its large gate, which was set in very high thick walls that would be hard to scale and that were topped with sharp barbed wire. We marched inside those walls in rows, each group following its trainer, to military music, moving our hands in unison with our feet till we reached the sandbags that had been arranged to shelter our bodies from injury while we aimed at fixed targets placed several meters in front of them. We stopped when we heard "At ease!" broadcast from loudspeakers placed in corners of the garrison's walls. All the rows of students stopped to receive important safety advice and then tips to assure our success in the shooting drill we had come to perform.

The moment I saw the other rows of students who had already completed the shooting drill and who had executed an order to retreat, my blood pressure rose. There was no way I could bear standing beneath the harsh sky and the intense sun that scorched my head—even though I was wearing a beret. But the moment I heard the words "Get set!"

shouted by the trainer, I rushed forward with the other girls in my group, barely conscious of the rifle I had been handed. After I assumed the prone position, I forgot completely how to secure the buttstock in the hollow of my shoulder. When I failed to do that several times, one of the young trainers tried to help me. I felt totally humiliated then and jerked the butt of the rifle to my shoulder so forcefully I almost injured myself. When he saw my agitation, he asked me to calm down, take a deep breath, and focus on the target before me. Then he took the rifle from my hand and easily set it in the proper hollow on my shoulder before moving away so I could demonstrate my skills. I felt the rifle become part of my body as I put my finger on the trigger and pressed it gently. The shot emerged from the barrel of the rifle and pierced the target, making a hole right in its center. On hearing the trainer praise my aim, I recovered my self-confidence. I took another deep breath and aimed a second shot at the target. It was also able to penetrate the sand-bag easily. Then the trainer shouted, "Well done," which he repeated after my third, successful shot.

We returned to the institute at three with memories that did not fit into the "happy" column but that we could by no means characterize as "sad." All the way back, we laughed at details of this unique day while also feeling hungry and thirsty, conscious of being covered with dust that stuck to our clothes, and reeking of gunpowder and the rank sweat of our exhausted bodies.

I ignored whoever opened the door of our apartment for me when I returned from the institute that afternoon and raced straight to the bathroom. The warm shower cleared all the clinging dirt and stinky sweat from the pores of my body. I then went to the kitchen to devour the leftovers the fridge had been saving for me since the family's lunch. My hunger was too intense to afford me the patience to heat up the food. Even so, I enjoyed every morsel of food that entered my mouth and praised God for the blessing of sustenance.

I did not confide to anyone my secret embarrassment about the young drillmaster and my confusion and fear of the weapon. I kept this secret from my family for fear my siblings would enjoy my humiliation too much—after watching me day after day easily take apart and reassemble my father's rifle and parrot the trainers' precise instructions that had been dictated to us for forty-five days and that we had learned by heart. It would not have been possible for me to convince them that memorizing information is one thing and its practical implementation another.

I merely informed them that I had excelled at shooting and had earned a perfect score for hitting the target three times in a row. Everyone was proud of me, and we all laughed about some of the issues between students at the military base. I told them as well that one of our teachers had refused the order to lie down prone to shoot and thus shot from a standing position. After that jolting experience, she lay down on the ground while all the students laughed loudly.

Ten full days following the conclusion of our military training—even though I was certain I had returned my military uniform, after washing and ironing it, to the school administration—whenever the teacher of our sixth-period class left our classroom, I automatically put my hand below my bench, which I shared with a classmate, and started to search for the bag with those garments—as if my mind were stuck on that moment and did not wish to abandon it for some reason I never grasped.

The sharp, acrid smell of gunpowder never left our nostrils, because after the conclusion of those drills, each student took a turn shooting five rounds from the rifle of one of the school guards as a salute to the Iraqi flag during the flag-raising ceremony each Thursday morning. I was the first student selected for this because I had been one of the students who had received a perfect score for target practice. I fired the rifle very cautiously and circumspectly, surrounded by students and teachers, after taking my position before the flag, which was raised on high. I offered two silent prayers: the first was that the rifle not fall from my hands and make me a laughingstock, and the second was that the first bullet to emerge from the mouth of my rifle not strike and slay one of the doves tranquilly circling over the courtyard. My two prayers were granted. I returned to my row after successfully completing my assignment and handed the rifle back to its owner, congratulating myself on the survival of the doves, which had flown back to their dovecote the moment the first bullet disrupted the sky's calm.

The year's remaining months brought tragic events comparable to those of the months preceding them. The beginning of 1985 saw a proliferation of black posters on the walls along the streets. Women's voices grew hoarse from keening behind flag-draped coffins, and Iraqi television continued to broadcast four things every day on the single channel: the president's speeches, a report on recent battles, military anthems, and battlefield images. We had lost hope of ever seeing the end of this war. Our ears had grown accustomed to hearing sirens, and it had become very natural for a person to stop when he heard a siren that warned of an air attack and scan the sky for some trace of incoming aircraft. If they flew past, he would bow his head slightly as if afraid of bumping the planes with it, and then proceed on his way.

Like most other men, my father scurried from his morning job to his nighttime chores while dreaming of a momentary, calm nap or a few minutes of simple relaxation when he could stretch his feet without military boots on them.

My mother visited the hospital so often that everyone working there—the physicians, nurses, janitors, guards—knew her, called her Umm Falah, and rushed to assist her the moment they saw her being brought in on a stretcher. She would not return home—smelling of

Dettol and medicinal potions—until she had spent a night or two there, accompanied by me and one of my sisters.

Only my friend Maysun could relieve me of my concerns about the terrors and disasters happening to me, with me, and around me. She would make me laugh wholeheartedly when she related weird tales about her experiences with her cousin who was madly in love with her.

My grandmother was preoccupied by the idea of journeying to the next world and had begun to prepare herself for it with all the means at her disposal. One day while I sat in the living room doing homework like my siblings, my grandmother asked me to accompany her to her room. I did, just as soon as I had put my book and notebook back in my bag, which I then placed in a corner of the room.

"Do you have a fountain pen?" my grandmother asked in a whisper once we entered her room.

"No, but I have a ballpoint pen, pencils, chalk, and colored pencils," I replied.

"No, those are not fit for this task. Could you buy me a fountain pen on your way back from the institute tomorrow?"

"Certainly, Grandma. There is a kiosk near the institute, and the proprietor sells every type of school supply. I can definitely find a fountain pen there."

She smiled at me and went to her wardrobe. She removed some money from beneath her folded clothes and placed it in my hand, saying, "Buy me an excellent fountain pen, and keep the change!"

"Should I buy you a bottle of ink?"

"No, just an excellent ink pen!"

I returned to the living room wondering about my grandmother's request. I had no idea that she would make me write an ending to her life.

I was afflicted with a murky feeling about the fountain pen I bought. I sensed that this pen was weighing down my backpack, which seemed to be carrying a concern, not a pen. When I reached home and handed the pen to my grandmother, she examined it briefly and then went to her wardrobe and brought out a medium-sized inkwell filled with dark-yellow ink. She screwed off the top and smelled the fragrance of the liquid inside it. She immersed the tip of the pen in the inkwell and then started drawing circles and lines on a piece of white paper she had also brought out of the wardrobe.

When she was satisfied with the color, she turned to me and said, "Tomorrow you will begin writing a prayer with this ink." As she said this, she took from the wardrobe a piece of white linen large enough to make a tunic. Then she drew from under her pillow a tiny book no bigger than the palm of my hand. Clearly written on its cover were the words: *Du'a' al-Jawshan al-Kabir*, or "the Great Cuirass Prayer."

"How can a prayer serve as body armor?" I asked.

"What better protection does a person have than prayer?"

As I fingered the piece of fabric she had placed in my hand, I asked her anxiously, "What is this ink? Why should I write out this prayer with it?"

With tears sparkling in her eyes, she said, "I hope you will do this one favor for me. If I knew how to write, I would not burden you with this matter." Tears streamed down her cheeks even as she smiled. "I feel my end is near at hand. This piece of cloth is a present a friend gave me after she brought it back from Holy Mecca, where she performed the Hajj pilgrimage to God's sanctuary. The ink is saffron mixed with water from the Well of Zamzam there. I hope you will write this prayer on the sides of this cloth, which is called a *hibra*, without telling anyone else in the family about our secret. What do you think?"

Wiping tears from my cheek, I told her, "Absolutely! I will certainly do this. But, Grandmother, you haven't told me whether you will make a tunic for yourself from this *hibra*. Have you finally decided to stop wearing black and wear colorful clothing again?"

At that moment I felt like an idiot, asking such inappropriate questions. If my grandmother had wished to resume wearing colorful clothes, she would have made a new shift without needing saffron ink and the Great Cuirass Prayer. But I did ask her, and perhaps she lied to me; she said she had decided to go to Mecca and wanted this fabric sewn into a tunic she could wear while performing the rituals of the pilgrimage. If she had been planning that, why did she tell me she felt her end was nigh and that the hour of her departure from this life was approaching? First and foremost, why was she weeping?

"Don't worry about the fabric now. Don't concern yourself with how or when I might use it. All I want you to do is begin writing out the prayer when you have time."

My grandmother told me this after she had dried her tears and placed the piece of fabric, the pen, the inkwell, and the tiny book back in her wardrobe. She then sat me down beside her, the way she did every day, to listen to me recount what had happened to me at the institute.

The next day I entered my grandmother's room after finishing my homework and began to write the prayer on the cloth. It took me ten days to copy out this prayer. My handwriting was not as beautiful as I would have liked it to be or as clear, because the fabric absorbed the saffron ink rapidly. As I wrote on it, the words merged to become a yellow block. All the same, my grandmother continued to encourage me and praise the speed and accuracy of my writing. The one piece of advice she offered was to focus on transcribing the words correctly without any errors.

Even though I grew tired of writing, I wasn't able to tell my grandmother that, so I kept transcribing the words. The task became even more difficult each time I had to fold the fabric to continue writing on it. Then the saffron-tinged sentences would bleed into each other, and occasionally I would need to rewrite a sentence from the beginning to figure out where I had left off the previous day. A prayer like this one, which contains a hundred stanzas, demands the total concentration of its scribe. Barring that, the textual and orthographic errors are blatantly obvious.

After each session of transcribing the text, my hands would be stained yellow. When I realized that soap and water didn't remove the stain, I tried using Tide detergent. When not even Tide worked, I had the bright idea of using toothpaste to rid myself of this color. I placed a little Amber-brand toothpaste on the yellow spots on my fingers and scrubbed them thoroughly. After that I washed my hands again with soap and water several times. The color of those spots started to fade a little, but when Maysun saw the yellow stain on my right index finger while we shared a seat on the bus carrying us home, she moved a little closer to me and asked in a whisper, "What brand of cigarette are you smoking?" Then she moved back, sat up straight, smiled, and winked at me.

I was infuriated by her stupid conduct; how could she have allowed herself to suspect me of that? How could she upset me without feeling ashamed—even if she were just kidding? I certainly did not like crude humor of this type. What if someone else on the bus heard her? He would think I was an ill-mannered girl. To express my anger, I scooted to the edge of the seat till I was about to fall off, leaving enough space between us for another passenger to sit. If I had possessed enough money to pay the fare again, I would have gotten off that bus and taken another one, letting her walk home alone. The moment the bus halted at our stop and a first passenger got off, I raced to disembark, almost leaping from the door. Then I sped home without saying goodbye to Maysun. She hurried after me, caught up, and asked, trying to provoke me further while laughing, "Won't you tell me what your brand of cigarettes is?"

"Are you an idiot? This is saffron."

She shot back incredulously, "Saffron? Why is it only on your fore-finger, then?"

Since Maysun wasn't a member of my family, to defend myself against her accusation of smoking, I told her candidly that I was writing out the Great Cuirass Prayer with my grandmother's ink—after making her swear by God that she would not tell anyone the secret I was sharing with her.

As the smile vanished from her face, she said, "Many people here believe in writing that prayer on their shrouds to mitigate their punishment in the tomb."

I did not believe what she said and asked, "Shroud? But my grandmother isn't having me inscribe this prayer on her shroud. I'm writing it on a *hibra*."

"A *hibra* is a shroud! What did you think it was?"

I headed home sobbing silently. My greatest wish then was that the distance from the bus stop to our apartment were longer—far enough for my tears to dry, even though they had now dampened my smock. I did not greet my brother when he opened the door for me; instead, I raced to my grandmother's room, where I found her seated on her prayer mat with her black prayer beads. I set my schoolbag next to my shoes by the door of the room, hugged my grandmother from behind, and began to wail loudly.

My startled grandmother was frightened and hugged me after drawing the abaya from my head. She asked me anxiously, "What's wrong with you? Why are you weeping? Has something bad happened?"

I was unable to reply and continued weeping. If I had been able to speak, I would have asked why she thought me strong enough to touch the shroud in which her body would be wrapped after she died.

My grandmother, however, knew me better than I knew myself and eventually grasped the reason for my tears. As she stroked my hair, she said, "We all die. Praise to the one who never dies!"

I embraced her even more forcefully and wished that she and I had been born on the same day of the same month of the same year so that we might die at the same time. I was bound to her by something like an umbilical cord and could not imagine surviving her even by a single hour. My grandmother was too sublime to be tormented by pain.

She was too affectionate for her face to be covered by dirt. She was too beautiful for her eyes to be extinguished by death.

When I had calmed down a little, I went to the wardrobe and brought out the *hibra*, the pen, the inkwell, and the tiny tome and began to finish transcribing the final stanzas of the prayer:

(93)
Allah, I beseech You by Your name:
Generous Provider,
Bestower of bounties and gifts,
Enricher, Giver of Shelter
Destroyer and Reviver,
Satisfier Who grants salvation,
(94)
The First and the Last of everything,
Lord of every creation and its Master,
Lord, Cherisher of everything and its
    Fashioner
Creator of everything and its Maker,
Clasper of everything and its Extender,
Origin of everything and its Return,
Originator of everything and its Estimator,
Creator of everything and its Destroyer,
Reviver and Slayer of everything,
Author of everything and its Heir.
(95)
Both Remembrance and Memory,
Best Appreciator and Appreciation,
Best Glorifier and Glorification,
Best Witness and Observation,
Best Host and Invitation,
Best Responder and Response,

Best Comforter and Counselor,
Best Friend and Companion,
Most Desired and Ultimate Goal,
Most Affectionate and Loved.
(96)
He Who answers His petitioner,
Friend of anyone who obeys Him,
He Who is close to those who love Him,
Protector of those who seek His protection,
The Generous One to those who rely on
    Him,
The Forbearing One with those who rebel
    against Him,
The One Who is Merciful in His Grandeur,
The Compassionate One Who is Great in
    His Wisdom,
The Almighty Whose Benevolence is
    everlasting,
God Who knows who seeks Him.
(97)
God, verily I entreat You by Your name:
First Cause, Creator of desire and
Of change, Avenger, Organizer,
Chastiser, Cautioner, Harnesser,
And Displacer.
(98)
God Whose knowledge is primordial,
Whose promise is sincere,
Whose grace is manifest,
Whose command dominates,
Whose Book is judicious,
Whose decree is unavoidable,

Whose Qur'an is glorious,
Whose rule is eternal,
Whose favor is all-embracing,
Whose throne is mighty.
(99)
He Who listens to one soul even while listen-
　　ing to all others,
Whose one deed does not preempt other
　　deeds,
Who pays attention simultaneously to one
　　speech and all others,
One request and all others,
Whose sight sees everything simultaneously,
Who never wearies of our plaintive cries,
Who is the ultimate aim of seekers,
The goal of recluses
And of wayfarers,
From Whom not a single particle in the
　　worlds is hidden.
(100)
The Forbearing One Who is not hasty,
The Generous One Who is never miserly,
The Truthful One Who never breaks a
　　promise,
The Munificent One Who never wearies,
The Victor Who is never overpowered,
The Almighty Who is indescribable
Justice Who is never injudicious,
The Bounteous One Who is never needy,
The Almighty Who is never small,
The Protector Who is never negligent.
Praise be to You,

There is no god but You,
Relief! Relief!
Protect us from the Fire, O Lord.

Once I finished copying out the last of the hundred stanzas, pleading with each word that death would not be too quick to steal my grandmother from me, fatigue overwhelmed me, causing me to forget my fear for my grandmother, especially because I hadn't had a moment to relax since I returned from the institute and felt afraid of parting from her but also hungry. So I stretched out on her bed, without changing out of my school clothes, and fell fast asleep.

I was panting while running over a sidewalk of skulls. Whenever my foot trod on one of those skulls, its spirit crept back into it, and the skull changed into a wild black stallion neighing behind me. Every time the neighing horse's head drew near me, I screamed loudly: "Granny, Granny!"

My grandmother came to me and shook me gently to wake me after she heard me scream several times. When I opened my eyes and found her standing before me, I secretly praised God and went off to the bathroom. When I returned, I found that my grandmother had put everything back in its previous place and wrapped the large sheet of clean plastic we had used to cover the prayer rug that was spread on the floor to keep the saffron ink from reaching the rug. As I was starting to leave her room again, my grandmother pulled out a tray of food I hadn't noticed before, and we both sat down on the floor and began to eat.

For the first twenty days after I finished copying the prayer, I kept my eyes fixed on my grandmother from the moment I returned home. She appeared to be in excellent health—as if my prayers for her to have a long life had been answered by the Unknown. Gradually my anxiety for her faded because I saw her before me, applying henna to her hair every week and bathing each Friday, performing the ritual prayers at the appropriate times, helping my mother prepare delicious food, telling us her entertaining stories, and answering my questions about matters that confused me.

But my relaxed feeling of reassurance about her did not last beyond those twenty days. One day I returned from the institute to find that gloom had descended over the entire household. Instead of asking why everyone was silent, I rushed to find my grandmother stretched out on her bed, showing no sign of life except that her chest was rising and falling as she breathed.

My mother seemed as surprised as everyone else that my grandmother was lying in bed in this unusual manner. It wasn't normal for a person to enter a trance without some clear precipitating reason, and my grandmother hadn't suffered any accident. The night before she had seemed in excellent health.

After I changed out of my school clothes, I went to my grandmother's room and sat down beside her on the bed, observing with amazement the change in her condition overnight to such a frightening state, which suggested nothing so much as her imminent demise. She sensed my presence and in a feeble voice asked me to call my mother. I ran to Mother.

When my mother entered the bedroom, she told my grandmother, "I'm waiting for Hassan. I phoned him, and he will be here shortly. Then we'll take you to the doctor."

My grandmother steadied herself and informed my mother that there was no reason to take her to the doctor, because her appointed hour had arrived and she would soon be reunited with her departed relatives. Then she asked my mother to listen carefully to her last wishes. She did not want the children to be prevented from watching cartoons on television in the evening. There was no reason to keep the TV turned off out of respect for her spirit, as was typical in Najaf during a period of mourning. She did not want us to wear black in her honor for more than forty days. She refused categorically for anyone—no matter how close a relation—to spend a single dirhem for her burial or wake, because she had set aside funds for that. She gestured with her hand to the wardrobe, where she had placed that money. I asked my mother to ask the woman who washed her body to use as her shroud the *hibra* on which the Great Cuirass Prayer was written.

Then my grandmother told my mother to contact my father again and tell him he needed to come—not to take her to the doctor but for something she thought much more important.

My father raced to my grandmother's room after my mother phoned him again. He stood near her head, and my grandmother told him it was pointless to take her to the doctor and asked him to have her buried beside my grandfather. Her tomb should not rise higher than his, and no heavy marble tombstone should be set by her grave. It should have a simple marker with only her name and age on it. She did not know precisely what year she had been born. The date on her birth certificate was not correct.

My father left her room unable to speak; her words had dumbfounded him. My mother started to follow him, but my grandmother's voice stopped her: "I want to perform my ablutions!"

I brought her a plastic basin and a bottle of clean water. First we helped her sit up on the bed. Then she slowly leaned her weight on us, moved to get up, and walked a few uncertain steps. When she realized that she could not walk farther, she asked us to help her sit down on the floor. Then she drew the empty basin and the bottle of water toward her and, with my help, began to perform her ablutions.

She said, "I resolve to cleanse myself with this water for God's sake."

I placed a little water in her right hand, and she washed her entire face with it, from top to bottom, as she whispered, "God, brighten my face on the day when faces are blackened. Do not blacken my face the day faces are whitened."

Then I poured a little water in her left hand, and she washed her right forearm with it from the elbow to the tips of her fingers as she said,

"God, give me my book in my right hand and immortal life in paradise in my left. Judge me lightly."

I dripped a little more water, in her right hand this time, so she could wash her left forearm from the top of her elbow as the water descended to the tips of her fingers, ending with the fingers. As the last drops of water fell into the basin, she said, "God, do not give me my book in my left hand, and do not shackle it to my neck."

Next, she ran the insides of three dampened fingers over her head from the crown down as she said, "God, veil me with Your mercy, blessings, and forgiveness."

With the moisture remaining on her hand, she rinsed between the toes of her right foot and beneath her right knee, then said, "God, set me on the straight path." Next, she did the same thing with her left foot. After my grandmother finished these ablutions, I took the basin, from which a few drops of ablution water had dribbled on the floor, and carried it carefully to the bathroom. I returned for the water bottle, which I also took to the bathroom. I spread out the prayer rug for my grandmother, facing Mecca, and my mother slipped her white prayer shawl over her so she could begin praying seated.

Once she had performed her prayer to the end, she sat up straight, took her black prayer beads in her right hand, and started to count the beads, moving them with her right thumb as she recited, "God, pray for Muhammad and for the Family of Muhammad as You prayed for Abraham and the Family of Abraham in all the worlds." Then she gave my mother a farewell look, after which she gazed down at the floor as she recited, "I bear witness that there is no god save God. I bear witness that Muhammad is the messenger of God. I bear witness that Ali is the friend of God. I bear witness that Hasan ibn Ali is my imam, that the martyr al-Husayn is my imam, that Ali ibn al-Husayn al-Sajjad is my imam, that Muhammad al-Baqir is my imam, that Ja'far al-Sadiq is my imam, that Musa al-Kadhim is my imam, that Ali ibn Musa al-Rida is my imam, that Muhammad al-Jawad is my imam, that Ali al-Hadi is my imam, that al-Hasan al-'Askari is my imam, and that al-Mahdi al-Muntazar—may God speed his release—is my imam." Then she prostrated herself, placing her head on the *turbah*—a clay seal—and died.

Chapter Six

I did not discuss with anyone the details of my grandmother's shrouding and burial. All I recall of the rest of the day she died was taking her small black transistor radio and secluding myself in a corner of our room. I turned it to a station that played boisterous music and held the radio up to my ear, hoping its noise would drown out the sounds of the chest slapping and wailing that filled the apartment. I did not believe my grandmother had passed and did not want those sounds to certify this tragedy for me.

Once the voices of women keening mixed with those of men, whom I had not noticed enter our apartment, I dropped the radio on the floor and went to investigate. My thought was that my grandmother had fainted and would soon come to and that my father had rounded up some men to help him carry her to the doctor. The situation, however, was not as my daydream had sketched it. After a brief pause, the wailing cries rose again when my father and three other men emerged from my grandmother's room carrying on their shoulders my grandmother's rigid body, which they bore away before I had a chance to cast a farewell glance at it.

My grandmother's final wishes were executed to the letter, except the proviso about wearing black for only forty days. My mother violated that and wore black for two whole years. At home I wore only black for an entire year but wasn't able to wear black at the institute for fear of being punished again by a barrage of questions launched by the head-mistress and the teachers.

Forty days after my grandmother's death, my mother prepared the commemorative feast that has been celebrated by our people since antiquity. Forty days after the death of a family member, women pre-pare a banquet consisting of forty different dishes. My sisters and I helped my mother prepare it, together with some of my mother's close friends. Men and women from the tribe were invited to this banquet. The women sat in my grandmother's room, and the men in the living room.

Since I dream the impossible, I nourished the hope that I would enter her room, which was crowded with women, and find her among them by the dinner mat, eating with them the way she always had. When I entered the room, though, those seated women were eating and discussing various subjects, but I did not find her among them. I began to scan their faces to see whether my grandmother had bequeathed her compassionate expression to any of them. Perhaps among these faces there would be one as compassionate as hers. When my eyes failed to detect anything of the kind, I felt scalded by the misery of her incendi-ary passing. I retraced my steps to our room, leaving behind me a trail of tears.

One day after attending classes at the institute, I checked my grand-mother's room before I went to bed; this was something I had done since her passing. When I entered the room, I was surprised to find none of her personal effects there save her prayer rug, which was spread out on the floor, and her wardrobe, which stood—empty—in a corner. I was enraged and rushed to my mother to ask what had become of my grandmother's belongings.

When she informed me that she had given them to one of the impoverished women who came to our neighborhood every week to collect used goods from people, I was incapable of composing a meaningful sentence that would have helped my mother understand why this had been wrong. Instead, I replied with a scream that drowned out her words.

The only response she could muster then was to pack all her force into a punch that landed on my cheek. Then I fell silent as blood dripped down the side of my lower lip. At that moment I was bereft of all my emotions, even my anger, and felt a tooth fall from my open mouth and hit the floor.

I bent over, picked up the tooth, and went to toss it down the drain in the bathroom. I returned immediately, even without thinking to wash the blood off my mouth, to the room I shared with the rest of my siblings. I pulled out my drawer of our bureau and gathered all my clothing and personal effects. Then I put everything in my grandmother's wardrobe and closed the door to the room behind me. I sat down on the floor, after pulling out my diary, and began to write a letter to my grandmother.

> *My precious grandmother,*
> *I am sad for many reasons. First is that I did not bid you a proper farewell that reflected the depth of what your passing meant to me. I would have wanted you to know that you were my refuge from all my fears concerning the war and news about it, about my anhedonia, about this, and that, and that. I will share with you now a secret that I would not like to reach the institute, which is no longer a healthy place to study—not since they turned it into a military facility. I don't like seeing my father dressed in the uniform of the People's Army. Whenever I open the door for him and find him standing there clad in that garb, I feel he's some stranger who has stolen my father's body and is now attempting to enter our house,*

after leaving my father alone in the wilderness, without a body. Granny, do you understand what I mean?

I was overwhelmed by terror and panic today because I had wanted to preserve your personal effects for as long as I live, because they are part of you. I believed that the scent of the fragrance of your bedding afforded me some trace of you. You know I respect my mother. Therefore, if my voice was raised to drown her out, that was not for some trivial reason. I felt that she had squandered you too easily. Thus I have decided I will not speak to her for a week. I hope she will not suffer an asthma attack during this period, because then I would be obliged to speak with her when I take her to the hospital. I pray that this does not happen.

You know, Granny, that I am astonished by my mother's punch, because I never remember being beaten or slapped by her, my father, or by you. My astonishment has subdued my anger.

You certainly are urging me to go rinse the blood out of my mouth. I want to do that too, because the taste of blood in one's mouth is very disgusting. I fear, though, that if I open the door, one of my siblings will enter this room and ask me to explain what happened between me and my mother. But I have no words they would understand. How could my siblings understand what I mean when I inform them that my mother severed the link between me and my security blanket? They would surely keep repeating this phrase for a long time and mock me, laughing uproariously.

Granny, would you mind if I live in your room? Please let me know.

I do not want to defile the purity of your absence with the commotion of my daily presence, but you know that I feel safe only in your embrace, which for the foreseeable future I can find only on the floor of your room.

Before I forget, I want to inform you that the tooth my mother's punch knocked out would probably have fallen out anyway.

I will fall asleep now and leave the door open for you. Perhaps you will come and lull me to sleep as you did long ago. The room, as you see, is empty, and I feel cold now.

PS: I will never stop loving you, Grandmother!

I wiped away the blood that had dried on my lip and chin with the hem of my tunic, returned the notebook and pen to the heart of the wardrobe, and stretched the rug out on the floor. When I started to feel chilly, I curled up, with my arms and legs together, like a fetus in its mother's belly.

The moment drowsiness flirted with my eyelids and I was on the verge of falling asleep, I sensed the door open quietly and someone enter, carrying a thick blanket and a pillow. I felt a pleasant warmth when the figure covered me and raised my head a little to tuck the soft pillow beneath it. I wanted to believe that the figure protecting me from feeling cold was my grandmother's ghost, but then I heard my father say to himself before closing the door and exiting, "I don't know how to sort things out between the two of you."

After what happened between me and my mother, everyone in our household understood that I would live in my grandmother's room. For this reason, I was able to prohibit my siblings from playing in Grandmother's room, where even her absence conveyed the beautiful sanctity of her presence. Naturally, I let them share the room with me when I helped them with their homework.

It was quite natural for my sisters to share the room with me frequently during the day, but they refused to sleep there for fear my grandmother's ghost might come at night to reassure herself about my welfare.

◆　◆　◆

For many days I was troubled by the presence of a young man who looked familiar. He acted as if he were waiting for me at the bus stop in the morning, and whenever I glanced at him, he smiled at me. The only thing that rescued me from his deliberate, ridiculous smile was Maysun's arrival. Once he saw her coming, he would look gloomy, and his face would become a wooden mask. On many occasions he would leave and move somewhere else down the street.

His repeated, daily appearance made me search my memory, wondering who he was. Finally, I did place him. He had helped my father and the other men carry my grandmother's body from the apartment. Even so, the way he waited for me every day made me furious, and I could not think what he wanted.

What reason did this idiot have for standing here every day? Why did he never stop smiling at me so impudently? Didn't he realize he was really upsetting me by doing this? What if someone who knew me happened to see him? Such a person would certainly think there was some relationship between the two of us. I wished I possessed sufficient courage then to discuss this matter with my mother and father, who might put a stop to it.

But a week after that young man had appeared repeatedly, he disappeared, and I felt relieved. What would have happened if Maysun had noticed his speedy retreat when she neared the bus stop? She would certainly have subjected me to hours of interrogation because her vast imagination would not accept the possibility that I did not know him—not even if I swore the mightiest oath.

This day passed with me feeling immense relief because I was not obliged to sense I was concealing an enormous sin I had committed. I returned home with a smile on my face while listening to Maysun's thrilling account of her latest trip to Baghdad, the places she had visited, and the restaurants where she had eaten with her family. We parted when the bus deposited us at the normal place, and each of us proceeded calmly to our homes.

My sister opened the door for me and, after I greeted her, moved closer and whispered, "We have guests."

"Men or women?" I asked her, closing the door behind me quietly.

"Just one woman. You know her. She came to Grandmother's wake."

I asked, "What does she want?" My sister, however, raced to the room without replying.

I found the woman seated beside my mother in the parlor and greeted her. I had slipped into a black tunic appropriate for welcoming guests in our home and washed from my face the fatigue of a day at the institute.

Once she saw me sit down with them, the guest immediately said, "God's will be done! You look like a teacher now!"

Feeling nervous, I replied, "Thank you, Auntie."

When she noticed my anxiety, she reached for her handbag and drew out a rectangular box wrapped in a piece of velvet. She held it out to me and said, "I bought this watch a long time ago and have never worn it. I want to give it to you as a present in honor of your entering the Teacher Training Institute!"

"It's a number of years since I entered the institute," I pointed out as I attempted to figure out what was happening.

"I know, my dear, but I only learned you had entered the institute when I came to your grandmother's wake."

She placed the box beside me on the seat. She rose then, after quickly pulling her abaya around her, said goodbye to my mother, and headed toward the door. I accompanied her to the door and thanked her. Once I was sure she was headed down the steps, I closed the door and returned to the parlor, where I found only the perplexing gift.

Even though I did not believe what that woman had said, I felt obliged to open the present before my siblings appeared and asked me why she had given it to me rather than to one of them. With few exceptions, they were all excelling in school every year.

I took the small present in my hand and went to my bedroom, where I sat down on my pallet to open the box. With extraordinary calm I undid the red satin ribbon that had been very carefully tied around the small box. Then I pulled away the red velvet that covered it. When I opened the box, I found a Swiss-made lady's silver Citizen-brand wristwatch with a rectangular blue dial, small numerals, and silver hands. I really liked its meticulous craftsmanship and beautiful appearance. When I tried to lift it from the cushion on which it sat, I had difficulty and was forced to lift the entire cushion toward me. Then it and the watch were in my hand while the rest of the pasteboard box fell to the floor, revealing a white piece of paper folded precisely to fit at the bottom of this box.

I reached down for the paper, which excited my curiosity by its unexpected appearance, picked it up, and read the following:

> *My dear Faleeha,*
> *I have found only this bizarre way to demonstrate the extent of my love for you. Since I first saw you, I have not been able to stop thinking about you. All I want from you is to believe the sincerity of my feelings for you. Just try to smile at me in the morning before you board the bus—that's all I want.*
> *Anwar*

My hand started to tremble nervously as I reread the letters on the page. Fearful that a member of my family would enter the room, I quickly closed the door. When I returned to where I had been sitting, I hastily folded the paper and tried to tuck it back in its hiding place but failed. I was obliged then to sit for hours trying to think of a place to hide this note, but the entire room seemed wide open to prying eyes. It lacked anywhere suitable for this difficult assignment.

This paper added one more concern to my list, because where could I hide it when everywhere was public and readily visible? Even if I put it in my schoolbag, what guarantee did I have that the hands of inquisitive students would not rifle through it on the pretext of looking for a pen, find the paper accidentally, and betray my secret?

If my grandmother had been here, she surely would have told me how to hide this paper or what to do with it. It was hard for a girl like me to survive without her grandmother. I was in perpetual need of her wisdom. I considered tearing the paper to shreds to rid myself of the problem but hesitated because the words were so sweet and I had never before received a message like this, filled with expressions of love.

After reading the note again, I genuinely felt that the words had been drafted especially for me and no one else—not only because the writer had begun it with my name but because I felt the sincerity of his words. Another reading instilled a greater degree of confidence in me about that paper, which had suddenly become an authentic, passionate love letter.

At that time, I wished my siblings were slightly less prone to go through my belongings; then I could have hidden this love letter in my wardrobe, which had no lock. I reread the letter again and scrutinized it—without fearing any sudden entrance into my room—because some strength slipped from those words into my spirit and quickly lent it maturity, something I needed to receive precisely at this moment.

I now felt certain that those words would breathe their enchantment on me even if I tore the paper into minuscule pieces, because I would remain enthralled by their impact. I could never be protected from the gleam of this magic, quite simply because this was my first love letter.

I put the very beautiful watch on my left wrist and began to admire its design, as if it were an extraordinary instrument of superhuman craftsmanship that had ushered me into the castle of love through its large portal without prior permission. I woke the next morning to find that I had left my silver watch on my wrist. When I glanced at it to check the time, its hands, numbers, and entire shape evaporated and became letters pulsing with passion: "My dear Faleeha, I have found only this bizarre way to demonstrate the extent of my love for you . . . Just try to smile at me in the morning before you board the bus—that's all I want. Anwar."

The letter seemed to tell me: "Now that you treasure my message and it is bound to your pulse forever, there is no need to burden your-self by retaining my secret as a wad of paper." To make sure my hunch was correct, I closed my eyes and saw those words surrounding me on every side and becoming a mouth that warbled to me my first love song. Then I placed my hand on the piece of paper, which had shared the bed with me that night, and squeezed it hard while pressing it to my chest—as if to extract from it all the juice of its words and slip that into the pores of my skin to penetrate my cells and then dissolve in my blood as it circulated.

After I sensed that those words had completed their journey to my heart and settled there as one of its beats, my fingers took turns tearing the paper into tiny, almost invisible shreds. The moment I left the door of our apartment building, I opened the palm of my hand and blew on those paper specks, which flew into the street. There was no way they would end up in a trash can, because they were imbued with the sanctity of love.

On this morning, everything was new. I had not eaten a morsel of food, because who needs food when satiated with delicious words of love? Instead of eating breakfast, I gazed at myself for a long time in the mirror after I washed my face repeatedly with perfumed soap and water and spent a long time brushing my teeth. Then, before I left the apartment, I checked to make sure my abaya was cleaner than usual and that my shoes bore no trace of dirt from the road.

I thanked my grandmother profusely when I opened the wardrobe to hide my watch there and found the gardenia perfume that she had given to me a long time ago. It was propped inside some folded clothes, where no one had touched it. I removed the cover from the slender flask and raised it to my nostrils to check that it still smelled fine. When I was convinced of that, I brought the bottle near my nose and rubbed some on it. Before the perfume could scent the room, I donned my one-piece school uniform, socks, and shoes, picked up my schoolbag, draped my abaya around me, and left.

Once I had finished watching the tiny paper remnants fly through the air and vanish somewhere along the street, I turned my gaze to the bus stop, where I found Anwar in his usual position. Then I walked shyly to my customary spot where I waited for Maysun and the bus. When he ascertained that no one else was there, he quickly approached me and whispered, "Did you like the watch? If so, where's your smile?"

I sank into the earth with embarrassment and continued to stare at the ground, smiling ever so slightly. Before he returned to his place, I heard him say, "That's beautiful perfume—your perfume!"

A few minutes later, I looked across the street and saw Maysun leaving the door of her grand house and crossing the street toward me. From the moment she saw me, she tried repeatedly to learn the twin secrets behind my smile and the perfume that wafted from my clothing. But I revealed nothing to her. I sought refuge in silence and allowed curiosity to consume her all day long.

The next morning, I wore my watch when I headed to the institute. I was at a loss, though, to know what to say when Maysun asked me where it came from. She wasn't satisfied when I told her a relative had given it to me. She demanded that I provide her with more details. For example, was this relative a man or a woman? Was there some ulterior motive for this beautiful present?

This made me angry enough to ask her, "Is there any ulterior motive behind all the fine watches that you rotate almost every week?"

But this question did not annoy her. She replied very calmly, "You know my father sells watches and antiques. Naturally, I can wear whatever watch I want when I want to!"

"Just because my father is an ordinary man, and I'm from a middle-class family, am I not allowed to wear a fine watch like this?"

When she noticed the anger flashing in my eyes, she replied, "No, of course not. Who said that? I just wanted to know whether a man was involved in this matter. I hoped you would share a beautiful secret like the one I have shared with you ever since I met you. There's no need for anger!"

I calmed down when I saw Anwar approaching and crossing the street to the bus stop. When our morning bus arrived, we all boarded it—not just me and Maysun, but Anwar too.

He sat down very calmly in the seat across the aisle from mine. I, however, was quite nervous and fearful, feeling everyone knew our secret. Despite all this discomfort, I did my best to make sure he saw his present, which was gleaming on my wrist. When I failed in that attempt and we were about to get off at the institute, I deliberately extended my left hand to Maysun after hiking up my abaya a bit as if I meant to take the fare from her and hand it to the driver, since we were sitting directly behind him. Then the band of the silver watch glinted, and as I was reaching to hand the money to the driver, I heard Anwar whisper, "I'll give it to the driver."

I adjusted my posture as his voice reverberated in my ear—sweet, soft, powerful, manly, tender, and unlike the voices I customarily heard. I closed my eyes as if living an everlasting dream that I hoped would never end.

I held the money out to him, and the tips of our fingers touched briefly as time stopped entirely. This moment made everyone else disappear and inscribed me as the only person in a time that would fade away momentarily. I appeared oblivious to my own existence or any actuality beyond this interval, which slipped from time undetected and which time did not shower with its blessing by extending it till it became complete. I paid no attention to anyone else around me in the bus; even Maysun's existence faded away. When I looked at Anwar, I found his eyes were still closed and trying hard to restrain the sigh that would have revealed his love for me. How I wished that the route would never end this day, that the bus would become lost or break down so that we would remain seated inside it while waiting for some mechanic to come make repairs or for some other bus to carry us on to our destinations. My hope evaporated, however, when I heard Maysun tell the driver, "I'm getting off, dear. Getting off."

Then the bus stopped. Before I rose to disembark with Maysun, Anwar's voice whispered to me with a melody that blended many varieties of soothing music: "Very pretty on your hand!"

I entered the institute feeling I was an entirely different person, someone I did not know, someone newly minted. Frankly, I wasn't walking normally. I was walking gracefully on the tips of my toes like a ballerina. I don't remember whether I said anything to Maysun before entering the institute or not, because I was busy watching Anwar's face smile at me through the window of the bus. That caused me to forget how to speak.

Everything looked great this morning: the students were extremely beautiful, and all the delicacy of the world graced the entire institute. The teachers seemed to speak in hushed voices when they taught our normal classes. The hem of my smock did not scratch the skin of my leg every time I moved—the way it always did, even when I was wearing long socks. I don't know how the traces of those scratches suddenly turned to faint lines that no longer itched.

At the end of the school day, I needed to hug Maysun but paused when I saw her standing at the door of the institute waiting for me to come out. I hesitated to embrace her for fear of falling prey to a trap her intuition had been weaving for me since that morning to lure me to confess.

Back at the apartment, everyone in our household noticed how absentminded I seemed and the faint smile that lingered on my mouth as I listened to my siblings' entertaining, varied, and unique narratives when we sat around the dining mat for lunch; we were eating the same dishes, but they suddenly tasted different. Ordinary discs of bread had acquired the flavor of crispy *shukr*, with its appetizing, sweet taste and the topping of sparkling sesame seeds, which my grandmother and I had purchased from one of the bakeshops every time I accompanied her to the Wilaya District.

From the afternoon tea, my nostrils inhaled the refreshing scent of mint and cardamom, and the grains of sugar in the teacup became melting silver cubes of rock candy.

When I entered my room that evening, I did not complete my school homework but hastened to pass the top of the bottle of perfume over my right palm so I could inhale the scent of gardenias. I put my watch on my left wrist, closed my eyes, and fell asleep.

I was sitting with Anwar in the rear seat of a small taxi passing through a tunnel that was dazzling with light and seemed almost endless. Gentle music was emanating from the vehicle's radio, and the blissful way our fingers intertwined obliterated all forms of meaning in the world. We were not conscious of the time, the place, or the destination of our secret journey as our fingers transmitted to each other a unique warmth.

What a formidable dream with such simple elements! Its taste concentrated inside me until it colored all my senses with a pleasure I had never experienced before—one I couldn't name.

As I had the previous day, I paid special attention to my appearance when I departed for the institute in the morning. Just as soon as I reached my normal place, Anwar quickly crossed the street toward me as if he had been waiting for me to arrive since dawn.

My problem was that I did not know where he lived and therefore could not estimate how much time it took him to be there first to wait for me. Even if I had wished to ask his address and other details about his life, it would have required incredible daring and careful planning to acquire this information. Since there was no official relationship between us yet, I should not vex my head brooding about such matters, especially since that knowledge might spoil the unfolding sweetness and the flow of these dreamy moments.

The important thing was that Anwar was approaching me after crossing the street. He was as tall as a basketball player, his body was manly and vigorous, and the features of his face were virile. He whispered delicately, "Good morning."

Without waiting for me to respond, he bent down and placed at my feet a rose I had not seen, since he was carrying it behind his back. Then he hurried away for fear people would see us together. I was amazed by this action, which far exceeded any romanticism I had anticipated since I had become acquainted with this young man. It had never occurred to me that such a tall, slender frame would bend down at my feet— like the prince bowing before Cinderella in the beautiful story that was shown on television before the war. I felt perplexed then—what could I do? My eyes were fixed on the dewy red damask rose, and I could not think what to do with it. When I looked for Anwar again, I found him standing in his customary place, like any other day. When he noticed my perplexity, he gestured with his index finger toward the rose, encouraging me to pick it up quickly. After hastily looking right and left to make sure the street was empty of passersby, I picked up the rose and shoved it in my bag.

When Maysun arrived, Anwar hailed a small taxi and climbed into it, departing while we boarded the bus heading to the institute, like any other day. Did I say: "Like any other day"? No, this day did not seem an ordinary day or like the previous ones I had experienced before I met this romantic young man who had a magical touch in everything he did. On this day the teachers seemed extremely elegant, and the school's hubbub dissipated, replaced by a pleasant calm.

I would not be lying if I said that the rose, which was snuggled tranquilly among my books, grew and became so large, with such extraordinary speed, that it filled the entire classroom. I, on the other hand, dwindled in an amazing manner till I became merely a living particle that love had deliberately forgotten on the anther of that rose.

I was amazed at myself when I realized that the unscripted and awesome entry of Anwar into my life had erased quickly all the war's fumes and now prevented its foul, noxious vapors from reaching my lungs. For the first time since 1980, I felt I was inhaling air imbued with peace.

I returned home and hid the rose in the wardrobe with my clothes after I breathed in its perfume time and again; it seemed that with every act I undertook that day, I needed to sniff that rose's perfume as a reward for a chore well done.

I wished then fervently that I truly had a room of my own, where I lived alone, a room with a door I could lock whenever I wished. In that case, I would have put the rose in a vase and placed it near my pillow. Then its perfume would have been the last scent I experienced before voyaging through sleep's pavilions.

This curious sensation soon faded, and I was instead seized by an almost total feeling of contentment. I thanked God repeatedly when I realized that I *did* have a room of my own with all my personal effects inside it and a wardrobe containing my clothes and books, a room where at the end of the evening I slept alone in my own bed. To assure its privacy, this room lacked only a lock on the door. Of course, locking my parents and siblings out of my room would have been not only inappropriate but reprehensible. How can you say you live with your family if you lock yourself and your secrets away from them?

On the other hand, I wished that someone else shared my rosy secret—not just any person but specifically a member of my family. But this seemed totally out of the question. My mother was sick all the time and irritable. There was no way she would allow a young man to give gifts and flowers to one of her daughters, even if his objective was marriage.

My father was always busy and worked two jobs to provide for us. What would he think of me if I told him what was happening? He would definitely consider this entire episode to be rash idiocy that violated the family's traditions. He would certainly regret his decision to allow me to complete my studies or would perhaps decree that I end my education. He might punish me by marrying me to his brother's son, who was a failure and an alcoholic who hadn't completed primary school and had recently volunteered for the customs police.

I would hurt even the feelings of my sister, the martyr's widow, if I shared with her my happiness over the presence of Anwar in my life, because even a passing reference to the engagement or wedding of one of our relatives upset her and reminded her of her all-too-brief marriage.

So I would keep my secret to myself and make a serious attempt to stop talking to myself about it in an audible voice whenever I was alone in my room, because my open door was a magnet for my siblings' curiosity, drawing them toward it. They would surely think me irrational if they heard or witnessed me talking to myself emotionally—as if I were a guest paying her only friend an amiable visit. How, then, would they gloss my sighs as I spoke to myself? Whenever I thought of him, I heard my heart hum a song that could be fulfilled only by Anwar.

◆ ◆ ◆

I felt annoyed by the commotion around me in the classroom and did not know why. Perhaps it was a Thursday, and the other students were anticipating their Friday holiday. Friday meant nothing to me besides staying home and performing household chores. I had to brace myself to endure another dull Friday and not being able to see Anwar. I prayed to God the minutes would pass swiftly with no painful consequences.

In fact the day was a total loss and left all of us tired from cleaning the house, doing the laundry, and preparing dishes that required extra time to prepare, like three types of kibbeh—with rice, with bulgur, and with potatoes—and some pastries like *kleicha* pastries stuffed with dates, which my siblings took to school with them as a morning snack every day.

Finally, Saturday morning, which I had been really looking forward to, arrived, but it also seemed lackluster. Where was Anwar?

By the time another week had passed, I felt a keen desire not just for Anwar but for the specific details he provided for my mornings. Gradually, I began to miss the little signs associated with him—like his shadow on the ground while he stood waiting for me; his voice, which at least four times reached my spirit before my ears; and the romantic gestures he improvised to bring happiness to my barren heart. The scent of the wilted rose among my books no longer sufficed to transport me to the realm where I imagined those particulars as it once had when I secretly sniffed it.

By the second week of his absence, that silver watch lost its sheen and instead became hard for me to bear, because whenever I looked at it I was reminded of the ignorance of the naive girl I was, the girl who had allowed a young man to amuse himself with her and then had cast her aside. The watch had simply been his bait, I thought.

I frequently considered smashing it but instead thrust it under piles of clothes in the wardrobe and slammed its door shut. The gardenia perfume that Anwar had liked I never used again, because a bad boy like him did not deserve even a whiff of perfume.

During the third week of his absence, the passing of each second and minute unnerved me. I felt drained—as if happiness were fleeing from me like a healthy female camel from a mangy male camel. I was totally incapable of smiling.

During the fourth week of his absence, my spirit returned to its prior condition before he had suddenly appeared in my life—as riddled with holes as a sieve. Anything related to the war easily penetrated it and clotted inside it.

During the fifth week, everything conspired against me; even the teachers once more became as harsh as they had previously been. Vitality deserted the eyes of the students. The military anthems became even more blaring, and I wondered privately whether hostile airplanes had launched more air raids after ascertaining that Anwar was gone for good.

I did not discover a proper and appropriate answer for this question, because by that hour, I was living outside of time.

During the sixth week I experienced a genuine, intense desire to die.

During the seventh week, everyone around me annoyed me. My siblings almost suffocated me with their deliberately hostile acts and by mocking my taciturn presence among them. When I observed them attack me and my withered existence in my chilly room, I would wonder when their innocent childhood had left them. I was afraid to examine my brothers' faces for fear I'd detect thick mustaches or long beards.

During the eighth week of his absence, I told my ego, after sitting her down beside me on the bed: "You're stupid!" I slapped her around several times without allowing her to respond. Then I screamed in her face: "The failure of a temporary liaison, which lasted only a few days, does not give you the right to judge everyone around you with a critical eye. Even more important than that—it does not give you the right to destroy *me*."

Then I dragged my ego by the collar of her tunic and tossed her among the books and school notebooks as I asked her resolutely: "When do you think you will complete these school assignments that have been piling up here for weeks?"

I screamed at her face as she tried to escape: "Do you want us to taste flunking out after swallowing a failure in love?"

Even so, my ego ignored all my anger and did not listen to what I told her. In fact, she ignored me for three days in a row. My increasingly urgent pressure on her, day after day, finally caused her to surrender and shake off the dust of loss and laziness that had coated her. Then she brought the books and notebooks near her and began to complete all the homework that had been piling up for almost two months.

My father and mother were unable to explain what had happened to me. One day my mother telephoned Maysun and asked her if I had suffered some situation that had made me turn into a different girl unlike the angel they knew.

Frankly, these weren't exactly the words my mother said to Maysun. On the phone, she asked her, "Has there been some falling-out between you and Faleeha? She doesn't talk to us anymore. She eats in her room when she's hungry. She sleeps for hours on end and starts screaming if her siblings enter her room."

Actually, since I was asleep in my room, I did not hear anything my mother said to Maysun, who told me the next morning when we were waiting for the bus. Maysun herself added, "Your mother is very anxious about what has led to all this. Tell me: Is something the matter?"

I was unable to answer Maysun, and hot tears flowed down my cheeks all the way to the institute. The only reason I stopped crying was my fear of questions if other students observed my tears. Even before I removed my abaya, I ran to the restroom and washed my face repeatedly with cold water from the tap. Then the redness of my eyes was less obvious.

After the end of the school day, I dragged my ego to our apartment and entered through the open door, where my foot bumped into a man's nut-brown leather shoes at the doorstep. This was naturally not one of my father's shoes; my father did not leave his shoes there because he believed that would bring bad luck.

These shoes meant we had a visitor, but I did not pay the matter any heed, because guests were always welcome in our home. They had a right to come whenever they wished to visit my father or check on my mother's health, which had continued to fluctuate between stable and concerning.

I went to my room and closed the door so I could change my clothes. Then one of my sisters came, opened the door, and said, "It seems this man will never leave. He's drinking his third cup of tea." Then she sat down on the floor and complained, "I'm not going to fix the fourth cup! I'm tired. You go fix the tea this time!"

I left my sister in that room and went to the kitchen. Then my second sister came to say, "Prepare a cup of tea for our guest. Do it quickly." After a brief silence, she added, "We'll die of hunger waiting for Dad to come home!"

I made the tea and walked calmly, carrying the tray. I entered the parlor with my eyes looking down at the floor. When my mother saw me coming, she told our guest, who was seated beside her, "Help yourself, dear!"

The man sat straighter and extended his right hand to lift the cup of tea from the tray as he said, "I'm wearing you out today!"

The moment that voice reached my ear with its familiar melodies, I looked at its source. I was motionless as I stared at a flesh-and-blood Anwar.

He took the cup, sipped a little, and then returned it to the tray, which I managed somehow to place on the table, without even being conscious of what I was doing. Then he looked at me with a formidable, yearning smile across his face. He quickly turned back to my mother, and the two sank back into the conversation I had interrupted when I entered.

Embarrassed at finding myself face-to-face with Anwar when I was wearing house clothes, I swiftly left for the kitchen, incredulous at what I had just witnessed. Could I really assert, authoritatively, that the person sitting on the chair in our living room was Anwar?

His voice, though, which he raised a little as he said goodbye to my mother at the door, confirmed that for me. Then I felt a joy I could not comprehend. I was also dumbfounded by how all the convoluted anger, sorrow, fear, deprivation, despair, and pain that had concentrated in the pit of my spirit for the last two months, like oil settling in an oil well waiting to be flared off, had all dissipated in a moment. Then a question popped into my mind: What was Anwar doing here?

My mother closed the door after our guest departed and came to the kitchen, followed by my siblings, who had begun asking her to prepare lunch at once. I, for my part, tiptoed to the door for fear someone might hear me and opened it to find Anwar waiting on the third step down.

When he saw me, he smiled more sweetly than ever. Then he lifted his pants leg to show me the bandage on his knee, which had white gauze wound around it. Once he was sure I had seen his wounded knee, he whispered, "I left you a letter tucked in the chair I was sitting in!"

I closed the door very quietly after I watched his shadow follow him down the building's stairway. Then I quickly returned to the parlor and drew the chair toward me. When his surprise letter fell from it, I promptly hid it in the wardrobe in my room and hurried back to the parlor, which was still redolent of his sweet cologne, the breath of his presence, and the charm of his words, which I heard echoing everywhere.

I opened the curtain at the window and began to watch his slow progress down the street. When he stood on the sidewalk and hailed a cab, before he climbed into it, he looked back at our window as if he knew I would be standing there.

My eagerness to learn why Anwar had come to visit was so great that I went to sit with my mother and siblings around the lunch mat even before they called me to eat. The moment one of my sisters asked my mother why our guest had come today, she immediately provided us all the details as she distributed discs of bread to us. I learned that he had come to give my father news of his paternal uncle's son's injury because they had fought together in the same battle. They were both wounded, but my father's cousin's injury was so very grave he might not survive it. Anwar would return tomorrow to take my father to see the wounded man in the hospital.

When I washed the dishes after we finished eating, my fingers seemed to be delightedly playing a song of joy that they had been missing for the last sixty days. Then I hastily completed my homework and helped my siblings with theirs. I braided my sister's hair after she finished bathing as we laughed a lot at my brother, who was attempting to speak literary Arabic—instead of our Iraqi dialect—imitating dubbed cartoons. Everyone, myself included, felt that I had returned today from wherever I had been lost for weeks.

After the household calmed down, and everyone else was napping, I turned off the lights and slipped to the parlor, where I fell asleep on the sofa, buoyed by the memory of Anwar's magical presence and inhaling the fragrance of his cologne, which lingered everywhere in the room.

I put off reading the letter until the next morning and left it dozing calmly among my folded clothes. Yes, I slept and dreamt of the magical nourishment of love's consonants, like a hungry person dreaming of a delicious plateful of sweets, better than any he had ever tasted.

At six the next morning, my father returned from his assigned guard duty, and I opened the door for him, welcoming him with a broad smile. He greeted me and went to bed. I, however, returned to my room, opened the wardrobe, removed the letter from it, and sat down on my bed. I began to examine each of its words, one syllable at a time:

Good morning, if it is morning. Good evening, if it is evening.

My dear Faleeha,

I don't know if you realize that I am serving as an infantryman. I am currently assigned to the Southern Brigade in Basra. Like many other Iraqi soldiers, I previously trained in the region of al-Mahawil in the city of Hilla. In Basra there are many cinemas.

After training, most soldiers go to the cinema houses once they have filled their stomachs with falafel and drunk a cup or two of tea bought from a roving vendor.

Soldiers aren't primarily concerned with watching films in these cinemas. Instead, they enter to take a nap after spending an extremely arduous day in strenuous military drills, obeying stern military commands.

These halls frequently reek of the stink of soldiers' boots, of the tired feet inside them, of the sweat that has dried on their khaki uniforms, and the sound of their snores, which drown out the atmospheric music of most of the films.

Once, though, when I did not fall asleep, I watched a war film, the title of which I've forgotten. The hero had gone off to war and left his sweetheart for a long time. When he longed for her, he wrote her a letter and sent it to her. But his letter, which he thought was top secret and would be read only by his sweetheart, made its way through many cities, where many high-ranking officers read it after it fell into their hands, before it finally reached the hand of its intended recipient.

I really loved the scene when his letter finally reached his sweetheart's hand and the way she began kissing the letter, sniffing it, and hugging it, even before she read its words.

At that moment I wished I had a devoted sweetheart who was waiting for me to return, a sweetheart to whom I could write letters I would post to her and then sit on a berm while imagining the postman arriving at her home.

Because God placed you in my heart the first time I set eyes on you, I am writing that letter to you now and delivering it with my own hand. Thus I am both the correspondent and the postman. I haven't been able to post you a letter in the mail for fear that such a letter would cause you problems with your family, if it fell into their hands.

I apologize for my lengthy absence from you. I and the other soldiers in my regiment have been actively repelling numerous attacks by the Iranian Army on the southern sector of Basra.

I have been lucky this time and survived by a miracle because many soldiers have fallen victim to these sudden and repeated attacks.

I was not conscious of pain in my wounded leg until I and many other soldiers reached another berm, after our berm was destroyed when it was bombarded by Iranian artillery. Once I was evacuated along with other wounded soldiers, I was thinking only of the two people whom I consider the two most important people in my life. They are my mother and you.

Before I forget: I have been granted a fifteen-day leave. You will see me every day in the morning—even on Friday. You will find me standing there, waiting for you. Perhaps I will see you somehow. Please don't grow bored by my presence, because a day has no savor for me, unless I see you.

Anwar

I wept for ever having doubted him and for my stupidity and ignorance of the terrors he was suffering on battlefronts while I, like a coddled brat, was venting my wrath on the innocent people around me and also tormenting my ego and helping it fall prey to suspicions that were unrelated to anything in reality.

I read the letter a second time, imagining myself to be the girl in that film as she read the letter from her true love, the soldier. To the scene of her reading the letter, I added many romantic details that I need not mention here.

Before 3:00 p.m. announced itself, I was turned out with the prettiest jewelry, looking my most beautiful, even though I was wearing a black tunic. Gardenia perfume wafted from my body with my slightest gesture. To appear totally natural, I took a history book with me and sat in the parlor, after I had checked repeatedly to be sure it was tidy. I sat facing the chair that had enthroned Anwar the day before. As I settled myself to await the moment his fingers rapped musically on the door, I hoped that only I would hear him knock.

By ten minutes after three, I heard, with my heart before my ears, his angelic steps ascend the stairs and stop at the door. His footsteps were so gentle and light that only a devoted ear and a loving heart would have noticed them or heard them tap the floor.

I sprang from the chair where I was sitting, a chair that had barely been able to encompass the expectant mass I had turned into since my intuition had confirmed his imminent arrival. I rushed to open the door, and then found him before me. He said nothing but extended his right hand to shake mine.

I did not hesitate to shake his hand, and intentionally forgot to retrieve mine, letting the touch of my fingers transmit to him both my desire for him and my pain during his absence. I have no idea how long I remained like this, with my eyes closed, trying to inhale his celestial cologne, with only the doorstep separating us.

When I heard footsteps approaching from inside the apartment, I withdrew my hand from his, and he entered as he said for everyone to hear: "Peace on all of you. Is Uncle Abu Falah here?"

I replied, "Yes. Please come in!" Then I retreated inside to inform my father that the guest we had been expecting had arrived. Anwar did not sit alone for long. Once my father appeared and the two men greeted each other, they left together to visit our injured relative, whose fate I never troubled myself to ask my mother about after that day, because the fact that my father had not attended another wake meant that the young man, whose condition had been described as "critical," had recovered.

Personally, I spent the next fifteen days in a state of rapture and perpetual emotion, as if I were a coddled girl living in God's heart.

My mornings were dew-struck from the moment I saw Anwar standing on the sidewalk waiting for me at seven thirty. By night I was plunged into a world of the imagination and frequently seated Anwar's apparition in my grandmother's spot, and he and I discussed many topics: love, war, the different scents we both loved, the titles of films we *had* to see together, the name of the school where I wanted to teach after I graduated from the institute, and still other topics that I would not have been willing to discuss with anyone but Anwar.

In the swell of every wave of love that swept over me, I never forgot my grandmother, although I felt somewhat nervous whenever her apparition faded during this period. I wondered if she were angry at me for some reason, perhaps at my not having been to visit her grave. I doubted that was the reason, because she certainly knew that I could in no way imagine her sleeping beneath the cold tombstone of her grave while I continued to live.

When I fell asleep, I found myself copying Anwar's steps as I danced with him in the moonlight while splashes of euphoria surged from the melody of an ancient, classical tune. I felt my braid turn green and grow so long it reached my feet. It extended so far, I almost tripped on it and fell. I don't know where my grandmother emerged from to take it and then disappear at that same spot.

I wasn't angry at my grandmother when I woke the next morning and attributed her odd comportment the night before to her discomfort with my recent behavior. She had not gone to such pains to raise me and been so vigilant about my welfare only to find me dreaming about dancing with a man in the moonlight.

That wasn't all, but I totally forgot the dream's details and implications when I saw Anwar advancing toward me with yet another present, which he offered to me as he said, "A jasmine morning to you!"

Before he hastened away, I whispered, "A luminous morning to you!"

I did not wait to return home to open his present; instead, I quickly tore off the wrapping to find a cassette entitled: "A Song by the Artist Abdel Halim Hafez: Where Should We Begin Our Story (Nebtedi Menien El Hikaya)."

Once Anwar returned to Basra, this song became my sole consolation, and I listened to it every time my desires exhausted me. I would collapse, alone, into a blaze of passion. Truth be told, I did not hear the voice of the Egyptian superstar Abdel Halim Hafez. Instead, Anwar's warm voice emerged from that cassette.

One day I returned from the institute to find my mother wearing a hijab, stockings, and abaya, preparing to depart. She informed me she was going with my father to console a relative whose son had been brought home from the front a martyr. She asked me to change out of my school uniform into a black dress and join them.

I did as she told me, and we descended from our apartment to the street silently. My father hailed a taxi, and my mother and I sat in the back seat while my father, as was the custom, sat in front with the driver. He engaged in no small talk with that driver. I attributed his silence to his fatigue, which was apparent from his body and attributable to his need to rest at this time of day.

The taxi took us to the Abu Khalid neighborhood. When we reached it, we found the neighborhood's streets jam-packed with the vehicles of people who had come to attend this wake. The closer we came to the martyr's home, the louder women's wailing grew, drowning out the voices of those arriving for or leaving the wake.

My father went to the male mourners' pavilion, which had been erected outside the house, and my mother entered the deceased man's house, which had a piece of black cloth pasted to the wall. I paid no attention to what was written on it, because in my opinion *everyone* slain in the war was an immortal martyr in his shroud. There was no need to remind people of that to encourage them to lament his loss or to increase their respect for him.

My mother entered the house, crying out at the top of her voice: "Yabuuu!" I followed her silently. The women inside responded to her scream with even louder shouts. Then they crowded toward her and began fervently beating their faces and chests.

At that moment I felt a painful sting in my heart and was struck by panic about something unfathomable except for its bitter taste, something totally black that was quickly invading my spirit with gloom and engulfing it.

I soon experienced difficulty breathing because of the crush of women and the way they were shoving against each other in that limited space. I turned to return to the street for a breath of air, but the very loud scream from one woman's mouth stopped me in my tracks as I observed the bodies of all those women swarm around that lady, whose voice grew ever louder, although she was already hoarse, as she shrieked, "My little boy!"

She was raising both her hands high, toward a large portrait inside a black frame, which she was trying to show to all the keening women around her.

I lost my balance and fainted when I saw the face of my beloved Anwar smile down on me.

Chapter Seven

When I came to, at home, I did not weep. I did not scream. Any emotional outburst would have forced me to explain it to my family. Oddly enough, by the morning of the next day, I felt, simply put, that a skillful surgeon had opened my body with his scalpel and entirely removed my vital organs, replacing them with dark ashes kneaded with clay after the entire earth and everything on it had been torched and scorched.

I lost any ability to savor even my sorrow over what had happened and gradually turned into a machine that performed its routine chores in an exemplary way. The most important of these was caring for my ailing mother.

My success in the fourth year did not wring even a phony smile from me. What was success worth when death stole my loved ones from me, one by one? I sincerely entreated myself to shed some tears over the corpses of the martyrs so that I would seem, even to myself, a normal girl, like any other. Those corpses were brought to their families to bid farewell before being taken to the cemetery for burial. People would transport them in pickup trucks to their houses as waiting mourners wailed.

I failed miserably at this, not merely because I had lost all my feelings but because the sight of those corpses entering a street leading to apartment blocks became very common—so common that it was unusual to go out on the balcony to hang clothes out to dry and *not* see a truck carrying the body of a martyr.

When you remember that the dead were victims and that each battle harvested thousands, you grasp that a single battle in 1985 created five thousand Iraqi martyrs.

Truth be told, some people saw their professions flourish brilliantly thanks to these battles. They became wealthy and had large houses built for them. As the saying goes: only people willing to stick out their neck acquire great riches. These profiteers included eulogists, undertakers, grave diggers, shroud sellers, ironmongers who produced the grilles placed on graves, and most definitely the coffin makers.

Perhaps all these profiteers and their crafts are common elsewhere except for that of the eulogist, the *mulaya*, who is, simply put, a woman who, with one or more assistants, recites in a loud, stentorian voice, using a megaphone at times, *latmiyat* verses, in Iraqi dialect, extolling the merits and virtues of the deceased and—if he was a martyr—his bravery at the front. This performance spurs women to slap their chests and wail for the deceased.

The fact is that these poems termed *latmiyat* are written by a eulogist only once; she simply substitutes a new name for the deceased each time she appears at a funeral. This profession dates back to antiquity among Iraqis, all the way to the Babylonians and Sumerians. This vocation is mentioned in the *Epic of Gilgamesh* as being reserved for temple priestesses.

Other trades unrelated to death experienced a slump. For that reason, my father, despite his numerous attempts to reclaim his restaurant job, which he had been forced to quit when he joined the People's Army, had no income besides his office job, which provided him only a modest monthly salary.

This year and subsequent ones exposed us to another threat even more terrifying than watching multitudes of processions for martyrs pass by our homes after every battle. This was exposure to the random bombardments of our previously secure cities once Iran began targeting Baghdad with long-range Scud missiles and what were termed land-to-land rockets. There was no way for these rockets to avoid passing over cities near Baghdad, like Najaf.

On October 13, 1987, Iran launched ballistic missiles that struck Bilat al-Shuhada' Elementary School in the Dora neighborhood of Baghdad, ending the lives of thirty-eight children and dozens of innocent civilians who lived in houses near that school. After seeing televised footage of the blood of those children covering the floors, and body parts scattered between wrecked school chairs, my family, like other families with school-aged children, needed many flowery sentences and honeyed words as well as empty promises to calm their children, first of all, and then to encourage them to attend school again.

For many days, my twin brothers held hands as they walked to their primary school, trembling as they proceeded as unsteadily as if walking over the twisting bodies of vipers, and training their eyes upward all the way, fearful that a cunning errant missile attack would in a split second reduce their bodies to smoldering ashes. My brother who was several years their senior refused to attend his middle school for days, informing my father that he would rather die at home than in his school. He said he wanted his flesh and blood to mingle with those of the other members of his family—not with people whose only tie to him was attending the same school. None of us blamed him for this decision. The point he missed was that we were embroiled in a war that would not allow us to choose an appropriate death.

Years passed during which every beat of their waking hours sounded like the drums of war. We matured without any goal or hope in life. We were just waiting for the end of a war that had begun for some reason that escaped us now. Nothing around us grew and multiplied save fear, and all those battles left nothing in our minds but the unfamiliar names of cities where they occurred.

It was not easy to forget names that were pronounced almost every day, that newscasters reported on TV, that teachers and students repeated at school and members of our family discussed at home, names like the Majnun Islands, al-Fao, Shalamcheh, Mehran, Dehloran, the Jasim River, and Khorramshahr. These aren't neutral names we remember nonchalantly now; they are names that have acquired in our memories a special resonance derived from all the blood that dyed those lands. Every mother of a martyr has a scorching memory of them, and time will never cool their fire.

On the evening of July 18, 1988, we were sitting down when Iraqi television announced on its one official channel that Iran had accepted UN Security Council resolution 598. This acceptance meant the end of Iran's war with Iraq, the exchange of prisoners of war, and the withdrawal of both sides to the internationally recognized boundaries. This decision would take effect August 8, 1988.

We exchanged questioning glances with each other. Had the war really ended? We could not believe this news even as we watched the presenter announce it. For eight years, we had never heard a single word about peace.

My siblings and I raced to the windows of our apartment to see what was happening outside because my father wasn't there to confirm this important news. When we rushed to the windows, we found the skies lit up with gunfire. People had become so addicted to gunfire that they were now using it to express their joy—after it had previously meant nothing but death.

My widowed sister began to cry and wept till midnight. Her sobs seemed to swell until they embraced all the widows of martyrs. This was the end of the Iran-Iraq War, which had caused a million fatalities and huge numbers of war prisoners and of men missing in action. In Iraq, that war became known as "Saddam's Qadisiyah," after the seventh-century battle in which the Sasanian Persians were defeated by the Muslim

Arabs, and in Iran, it was called the "Sacred Defense," *even though it changed nothing* in the region where it occurred and *had no winner*.

It was in this year, too, that I graduated from the Teacher Training Institute and realized my father's dream by becoming, in the ninth month of that year, the first woman teacher in our entire tribe, though I did not feel even a second of joy from my achievement. Simply put, I was no phoenix, which, legend says, shakes off its ashes and lives again. I was just an ordinary girl who had not experienced a typical adolescence or youth like those in the rest of the world.

I acquired my first job as a teacher in an elementary school in a distant region outside Najaf, in the direction of al-Qadisiyah. I was supposed to work there for two years before I was transferred to a school in our city. This was the operative plan of the Department of Education: new teachers served first in outlying schools in rural areas before they were transferred to a city's schools.

My first day on the job, my father accompanied me on the commute. We had to take two different taxis. The first transported us to al-Meshkhab, thirty-five kilometers south of Najaf, and the second took us to the school to which I was assigned. I remember seeing many new women teachers that day—all approximately my age—waiting for taxis to take them to the school where they had been assigned.

My father and I entered the school and greeted its principal, who was an elderly man, many years older than my father. He informed us he was requesting retirement that year. After we listened to his instructions, which he delivered in a calm voice lacking the severity typical of many principals, he gave my father the names of dependable taxi drivers who transported female teachers from the bus stop in the center of the municipality to the local schools.

At the end of our visit to the school, which counted as my first day on the job, I joined with four other teachers to hire a local, middle-aged driver to drive us daily—except naturally not on Fridays and school holidays—from the center of al-Qadisiyah to this school for a monthly rate that we would split among us. No bus serviced the school, since the roads weren't paved in these regions—they were dirt roads. Because there was so much dust, each of us women teachers brought two abayas. We wore the first from our homes to the center of the municipality and switched into the other one in the taxi.

The location of the school required us to enter it by walking on a palm trunk that ran at right angles to rows of palm trunks from the place where we were dropped by the car because a river separated the school from the community in which it was located. Inhabitants referred to these trunks as a bridge. During my first difficult experience crossing it with my father while I was wearing black high-heeled shoes that I had purchased especially for my career, I was forced to remove them for fear of falling into the river. So I began wearing flats every morning and changing into my high heels in the teachers' room once I entered the school.

One strange thing about this school was that a single class contained students of different ages. In sixth elementary, for example, there were thirty pupils, and you would find some students who were over sixteen. Their manly features were obvious, and they would address you respectfully, but with a low, masculine voice.

One unexpected experience occurred at a meeting between the teachers and families of the students before the end of the first term. An extremely beautiful young girl attended the meeting and asked for me shyly. When I met with her, she inquired about Ja'far Muhammad, who was one of my pupils. I discussed with her his academic achievements and told her he was absentminded, had trouble focusing, did not seem interested in the subject matter, did not complete all his homework, and frequently forgot his book or notebook at home. Therefore, he needed a lot of help. If he did not receive this assistance, he would not pass that year. The girl, though, fell silent and blushed. She felt very embarrassed speaking to me. When I noticed that, I asked her, "What is your relationship to Ja'far? Is he your brother?"

She moved a little closer to me and whispered, "No, miss, he is my husband."

In this awkward situation, all I could do was to amend my remarks and say, "I will try to work much harder with him. God willing, if he cooperates with me, he will pass."

Because we were novice teachers, we needed to listen frequently to the principal's suggestions and the advice he continually offered us. But we also had to seek the advice of other teachers older than we were when preparing our lesson plans for the day, the week, the month, the semester, or the year. After I had spoken to one of the older female teachers more than once, I developed a relationship of camaraderie and respect with her. But this teacher, who was about to get married, when she saw I was incapable even of faking a smile in the funniest situations, realized how badly I needed love and told me, "You don't have a heart in your chest, just a dead organ."

Her comment frightened me, even though it was true, because how could I resuscitate this inanimate object without any help? I pretended to ignore the matter for some days—until a student from the first primary class placed in my hand a piece of paper, which, he said in an innocent, angelic voice, was "From Mr. Hisham."

I accepted the paper and put it with my books. After I finished teaching the class, I went to the break room and read:

> *Hello, miss . . . , the amazing thing is that even though I have not yet achieved the honor of learning your noble name, when I entered the room for the parent-teacher meeting, I saw a halo of light surrounding your chair. It almost blinded me. I left but later regretted doing that and feared my day would end without you knowing how*

lucky I feel to have seen you today. All the same, I'm afraid you will think I am demented or rash to reveal all this to you. Act as you see fit, choose the worst possible sobriquets for me, but I hope you will cast one glance at the closed door of the classroom opposite yours because behind it there may be a man who feels ignited by your presence, and I am that man. I pray I will receive an answer from you.

"You know what: you really are demented," I told myself as I folded that piece of paper and placed it in my handbag. When I was returning home, I read it a second time, without his words evoking the least sensation in me, and placed it back in my handbag, which my siblings would not dare examine or mess with now that I had become a teacher—in other words, an adult woman.

That remained the status of things for two full months during which Hisham sent me other letters like this one:

Today I discovered that the sky and the earth are conspiring against me. The sky allowed you to escape from the cage of angels without trying to stop you, and the earth spread its gravity beneath your feet, allowing you to tread on the man you do not favor. Although I am a man who normally pays no attention to the colors and proportions of women's shoes, I now listen for the tap of your shoe on the floor. Then perhaps you are passing by the closed door of my classroom. This is a very frightening observation for someone you are ignoring.

I did not even try to glance at him as he passed near me, whether intentionally or accidentally, but another letter from him did provoke a strange feeling inside me and made me smile for a moment.

I have learned that you will not reply to my letters. How can a lonely stranger ask the sky to rain its blessings down on him when he does not possess a tongue fit for prayer? I apologize again, but here's an observation: feel free to ignore this letter as you have those before it, but please do not ignore the little heart I drew on the blackboard of your classroom this morning before you arrived. It's not children messing around. It is my heart shrinking to this small size since you ignore its pulse.

When I had erased that chalk heart from the blackboard, it had never occurred to me that a grown man had drawn it. For him to confess this meant he was either insane or truly in love.

I allowed myself another chance to fall in love and admired his long letters, which revealed he was an educated man and a big reader of romantic books. I started to reply to him in terse phrases that did not suggest a great, forceful love but did hint at my admiration and respect for him. Ten months later, precisely on the final day of the sixth month, a collection of his letters reached me. It contained almost three hundred letters, each pulsing with passion and affection.

He asked me in one of his letters to inform my family that he intended to visit, along with his mother, in the middle of the seventh month to ask them for permission to marry me. His father had died many years earlier, he informed me, and Hisham now occupied the rank of *shaykh*, or chief of the dominant tribe in his region. He was responsible for the direction of all its affairs. I was delighted by the seriousness of Hisham's concern for me but did not tell my family he intended to visit them to ask for permission to marry me.

Before this school year ended, a teacher named Miss Awham was transferred to our school. Miss Awham had long hair and a light complexion, but her lower jaw was large, and she could only close it with difficulty because her teeth were long and irregular. If that weren't enough, the prominent hump on her left shoulder exposed her to the pupils' mockery during her first days in our school. Their mockery quickly ended, though, once they grew accustomed to seeing her every morning.

I reached out to her to discuss school-related topics. Within a few days we exchanged phone numbers, after it became clear she also lived in Najaf. Although she did not visit our home, I received numerous phone calls from her, and we discussed various topics related to our lives.

July ended without Hisham coming to ask permission to marry me. I felt disappointment hover over my spirit again. I called Maysun and asked her to accompany me to my school to pick up my monthly salary payment. She accepted on condition that I go with her to her school for the same reason.

We had trouble reaching the school and found the principal waiting for us. He had stacks of bills sorted out on the table for each teacher. When I greeted him and the other teachers present, he asked me to sign the ledger. Then I deliberately looked for Hisham's name and saw that he had not signed for his salary yet.

I sat down and began to count the bills slowly while listening to the chatter around me, thinking that someone might mention Hisham and I would discover why he had failed to honor his promise to me. I hoped the explanation would be that he was ill or had suffered some accident. When I had sat there for some time, I sensed that Maysun was fidgeting, and I rose to say goodbye to everyone. Just then I heard a male teacher tell the principal, "Mr. Hisham asked me to pick up his salary for him as well as Miss Awham's because they can't come to school today."

The principal smiled and said, "Who would expect them to come today? Take their salaries after you sign by their names."

I felt like a dunce when I learned that Hisham and Awham had been married just two days earlier and that all the male teachers had attended their wedding while the other female teachers had attended a henna night at the bride's house.

I did not shed a single tear at my loss in my second and final round of love. I felt certain then that a woman in Iraq, regardless of the ranks to which she ascends and the degrees she obtains, will never be granted the love of a fair-complexioned man if her complexion is even slightly darker than his. Since she had been born with light brown skin, it would be extremely easy for an ugly woman who looked like the Hunchback of Notre-Dame to steal her man's love.

When I reached our house, before I handed my father the money I had collected, I informed him that I wanted to transfer to another school, to any other school, and that I did not care if this new school was far away or we had to ride a donkey to reach it.

My father's friends acted as mediators for me and transferred me to another school that was much closer, in rural Meshkhab. This new school and its female principal shared the same name. When I entered that school, I learned that the principal was a domineering woman. Her commanding voice and superior way of speaking clearly revealed this. The moment she saw me, she began to address me as if she owned me. The first week passed uneventfully, but the first day of the second week brought a surprise. When I finished teaching my first period, I went to the teachers' room but found none of the female teachers there. I asked the janitor, who had entered to check whether the room was clean, and she told me the teachers were currently in the principal's office.

Thinking there must be an emergency meeting they had forgotten to tell me about, I hurried to the principal's office. All the women teachers were seated in groups on the floor, leaning over a large pile of green broad beans, removing each shell and popping out the beans inside.

This pile of beans reminded me of the banquets given to celebrate large family occasions. Before I had time to ask what was happening, one of the teachers rose and introduced herself to me. "My name is

Miss Mi'ad, and I've taught at this school for three years. Please sit down with us."

"With you? Where? Here?" I asked in amazement.

"Yes. With us," she replied sarcastically. "Are you more important than us?"

I did not like the way she was talking and left the room, incredulous at what I had just seen. Before I could even sit down on the sofa in the teachers' lounge, Miss Mi'ad followed me there and walked right up to me. She said, "There have been many teachers before you who did not like the idea, but they reconciled themselves to the dictates of reality. Listen, dear, the principal is a woman who appreciates those who appreciate her and cooperate with her wishes. As for anyone who doesn't, well, you can kiss them goodbye!"

Trying to comprehend what was happening in the school and what kind of cooperation she meant, I asked, "Miss Mi'ad, please explain to me what is happening. Have we been invited to a banquet, for example? Is something happening that relates to the students and their families? And what do you mean by 'cooperating' with the principal?"

She replied rather sharply, raising her voice, "My dear, there's no banquet, and the matter definitely has nothing to do with the pupils. The fact is, briefly put, that occasionally the principal asks us to help her with chores and everyone pitches in. Today, for example, she has some beans to shell. So she brought several kilos to school and asked us to help her with this chore. Our compensation for helping is permission to come to school later the next day!"

"Several kilos? Miss Mi'ad, do you wish to convince me that the huge pile of broad beans I saw is only a few kilos? Doesn't the principal have any daughters to help her with chores like this? Permit me to say, my dear, that what is happening here is not cooperation but conscript labor. It cannot be described in any other way!"

Her anger was evident, but she gained control of herself and said more calmly this time, "I don't think the subject deserves all this debate.

Even if you do not want to help us, you should remember that the principal assists those who assist her!"

I could not play along with this teacher who was trying to construe what was false as true and say that the servitude the teachers experienced was merely "cooperation" or that their forced labor was some form of group work. I stopped debating with her and looked in my handbag for something to distract my mind from brooding about these upside-down priorities. When Miss Mi'ad saw that I was intentionally ignoring her, she calmly left the room, all the while threatening me with every motion of her body, no matter how hard she tried to disguise it.

During my first three months at this school, the teachers, the cleaning staff, and the school guard's family, who lived in a room at the school, were continually busy with chores the principal assigned them. Everyone appeared to be performing the principal's tasks. I could not restrain myself when I saw the principal and her daughter, who worked as a teacher in the same school, treat the school's teachers with haughty disdain, as if they owned them. Then I began discussing seriously with some teachers the poor working conditions at the school and the need to reject these rules put in place by the principal herself, who was blind to the fact that the job of the teachers was to teach and to complete the year's instructional program in the best possible way. We needed to concern ourselves with the pupils—not with someone else's chores.

The other teachers, though, seemed oblivious to the matter, and their excuse was that this situation would last only till the end of the current school year, when they would be transferred to other schools back in the city, as stipulated by law. They told me this, all using the same language: "We wish to end this year tranquilly, without any problems, so please focus on your own affairs."

I did not feel disconcerted when they told me this, because my duty was merely to offer advice. Acting on it was left to them. Only one other teacher sided with me in rejecting everything that was happening in the school that was not related to teaching or instruction. She was called Miss Khadija. She had also refused to perform the tasks the other teachers were forced to do. She and I would sit together whenever we could and discuss various books we were reading while we spent most of our time completing our lesson plans, reviewing and explaining difficult school subjects, and filling in gaps left by the neglect of the other teachers in their lessons.

As the first semester drew to a close, external examiners began to visit schools to evaluate the performance of teachers and administrative staff and to reassure themselves about the progress of "the educational initiative," as it was called. During each of these visits, the principal praised only Miss Mi'ad, her dedication to the instructional program, and how competently she utilized her instructional expertise to convey the educational materials to the pupils in the desired manner.

Matters progressed to the point that the principal recommended Miss Mi'ad for promotion to the post of assistant principal after the current assistant principal submitted a request for retirement due to a health condition. None of the rest of us, however, paid any attention to this, because our common goal was to transfer out of this school at the end of the academic year.

One day, one of these visiting external examiners asked for a teacher to present a model class with the pupils of her class, to which male and female teachers from different area schools would be invited.

A model class in Iraq is a sample class a teacher presents on some subject. It lasts approximately an hour, and the first forty-five minutes are dedicated to presenting the topic. The subsequent minutes are reserved for discussion and for a dialogue between the teacher and the guests invited to attend this class. An instructional supervisor, who is an expert in the subject matter in question, evaluates the work of the teacher and her performance and points out strong and weak points in that teacher's performance. This is done in a written evaluation, a copy of which is sent to the Department of Education. Another copy is sent to the teacher's school, where it is preserved in that teacher's personnel file.

The principal summoned us to her office and informed us in a commanding way that she had nominated me and Miss Khadija to offer this class. We did not decline this nomination, contrary to her expectations. Instead, we devoted every effort to preparing and readying the pupils for this class.

We began more than ten days in advance and strategized as if we had been assigned a military foray: My colleague and I took turns providing the pupils we had selected for this expedition the necessary information so presentation of this sample class would proceed in a satisfactory fashion. We drilled the pupils till they understood the information and how to apply it.

On the day scheduled for the model lesson, the principal came and asked me to show her the lesson plan. So I handed her my notebook containing my daily plans, and she took it to show to the male superintendent, who was sitting in her office waiting for the teachers to arrive from the other schools.

I searched for my colleague but did not find her. I began to feel nervous when I saw groups of male and female teachers arriving from other schools. But I got control of myself and hurried to check that the classroom was sparkling clean and that the pupils' chairs were arranged properly. Then I ran through a quick review of the lesson with the pupils. Once I was satisfied that everything seemed to be in good order, I went to the principal's office to see if Miss Khadija was there.

When I did not find her there and instead found the principal and the superintendent discussing details of the plan for my class that was moments away from being delivered, I asked why Miss Khadija was late. The principal rose and asked me with a nod of her head to follow her out of the room. I did, and once we were a short distance from its door, she suggested to me in a hushed voice that I teach the class with Miss Mi'ad instead of Miss Khadija.

I refused, saying, "I can teach the class by myself. I've never needed another teacher with me in the class."

Her face became red. She had grown used to hearing nothing but obedient acquiescence to her commands, even insane ones. She had never imagined that I might reject this suggestion of hers.

The class went brilliantly, and those present praised me. Even now I remember a sentence the superintendent said to me, vaunting my perfect presentation of the lesson: "Miss Faleeha, I congratulate you on your presentation of this splendid lesson. I will recommend to the authorities that they have you present a model class at the governorate level. God bless you."

The principal was annoyed by that and looked jealous. Then she left the classroom swiftly without offering any excuse for her abrupt departure. I stayed with my class, greeting my guests and offering them sweets and bottles of juice I had purchased from the school store that morning. After the guests left, I rewarded the pupils by offering them the rest of the sweets and juice as well as colored pencils.

Miss Khadija appeared the next morning, and when I asked why she had been absent the previous day, she replied that she had not wanted to get into trouble with the principal! I did not ask her to explain herself; it was very clear to me: I was now the sole enemy of our excellent principal.

In fact, I started to notice that when we turned in our daily or weekly lesson plans to the principal to examine, my notebook lacked the principal's signature when it was returned at the end of the day. The principal would frequently add to her signature words of praise for the plan submitted to her. I never found anything of that kind in my notebook but did not feel anxious about the matter. Instead, I continued to write out a detailed lesson plan every day, without fail.

At the start of the second term, I entered the teachers' room after the second period and found the other teachers divided into small groups. Each group sat around a stainless-steel tray covered with rice. The teachers were cleaning the grains of rice of any dross, like unprocessed grains, weevils, and tiny pebbles.

I shook my head incredulously when I saw this. I felt a stifling anger when I saw two large sacks of rice, each weighing fifty kilos, leaning against each other at the center of the room. I immediately returned to the classroom where I had been teaching and asked one of the pupils to collect their notebooks so I could begin correcting them. Once he did, I took them from him and returned to the teachers' room, where I sat on the sofa and started reading through them in an attempt to restrain my anger.

When the principal entered the room and found that I was not participating in her "teamwork" task, as these chores were referred to, she cast me a look that I understood to mean she was threatening me with an impending evil. In fact, just as I expected, the next day brought me an unhappy surprise. My colleague Miss Khadija and I were summoned to attend an inquiry that same afternoon on an official complaint presented by the headmistress of the Teachers Association.

My father was very surprised when he read the summons the principal had handed to me with a victorious smile. My father told me that—to the best of his knowledge—inquiries into violations and errors committed by teachers were investigated in the Department of Instructional Supervision by a committee composed of some individuals from the Department of Education and instructional supervisors, and that there was something fishy about this summons. But he also asked me to be courageous and resolute, no matter how hard the investigators tried to make a big deal of the case, because I had done nothing wrong that would put me in a weak position.

At 4:00 p.m., my father and I went to the Teachers Association, which was located on the far side of the residential area. On entering the building, we found Miss Khadija and her father seated in the waiting room.

Some minutes after we arrived, the secretary for the director of the Teachers Association invited us to enter his office with its fancy furniture and luxurious décor. After greeting us and before sharing the details of the case with us, the director asked his secretary to order us cups of tea from the cafeteria. In just minutes, a young man brought us a tray of hot tea fragrant with cardamom. He placed the first cup on the director's desk and then distributed the other cups to us. After taking a sip of tea, the director opened the case folder and began to look through its contents after asking us our names, the name of our school, and the name of the principal.

As he continued turning the stack of pages in front of him, his expression began to change. He soon stopped reading and looked at us again. He asked us our names once more to make sure he was really reading our files and not the files for some other case.

After shaking his head in amazement, he looked at us and said, "Miss Faleeha and Miss Khadija, your principal says that you are unfit for the occupation of teaching because you do not take this employment seriously, that you do not present your lessons properly, that you abuse the pupils, punish them by beating them with a stick, use filthy language, wear immodest clothes, and discuss obscene subjects, and that you, Miss Faleeha, have failed to turn in your daily lesson plan for many months, and that Miss Khadija failed to attend the model class without presenting an acceptable excuse for her absence."

I was enraged when I heard these accusations rain down on us, even though we were not guilty of a single one of them. I was about to release a cataract of screams at the face of this man, who was struggling to understand all these lies that an angry, domineering woman had fabricated against us. But my father sensed my anger and took my hand as if to say: Calm down, let me represent you.

In fact, my father did just that. He began speaking in a relaxed way: "Mr. Director, as I listened to Your Honor, I heard my daughter charged with a number of offenses. One of them was that she did not write out lesson plans. I would like to ask Your Honor to look at the notebook of lesson plans presented to you. You will notice that my daughter was not tardy in writing these plans. If she had been, she would not have had enough time since noon to write down all these lesson plans. As a matter of fact, my daughter has informed me that the principal stopped signing her notebook several months ago. With regard to the accusation that she has been remiss in her teaching, I place before you a copy of the book of thanks presented to my daughter from Instructional Supervision after the success of the model class she taught at her school a few months ago. If you will check the examination scores of her pupils, you will see they excelled. With reference to the charge that she wears immodest clothing, my daughter has always dressed like the other teachers in long skirts and long-sleeved blouses with high collars. As far as the other reports of inappropriate behavior—I know my daughter very well. I cannot imagine her wading into such unseemly conduct. I believe that all the charges the principal has made against these two teachers are false and unsupported by reality."

Before my father finished his statement, my colleague's father quickly spoke up in a voice tinged with anger. He made clear to the director that it was the principal herself who had asked his daughter to skip school that day so Miss Faleeha would be forced to present the model class all by herself.

This inquiry lasted for hours after a representative from Instructional Supervision and another from the Department of Education joined us. We had an excellent opportunity to narrate events occurring in the school with no link at all to instruction and explain how that woman treated everyone who worked at the school as her personal servant and offered bribes to her supervisors to retain her position.

By the end of the inquiry, all the charges lodged against us were dismissed, and the Teachers Association director asked us to return to our school the next morning, to continue working there till the end of the academic year, and to avoid escalating matters between us and the principal so that a bad situation would not become worse.

During the session, a few unintended remarks escaped from the mouth of a committee member. These disclosed to us that the principal's extraordinary powers were not limited to making false claims and fabricating accusations. Instead, she had the raw power to enforce them when she wished. After shaking his head sympathetically as he heard some of the fearful actions occurring at the school, he said, "This woman has an iron support system: her brother is head of a tribe and also a member of a branch of the Baath Party. I leave what she is capable of doing to your imaginations."

We looked at one another without any comment, said goodbye to the members of the committee, and left the association building, heading our separate ways.

I could not stop weeping noiselessly after my voice had been silenced and a stream of false accusations and lies were poured down on me *because* I had refused to conform to the herd. My father, for his part, suggested contacting some of his acquaintances and friends to have me transferred to another school, the way he had the previous time, but I thought that would threaten my self-esteem. So I politely rejected his suggestion.

I went to school the next morning and ignored the whispered conversations around me the moment I entered the teachers' room. When one of the teachers sidled up to me and naively asked about the accusations made against me the previous day, I replied in a voice loud enough for all the teachers in that room to hear, as if I were giving a speech from a dais: "We were accused of telling the truth, and anyone who refrains from telling the truth is a mute demon!"

All the same, each day when I returned home from the school, my mother would entreat me to quit this school and its evil principal.

In fact, in 1990, I was accepted as a student in the women's Faculty of Education in the University of Kufa, and while I was enrolled there, retained all my rights as a teacher, including my monthly salary. My time there also counted as part of my teaching career because I obtained academic leave for four years. I also retained my title as the first woman of our tribe to become a teacher and *now* to enroll in a university.

I had learned from the registrar's office at the University of Kufa that enrollment in this newly created program was limited to women and that only twenty women had matriculated the previous year. The number admitted in my year was only slightly larger. I was in the second cohort of students to enroll, and the students registering came not only from Najaf but from other cities nearby, like Karbala, Diwaniya, and al-Hilla. Although there were universities in those cities, these coed students preferred the University of Kufa for its reputation, since this university was considered one of the most important in Iraq, second only to al-Mustansiriya in Baghdad.

Once I learned I had been accepted into the Arabic Language division of the Faculty of Education, I felt much more self-confident. Despite all my suffering during the war and its aftermath, I had been able to realize not only my father's dream that I become a teacher but also my own dream of pursuing my studies in a university, where I might earn a master's degree or a doctorate.

My mother was relieved to learn from my father the details of my enrollment in the Faculty of Education, Arabic Language division. He assisted me in my application and registration, step by step. I had constantly heard her pray that I would be quickly liberated from "that ill-omened school." My mother realized the amount of harm this evil woman could inflict on all of us if she continued her hostility toward me. My mother's prayer seemed to have found a receptive ear in the heavens above, because the principal forgot all about us after her son was in a terrible traffic accident when he was driving drunk at night. He miraculously survived but needed to stay in bed for months. Then the Department of Education appointed one of the teachers who had many years of experience as the interim principal of our school, and the current principal was granted a lengthy leave to care for her son.

Thus we gave our final exams without ever seeing the face of our former principal. When we were correcting the exam booklets, our new principal sat in the teachers' room and cracked jokes with us. The louder our laughter rang through the room, the grimmer Miss Mi'ad's frown grew and the more the face of the daughter of the principal, who kept company with Miss Mi'ad, as if she were her shadow, clouded over. Their resentment for everyone else showed only too clearly then.

During those days, I asked my father if he would tell al-Fartousi about my journal. He taught my brother Iyas in the technical training school and was also a poet and a member of the Writers and Artists General Union in Najaf. My father agreed, especially since al-Fartousi lived in the apartment building next to ours and had a small shop where he sold paper and school supplies.

One afternoon, my father took that journal with him and sat down for a discussion of my writing with al-Fartousi. The man asked my father to leave my journal with him until the afternoon of the following day. When my father was too busy to go back then, I asked my mother's permission and went with one of my brothers to the stationery shop to retrieve my journal from the man.

Al-Fartousi, who was slightly older than my father, greeted me and said, "You really do have a gift for creative writing." He said he planned to suggest that my father allow me to attend the union's literary meetings that were held one evening a week, if I wished to. I was overwhelmed by an indescribable delight at his important invitation, because it wasn't easy for a girl who came from an ordinary family like mine to attend these sessions. Indeed, they were actually highly significant events, socially and culturally.

I waited impatiently for my father to return home and then told him what had happened. I expected him to reject the suggestion of me going to the union and attending those sessions, especially since the cultural meetings began at six and might last at times till nine or slightly later. When he discerned my intense desire to attend, however, he promised to contact al-Fartousi and ask him for more details. What most concerned him was my personal reputation, which could be affected by associations with men.

My father did go one evening to al-Fartousi's shop to share his concerns about me fraternizing with men. The other man informed my father that several women attended these meetings escorted by their husbands or brothers, and that there was absolutely no harm in my father or a brother accompanying me.

My father was my escort the first time, when the program, which was devoted to pre-Islamic Arabic poetry and criticism of it, was presented by Professor Abdullah al-Sa'igh. I felt enormously proud to find myself seated amid this large group of researchers, literary figures, and scholars of jurisprudence and of language. I continued to attend programs at the union once my father was satisfied that those sessions afforded me intellectual benefit and that I would not be the only woman, because two older women writers attended as well.

After only two weeks, I asked the president of the union, Mr. Makki Zabiba, for a copy of the printed schedule of events, first of all so I could read it and second so I could prepare for a discussion of the lecture to be presented. I prepared for each session by reading books related to its topic and relied on my father's help to obtain those books by borrowing them from the library of the Department of Education.

I gradually worked up the courage to ascend the dais and participate in the literary debates. After joining the union, my cultural personality was quickly burnished, and I again felt a pressing need to quench my thirst for reading after it had remained dormant for some time.

With each book I read, though, the gap between me and those around me grew wider, and I daily became aware of the lack of consciousness of those in my circle. I am indebted for this acquisition of new knowledge to my father, who despite his lack of higher education was distinguished by an open mind, which prompted him to allow me to transform myself from a naive girl to someone with a deeper consciousness than most other young women of Najaf.

In my choice of books to read, I relied on a standard of excellence that I devised for myself with the goal of achieving a level of knowledge that would allow me to at least call myself "a cultured woman," or *muthaqqafa* in Arabic.

I began by asking who the best Iraqi novelists were, the best Arab novelists overall, and the best Western novelists. Once I had compiled a list of those names, I asked which was the best novel by each of these writers. Then I drew up an excellent reading list. Thanks to God, my father cooperated with me, and in several months I read dozens of Iraqi and Arab novels as well as international novels translated into Arabic.

The moment *One Hundred Years of Solitude* by Gabriel García Márquez landed in my hands, though, it took me from the world of reality in which I had been living to the surreal realm portrayed uniquely in those novels of his.

I frequently praised God for the existence of an award like the Nobel Prize for Literature that recognized the literary merit of Márquez. He won this award in 1982 in appreciation for his singularly brilliant writing. Without that award, his works would not have been translated into so many languages, allowing me to become acquainted with him. I did not let up till I had read all of his works available in Arabic. I read the novels *No One Writes to the Colonel, Chronicle of a Death Foretold, Love in the Time of Cholera,* and *The General in His Labyrinth.* I soon read all of his essays, short stories, and the interviews that had been conducted with him; these were loaned to me by local authors who loved his work.

My passion for what he wrote was not limited to reading; it extended to the idea of preserving and making myself a copy of those novels, which were very difficult to obtain, borrow from public libraries, or purchase from bookstores. Instead, they circulated almost in secret.

Each time I borrowed one of his books from a member of the union, I would use a ballpoint pen to copy it out by hand into hundred-page school notebooks. You will realize how weird but also special this situation was when I tell you that all these handwritten copies of his novels were transcribed into notebooks with a picture of President Saddam Hussein on the cover.

You can imagine the number of notebooks and pens it took to copy out those novels. For example, *One Hundred Years of Solitude* in its Arabic translation runs 506 pages. I will also let you guess how many nights that transcribing took.

Even though I reread the novel after I finished copying it by hand, its magic held sway over me as I relived incidents in it, feeling that I was writing about them or that I was each of the major and minor characters.

Truth be told, even now, I can savor the taste of the satirical, surreal picture Márquez drew of the death of the dictator in *The Autumn of the Patriarch* when he described a cow on the balcony. For numerous reasons, this image of the cow rang true to me. We really did aspire to wake up one morning to find cows lowing from the balconies of our dictator's palaces.

There were only two times that I thought Márquez had let me down. The first was when I read *Memories of My Melancholy Whores*, which was published in 2004. It did not appeal to me at all. Perhaps that was merely a matter of my personal taste. The second was when Turkish television showed a film version of *Love in the Time of Cholera*, and I attempted to find then the same delight that this masterpiece had provided me when I read it. To my immense regret, I did not find either love or cholera in that film.

While I was preoccupied by reading novels I borrowed from acquaintances who loved reading and learning, Iraqi soldiers, my brother among them, were preoccupied by executing orders dictated to them by their leader, while destiny seemed oblivious.

With the same mixed feelings of astonishment and terror that dominate Kafka's character Gregor Samsa in *The Metamorphosis*, when he wakes from sleep to find himself imprisoned in the body of a huge insect, we awoke from our slumbers the morning of the second day of

August to the terror of the events caused by the entry of our Iraqi Army into Kuwaiti territories.

Yes, without any real introduction, the Iraqi news presenter Miqdad Murad announced on the official Iraqi TV channel that our army had entered Kuwait at two that morning. In the bulletin, which lasted fourteen minutes and eleven seconds, he announced that the Iraqi Army was backing their illustrious Kuwaiti brethren in the revolution that *they* had announced to liberate Kuwait from the corrupt cabal of collaborators that ruled them.

He naturally did not address the real reasons for this invasion; the most important of these were deep-rooted disagreements between the two nations about their shared boundaries and about pumping oil from wells in those disputed regions.

In a lengthy statement, he announced the formation of a government called the Free Provisional Government of Kuwait, which itself had issued a statement. Just as all the military press releases broadcast throughout the Iran-Iraq War were preceded by the religious invocation "In the name of God, the Compassionate, the Merciful" and recitation of a verse from the Holy Qur'an, this news bulletin also began with an invocation of God and recitation of one of the many verses in the Qur'an about the need to trust in God.

The anchor, in a determined tone, spoke:

> Television of the Iraqi Republic, broadcast by Baghdad and the voice of the masses: You Arab brethren, you brothers in dear Kuwait, the broadcast service of the Free Provisional Government of Kuwait released today, at noon, bulletin number one, which was issued by the Free Provisional Government of Kuwait. For dozens of years, since the daybreak of freedom and independence in our Arab regions, the people of Kuwait have aspired to freedom and participation in realizing the goals of the Arab people for

liberation, unification, and revival, sharing with their fellow Arabs their feelings and noble national aspirations for the honor of the Arab world and the recovery of plundered rights, especially in dear Palestine. Zealous Kuwaitis hope that the independence we have achieved after a taxing struggle and massive sacrifices made by the sons of the people and by sincere nationalists will be the beginning of the road to acquisition of these hopes and goals. Unfortunately, a foreign, colonial power has ruled this land, plundered its riches, and humiliated its people both before and after independence, either directly or indirectly through its agents, including members of the Al Sabah, who were granted power to rule the country after independence. This coterie established a corrupt, dictatorial, family rule. The cosmetic protocols they established to disguise the reality were seen through by the people from the start, because these protocols, which are devoid of any true content, were a fraudulent cover for a tyrannical, family-type government. The people realized that this coterie was resolved to monopolize the reins of power and to ransack the country's revolution by cooperating with a limited and isolated number of mercenaries and massive support from foreign powers. These truths were demonstrated over the course of years through successive experiences because rigging of elections, the imposition of the government's henchmen, the pursuit of nationalist personalities, and limiting their freedom and ability to make a living were always a distinctive characteristic of the rule by the Al Sabah. When the people were able to impose some of their free will in the last elections for the parliament, establishing a powerful bloc of impartial, nationalist deputies who cast light on the regime's tyranny, corruption, its deviant and suspect policies, its actions to squander the riches of the nation, and its links to imperialist and even Zionist interests and circles; and its distribution of the spoils of government to their children, relatives, and henchmen, the oppressive authorities did not tolerate the will of the people, the voice of its earnest citizens, or the truth. Instead, it resorted to intimidation and threats. When these attempts failed to silence the voices of the representatives of the people, they resorted to disregarding the constitution and dissolved the parliament to impose a total reign of terror, repression, and suppression of liberties as well as interference with the right to earn a living. Honorable men, fellow countrymen, noble sons of Kuwait, this oppressive ruling faction and its enablers served foreign interests before independence and continued after independence to serve all the greedy foreign forces in Kuwait and the region. This suspect faction made all our national interests and the wealth of the country subservient to foreign interests—even to some overtly Zionist interests— and moreover to the outright plunder of the country's riches and their distribution as booty among them and their aides, wasting them to feed their appetites and whims in ways that brought dishonor to the proud people of Kuwait and to their deep-rooted Arab, Islamic customs, by, for example, depositing tens—no, thousands—of billions in foreign banks. They tied their investments to shady interests linked to Zionist circles. They did not conceal from the proud citizens of Kuwait the fact that numerous individuals of this oppressive faction, men who were among the individuals known for their excesses in their slide toward the monopolization of power and corruption, including men like Emir Jaber Ahmad Al-Sabah, were among those individuals most trusted by the imperialists, not only in our country, but in the entire region. Imperialists aligned with him and wove conspiracies and plots with him—by foul and innovative means that broke the heart of the free, honorable Kuwaitis—against their proud Iraqi brother, who had borne the bitter responsibility for proudly defending the eastern flank of the Arab world and also that of Kuwait and the entire Arab Gulf while offering huge sacrifices to preserve land, status, and honor. With this detestable conspiracy, which served the goals of imperialism and Zionism by severing the bonds of relationships with family and brethren and in weakening the Arab entity and the Arab resistance against Zionist aggression, that group from Al Sabah and the mercenaries in their retinue disclosed not only their hostility to Kuwait and the Arab people but their treasonous cooperation with imperialism and Zionism. Fellow citizens, the political, economic, security, and social crises that afflict our people are the result solely of a plot concocted by this oppressive faction and their mercenaries with the goal of weakening Kuwait, keeping it a weakling that greedy foreign forces can toy with, while Kuwaitis struggle in a perpetual whirlpool of fear, anxiety, and chaos—so that they will not notice the corrupt deeds of the government and its despicable machinations and will remain subservient to the rule of the oppressive faction and so that Kuwait will continue to be held hostage by foreign powers: politically, militarily, and economically. Illustrious sons of Kuwait, to hell with anyone who does not understand that the proud Arab, Kuwaiti people cannot accept this vile procedure or the continuation of tyranny. They will not stand by while their country remains a pawn of foreigners and a plantation where corrupt rulers and their mercenaries frolic. The people have made known their views with various forms of rejection and legal opposition, and the conferences that have been held in assembly halls and the demonstrations that have emerged from those assemblies, which included most of the enlightened sons of the people, are the best expression of the true will of the people of Kuwait. The oppressive ruling faction, however, which has grown used to tyrannizing and dominating the citizens, relying on their allies from imperialist and Zionist powers, resorted once again to the use of terror, oppression, and distortion of the will of the people and presented that manifest farce dubbed the "National Council," which was met by the people with a boycott and scorn. Fellow countrymen, dear sons of Kuwait, the matter has come to a head, no far-flying arrow remains notched at the bow, and our people are no longer capable of enduring this degree of oppression, corruption, dissimulation, and conspiracy. The nationalist forces, which have rejected oppression, tyranny, and corruption and have opposed the regime that is allied with imperialist and Zionist circles, have decided, placing their trust in God and on the freely expressed will of the people and their benevolent representatives, to assume the reins of responsibility and to depose the corrupt, tyrannical, complicit regime. Dear Kuwaitis, we announce the formation of the Free Provisional Government of Kuwait, which assumes all the responsibilities, legislative and executive, of the country during the transitional period. The Free Provisional Government of Kuwait, once the necessary stability has been assured in the country, will conduct free and fair elections to elect a parliament that is representative of the people to take charge of establishing a ruling regime and essential concerns in the country. First among the duties and national, state, and civic responsibilities of the Free Provisional Government of Kuwait will be to address the harm and damage inflicted by the former corrupt regime on our citizens and on our Iraqi brothers, who have been our support and succor in calamities, based on the brotherhood that unites us and the fidelity of honorable men in regard to their responsibilities. We will work to resolve the issue of our borders and our relationship with dear Iraq on the basis of our shared brotherhood and according to the requirements of the supreme national interest. Oh, free fellow countrymen, on this glorious day of the blessed month of Muharram, a new era begins, an era of sincere and earnest effort to anchor the fundamentals of freedom, democracy, justice, and genuine prosperity for society. Arab brothers living in Kuwait, the Free Provisional Government of Kuwait salutes you and invites you to comprehend and support this blessed uprising, which your free brothers have undertaken, because you have the same rights and responsibilities that we do. As for foreign nationals living in Kuwait, the Free Provisional Government of Kuwait affirms its total dedication to protecting their rights and interests, their safety and honor, and invites them to heed and obey the decisions, instructions, and orders issued by the government. The government also warns them that it will strike with an iron fist anyone who grants himself permission to violate security and social order and execute the plots of greedy foreign powers. The Free Provisional Government of Kuwait affirms its adherence to all the pacts that are harmonious with our Arab, Muslim, and international affiliation— especially the Arab League pact and the joint defense and shared economic cooperation pact between Arab states, the United Nations treaty, the pact of the Organization of the Islamic Conference, and the Gulf Cooperation Agreement. The government also affirms its adherence to all compacts concluded with all other states, except for any secret ones that conflict with our sovereignty and our national obligations and on the basis of adherence to ideals. The government also affirms its adherence to all financial obligations to states and associations on the basis of the cooperation with peers and observance of reciprocal obligations as well. The Free Provisional Government of Kuwait warns vigorously against any form of foreign interference in our internal affairs by no matter what means and against these foreign powers that collaborated with the deposed oppressive faction, knowing that the people of Kuwait together with the sons of pan-Arabism who live in our country will defend the land, honor, and revolt of the blessed people to the last drop of their blood. They will not be frightened by the threats of foreign forces or by their machinations and conspiracies. In this context, the people of Kuwait and its Free Provisional Government reject any pretext or cover that might be used to raise the hopes of shady forces to intervene directly or indirectly, whether with their armies, fleets, or any other means. Any powers that might talk themselves into aggression against our country and the imposition of guardianship over it should realize that the people of Kuwait form part of the Arab world and have illustrious, tried-and-true brethren who will stand beside Kuwaitis should they be exposed to any harm, aggression, or foreign interference. Dear sons of Kuwait! This is your day. This is your era, and an era for all Arabs, an era of freedom, honor, and might. As God revealed to the

Prophet Muhammad: "Say: 'Act, and soon God, His messenger, and the believers will see your work.'" God's word is true. God grants success. God's peace, mercy, and blessings on all of you.

Free Provisional Government of Kuwait,

Muharram 11, 1411 AH

At the time that this news bulletin was being read out to us on TV, one hundred thousand soldiers of the Iraqi Armed Forces with three hundred tanks had seized control of Kuwait City after its ruler, Emir Jaber Ahmad Al-Sabah, fled to the Kingdom of Saudi Arabia and his brother Shaykh Fahd was slain.

On the fourth of August, an official government was formed for Kuwait, which was renamed the Republic of Kuwait. On the ninth day of that same month, Kuwait was proclaimed to be one of the provinces of Iraq, after all the embassies, Arab and non-Arab, in Kuwait were closed. In what seemed no time at all, the name of Kuwait City was changed to al-Kadhima.

In a situation duplicated in most Iraqi families that year, my brother Iyas, who had recently turned eighteen, was forced to participate in those battles, which commenced before we had time to enjoy inhaling even a sniff of peace.

He was summoned to enlist in the infantry of the Iraqi Army. We all believed that he was stationed in Basra, but when I searched for him there, I found this was absolutely not true.

Chapter Eight

My enrollment in the women's branch of the Faculty of Education in the University of Kufa was delayed to the end of October 1990 because of the long time it took me to obtain academic leave from teaching for four years at full salary while I was posted to the Department of Education with the title of teacher.

It is no exaggeration to say that the moment I entered the Faculty of Education was one of the most beautiful of my life. I felt then that life was trying to placate me and reconcile with me after all the atrocious offenses it had committed against me—like the woes of the long war, my mother's incurable illness, and my loss of loved ones before we had fully expressed our affection for each other.

The moment I set foot on the long walkway lined with damask roses, I felt like a queen with a crown on her head passing down streets decorated for her. The faculty's large building differed in both its overall appearance and architectural details from the Teacher Training Institute, where I'd studied. Its size was much grander than the two primary schools where I had taught; that would have been true even if those schools had been merged.

The faculty consisted of several separate buildings, each with its own library. The faculty's main library was located on the top floor of the Geography building, which occupied the other side of the campus.

The year I was admitted, the faculty seemed almost deserted, especially in sciences. The Arabic Language department, which had admitted me, was located on the second floor of the main building. The ground floor contained many laboratories for the Chemistry department, which did not fully move in until two years later. The women's Faculty of Education, even though it had a massive building, contained only three departments: Arabic Language, Geography, and History.

The Arabic Language department also seemed rather empty, and only two of its classrooms were in use. The first was reserved for students in the cohort a year ahead of mine, and the second was for the first-year students, of whom I was one. There was no need for a large lecture hall, and each professor was obliged to come to our classroom to deliver her lectures.

On my first day, I went straight to the library and obtained a card that allowed me to borrow books—even though this library was newly established and did not contain the novels I loved or even the books we were required to review in preparation for the lectures.

On my second day, I stopped one of the students in the cohort a year ahead of us to try to learn something about the way courses were taught, the names of the professors who taught in our department, and other useful tips. During our conversation, which was long and touched on all sorts of other matters, we were approached by a beautiful tall girl whose black hair flowed to her waist and whose eyeliner was expertly applied. When she stood between us, she asked me in an angry voice, as if preparing to strike me, "Are you Faleeha Hassan?"

I calmly said I was, puzzled by her way of introducing herself.

She proclaimed in a voice more like an angry scream than a normal conversation, "I hate you!" She was silent for a time, collecting her breath, and then added, "I hate you because our teachers are always talking about you!"

Then she walked away, stamping her shoes on the floor, as if she wished to convey a message to me with her high heels: "Don't count me out! I study here too, and I'm powerful."

Anxiety had stilled my tongue, and I did not ask her what had sparked this hatred. I had never met the girl; she wasn't in our year. When the other girl observed my astonishment and nervousness about this encounter, she looked at me, smiled, and said, "Don't blame yourself. Most of the other students here share her disdain for you—because our professors talk about you so much. They discussed your enrollment in the program almost joyfully and praised your preparation and your talent. That made it very easy for jealousy to spread among us students."

What this student said made me feel proud. I did not feel hatred or anger at the other student whose chest had been so burdened by loathing for me that she had not been able to bear it and had vented her fury in my face like a cobra spitting venom at its victim.

I returned to my classroom wishing I had a close friend with whom I could share the details of this moment and explain myself, especially since I was experiencing a wide range of emotions. Not even Maysun would have been interested, though, because she had not encouraged me in the decision to enroll in the university when I consulted her. In her opinion, life was an opportunity to enjoy and should not be spoiled by pursuing an education.

By the end of that day, I learned that all the creative, deliberative contacts I had made at the writers union with professors, creative writers, philosophers, literary critics, and cultured people had actually been with members of the university faculty here.

The professors did not treat me like the other students—I admit this. They treated me as if I were one of them. So it became natural for me to enter the offices of professors whenever I wished to discuss topics that were not covered in the formal lectures, and more than one professor asked me to substitute for him and deliver a lecture when he was busy with other matters.

Many of these instructors presented me with copies of their essays, books, and translations—within earshot of the other students. Thus Professor Abdullah al-Sa'igh gave me a copy of his book *Time in Jahili Poetry*, which was published by Dar al-Thaqafa in Baghdad; Dr. Hasan al-Bayati gave me a copy of his novel *Iron Dross* and of a play he translated from Russian as *Those Down Below*. There were many other books they shared with me, but the war erased those titles from my memory.

The flush of happiness I enjoyed during all the hours I spent in this program was dissipated the moment I set foot in our house and saw my sick mother, who was now a nervous wreck because my brother Iyas had disappeared; we had not heard a word from him since he enlisted in the Iraqi Army in Basra. Whenever my mother heard anything about Basra and events occurring there, she would retreat to her room and begin wailing.

I was exhausted from watching my mother suffer emotional pains in addition to her physical ones. Her separation from my brother was accentuated by the woes she had suffered when my father was posted to many different battlefronts.

I had a wild idea and shared it with no one for fear they would dissuade me from acting on it because it was so weird and dangerous. After I heard that the Iraqi Army was headquartered in Basra, I decided to go there to search for my brother, who had no street smarts and no true friends in the army. His social circle was limited to us, his family. We were his household, and I had always been the person closest to him. I was his favorite because I was the oldest sister with whom he had sought refuge in the most serious and grave circumstances. I felt I had a duty to investigate because being away from Najaf, with people he did not know, would be extremely difficult for him.

It also occurred to me that my brother would not have been able to receive his military salary throughout this period. Thus, he would not have enough money even to pay for transportation back to Najaf. Moreover, he might have been wounded in a battle. He might have been so severely wounded that he was now unable to speak or remember. *He might need me to recognize him.* Truth be told, I derived all these ideas from novels I had read.

For ten days straight, I could not rid myself of the silly notion that I would spot my brother wandering aimlessly in the streets of Basra after he had lost his memory and was unable to find anyone to show him the way home.

For this reason, I armed myself with towering courage while concealing my secret from my family. I woke at five, at dawn, and slipped out of the apartment without anyone noticing. Since I had enrolled in my program, everyone was used to me skipping out before breakfast.

Dawn's light was starting to stretch across the sleeping city, and only construction workers were heading to its bus stops. Their tattered clothes were dirty with dried splotches of concrete and plaster; their eyes, which had not enjoyed a fair share of sleep, were barely open; and their steps were heavy. On their shoulders they carried the tools of their trades: mattocks, pickaxes, coils of rope, and basins for mixing concrete or plaster.

I boarded a bus together with many of these tired construction workers, and that bus proceeded to Najaf's Union Station. Once we arrived there, I found many women and men thronging into it, in search of transport to many different locations.

Since I was an inexperienced traveler and had never traveled alone to any of Iraq's other cities, I approached a middle-aged woman and asked her shyly how to find a vehicle to take me to Basra. She informed me that this was rather complicated. I needed to take a bus to Najaf's southern terminal first and inquire there about heading to Basra. Then she told me that she and her husband had been visiting Najaf and lived in Basra, and if I wanted, I could accompany them on their trip home. I was truly delighted and felt that God was facilitating my reunion with my brother.

The bus, which was exactly like my previous one, arrived, and we boarded it along with the other passengers. When we reached the southern terminal, the place seemed almost empty. Even though it was a large building, there were very few vehicles. Each driver stood in front of his vehicle with its doors open and called out to passengers entering the terminal, encouraging them to climb in. The three of us walked quickly almost to the end of the terminal and headed toward a GMC. Its driver, who wore a white dishdasha and black leather sandals, began to call out very loudly, once he saw us heading toward him: "Just three! Three passengers, and we'll depart!"

I began to hasten toward him, almost running, but the woman, who was walking near me, moved close enough to take my hand, as if to pull me toward her, and said, "Not so fast! Don't believe what this man says! All the drivers say that same thing but don't depart till they've filled all the seats."

In fact, we climbed into the vehicle, and it did not depart until every seat was filled. Then the vehicle sped off, and signs of human activity gradually disappeared. I trained my eyes on the little side roads that reminded me of the villages I had grown accustomed to passing when I commuted to teach in rural schools.

After more than an hour, I grew fidgety and was tired of sitting. I asked the woman, who was sitting beside me, how long it would take to reach Basra. She replied that the length of the trip depended entirely on the will of God, but that if the vehicle maintained its present speed, it would take us approximately four hours and twenty minutes to travel from Najaf to Basra. She added that, if the driver did not stop at one of the roadside restaurants, we would arrive there around ten.

I had never imagined that I would travel such a long distance by myself. When the money for the fare was collected and I learned how much it was, I praised God that I had brought enough money to go *and* return.

The driver did insist on stopping at one of the roadside restaurants that adjoined a gas station after we had gone about halfway. His argument for this was that he needed to buy enough gas to get us all the way to Basra and that there might be passengers who wanted to visit the restroom.

The reality was, as the woman who was now my companion informed me, that the owners of these restaurants provided fancy free meals to drivers who stopped with their passengers. Without this ploy, these restaurants would not have been able to survive.

This woman and I headed to the ladies' room and then shared a table with her husband, who was a portly, unpretentious man. He asked the waiter to bring us two servings of kebab, a serving of grilled tomatoes, rounds of flat bread, green salad, and some water. The waiter did that so promptly it almost seemed the food had been prepared for us in advance.

I ate a few kebab and some of the grilled tomatoes with the bread, reasoning that most of the germs on the food had been killed by the fire that had cooked them. But I did not touch the green salad because I did not trust restaurant food, no matter how spic and span a restaurant looked from the outside.

We ate quite rapidly and drank the water quickly. The driver came to inform us that he was ready to depart. I handed the woman the money for my food, and she gave it to her husband, who paid the waiter. Then we returned to our previous seats in the vehicle.

The woman sitting beside me summoned her courage and broke through the curtain of silence between us to ask why I was going to Basra alone. But I wasn't able to tell her the truth. I merely replied, "I'm a teacher." Then I fell silent and looked out the car window at the endless sand dunes that extended away from the highway on both sides. I left it to her imagination to weave a story based on these few words.

She responded as happily as someone who had just found a map to an ancient treasure: "I knew from your appearance and conduct that you were a teacher! And now you are going to your new school. That's right, isn't it?"

I realized that I could protect my reputation by playing along with her narrative. She would never believe my simple story—not even if I swore to its veracity using the mightiest oaths. For this reason, I replied, "Yes."

Then she asked, "What's the name of your new school?"

It occurred to me to invent the name for "my school" and derive it from some famous landmark in Basra. Most Iraqi cities have such epithets. My city, for example, is referred to as al-Najaf al-Ashraf, or "the Most Noble Najaf"; Mosul is referred to as Leaning Mosul, which is a reference to its famous leaning minaret; Baghdad is the City of Peace; and Basra is called al-Basra al-Fayha'a, or "Far-Flung Basra," after words in a poem by the Umayyad poet al-Farazdaq: "Were it not for Abu Malik, whose favor is desired, far-flung Basra would not be my home."

After I pretended to be trying to remember the name of the school, I told her, "Al-Fayha'a."

She nodded her head approvingly, smiled, and said, "I wish I had a child in primary school. If I did, I would send him to your school. I know where al-Fayha'a Primary School is located. It's wonderful to know a teacher at a school. She will definitely look out for your child—won't she?"

"Definitely," I replied. Then I looked out the window again and gazed at the endless highway, which was empty of vehicles except for ours, speeding so fast it seemed to burn through asphalt as if challenging itself in a grand prix.

We entered Basra, where our shared taxi stopped in the Sa'd terminal, which had a large mural of President Saddam Hussein by its entrance. When I got out of the car, my feet tingled from sitting for such a long time. I dusted off the end of my abaya with my hand and then turned toward the woman who had disembarked before me with her husband. She planted some kisses on my cheek and said, "Have a wonderful morning! God willing, we will meet again, since you'll be living in Basra!"

I smiled and replied, "God willing! *Insha' Allah!*"

Then, before he escorted his wife away, the man said to me, "*Ma'a salama.* Take care of yourself."

I responded, "Goodbye."

My eyes were trained on the backs of the man and his wife while I watched them depart with a mixture of anxiety and desolation. I asked myself: "Where do I go now? What streets should I follow to achieve my goal?" The place was totally unknown to me, and its unfamiliarity made me feel as if I were wandering aimlessly in the middle of a sea of clashing waves of humanity. Even the voices I heard now—issuing from the mouths of the taxi drivers and those of the children carrying wooden boxes fastened to their chests with black plastic suspenders, kids trying to sell cigarettes and chewing gum—sounded really different from those in the Najaf dialect I was accustomed to hearing.

I walked along slowly while glancing at the faces of women who sat waiting for buses with their abayas spread out on the ground beneath them. While I proceeded, my gaze fell on two women who sat on a large bench at the entrance to the terminal. Each woman held a hand to her cheek, as if they were flesh-and-blood statues. I approached them and greeted them. They both moved slightly, greeted me, and made a place for me between them, inviting me to join them. So I sat down.

These two ladies were elderly, and each wore a black turban bound with black ribbons that hung down the back. The woman on my right removed her turban and sat with a straight back without uttering a word. The three of us resembled islands in a swelling sea of humanity.

My patience was reaching its limit, and I was about to break my silence and ask the two of them which way I should go to search for my brother, when the woman seated to my left shifted her position and waved to a man who was carrying two teas, one in each hand.

"Here, Abu Muhammad. We're here."

The man greeted me and handed each woman a tea. Each took a sip while the man remained standing in front of us, as if to encourage the two women to hurry up and drink their tea.

The man, who was also elderly, wore a nut-colored dishdasha and sported a white headcloth with black stripes and a thick black cord on his head. His brown cloak descended from his shoulders to his feet, which were clad in very dirty black leather sandals. The moment the women finished drinking their tea, the man took the cups from them and said, "I've found a car that will take us to al-Fao. There it is. Come on, get ready."

Then I turned to the woman beside me and said, "Auntie, my brother is a soldier in Basra and hasn't had leave for months. So I've come to search for him. Where do you think I would find him?"

My words surprised the woman, and her face clearly showed her astonishment. All the same, she quickly replied as she stood up, "I believe he's in al-Fao. Many soldiers are in al-Fao now. Most of its population has deserted al-Fao since Saddam's war with Iran. We have important business in al-Fao and have been looking for hours for a driver who will take us there. Most drivers have refused. They say the road is long, and dangerous too."

The other woman interrupted her, saying, "It's south of Basra."

I did not hesitate and at once asked them, "May I go with you to al-Fao?"

"My God, Niece, the matter's not that easy. You are welcome to come with us, but what I ask you is whether you can approach the military units all by yourself? The situation is very dangerous. We're at war, and death is certain!"

I did not want to listen to the advice of that woman, who had started to warn me against the dangers of death and war while *she* was risking her life, her husband's life, and her sister's.

The man returned quickly, and his wife told him about my situation and my desire to accompany them to al-Fao. He seemed not at all troubled by the matter. So we three ladies followed the man as he sped away. A moment later the man pointed to a little old taxi and said, "That's the car."

We climbed into the dilapidated taxi. The man was in the front seat, and I sat with the two women in the rear. Before we departed, the driver asked all of us to pray to and for the Prophet Muhammad, may God bless him and grant him peace, and to recite the Fatiha, the opening *surah* of the Qur'an, to facilitate our trip. After we had done that, he launched into a discussion with the elderly man about current events in Iraq while the two women chatted about family matters almost in a whisper. I looked out the window at the deserted road the vehicle was trying to traverse. Signs of devastation were clearly apparent in the remains of military machinery abandoned beside the road. There were rusty carcasses of trucks and the large tops of tankers. Huge wheels were scattered here and there in addition to sandbags that soldiers had used as berms to shelter behind during bombardments.

We seemed to be approaching a land where many battles had been fought. I don't know how far we had penetrated into that region by ourselves when a military truck appeared like a mirage on the horizon. When that truck drew nearer, we found that it was filled with soldiers. One of them noticed our vehicle heading in the opposite direction and gestured to us, signaling with his hand to turn around: "Go back where you came from!"

But the driver was busy talking to the passenger seated beside him and did not notice that soldier. So he drove on in the same direction. I started gazing at the departing truck with astonishment because all the soldiers sitting in it looked identical. Someone seeing them from a distance would think they were all a single soldier with multiple incarnations.

Only a few minutes later, another truck appeared on the horizon carrying soldiers—fewer than there had been in the previous one. The moment those soldiers spotted our vehicle heading their way, most of them began waving at us, asking us to turn and head back where we had come from.

This time the driver did notice and slammed on the brakes, stopping the car immediately. His head, and that of the passenger beside him, almost collided with the windshield. As for the three of us women, our backs and heads swayed several times in the air in reaction to this abrupt stop before settling back down on the seat.

The vehicle sat where it was for some moments before the driver attempted to turn it around and head back where we had come from. Then everyone inside the car seemed to be speaking at once, and I could not distinguish what was being said, except for the emphatic words that leapt from the mouth of the woman beside me: "Turn, take us back. We don't want to die here!"

The driver's anxiety increased then. He wanted to turn the vehicle around as quickly as possible and began talking to himself in an audible voice. "I knew that coming here was hugely dangerous. Lord, shield us and forgive us. Save us!"

Meanwhile the man sitting up front was trying to calm the driver by repeating, "Say, 'Oh Lord.' Say, 'Oh Lord.'"

The woman on the far side of the rear seat did not stop saying, "Oh Concealer, Oh Lord, Oh Concealer, Oh Lord!"

For my part, I experienced moments of sheer panic, but silently. My sense of myself as an educated woman may have restrained me from displaying my fear openly, even though it had shriveled up my body. I convinced myself that—if I died and was buried here in this land—any surviving passenger would testify to the courage I had displayed, even if that courage had been phony and superficial.

The wheels of the vehicle turned very rapidly to the left, and the entire vehicle tilted to the side I was on. The door beside me swung open all by itself, and I would have fallen out if the woman next to me had not grasped my body with both hands as she shouted angrily to the driver, "Watch out! We'll die! Allahu Akbar!"

It took several minutes, but eventually the driver was able to turn the car around and stop in the middle of the road. He jumped out and closed the door that was hanging open while my trembling body was curled up in a ball, adhering to the body of the old woman who had saved me, with her vigilance and courage, from being crushed to death.

Once the driver shut the open door, we all required a moment of calm, a time-out from thinking about what had happened or still might happen. The driver needed this most. He rested his elbow for a moment on the hood of the car. Then he began searching his pockets futilely for something. I deduced from the agitated motion of his fingers that he was looking for a pack of cigarettes in hopes of setting fire to this moment and turning it into a puff of smoke.

But a reverberating sound punctured our eardrums and shook the car as violently as if the ground beneath it had been rocked by an earthquake. The driver was panic-stricken. But before he climbed back into the vehicle, he ran around it once more to check that my door, which he had just shut, was still firmly closed. Then he tried to start the engine, but nothing happened. He tried again, and it refused to turn over.

The sounds of reverberating explosions were repeated several more times while the two women's screams rang out. The two men were not silent either. They began to curse the war and those who had ignited it. For my part, I began praying to God, silently, to save us from this trial, even as a feeling tormented me that I can summarize as a sense that this car had stopped in the middle of the road here to force me to witness some mighty event, which I hoped would not occur.

The driver asked all of us to get out of the car and push it while he remained inside and tried to start it several more times. We pushed it with all our might as the driver poked his head out the window and shouted, "Harder! Push harder!"

The moment we heard the engine start again, before we climbed back into our seats, we noticed in the distance another truckload of soldiers trying to retreat on our same road.

The driver asked us to be quick about climbing back in, but another terrifying, reverberating sound caught us off guard and shackled our feet to the ground even as the reverberation continued to deafen our ears. An artillery shell flew high overhead and landed on that truck, turning the soldiers into body parts dispersed in every direction.

I do not know how I climbed back into the car or how it shot off with us to return. The only thing that sticks in my memory is human remains flying through the air while the two ladies pounded their heads and wailed. The man removed his headband and sank into silence as our car put a lot of distance between it and the scene of the disaster we had witnessed. All the same, I turned to look back and found the truck had become a terrifying ball of flame.

The veneer of culture I had wrapped around me did not help me to appear any stronger than I was, and from my spirit burst a splinter recognizable only to me and not to those who knew me. I began to keen silently, continuing all the way back to the Sa'd terminal.

We were incapable of saying goodbye to each other. The terror of what we had witnessed did not allow us to congratulate one another on our safe return. What was the point of witnessing death and wishing someone else life? We merely paid the driver the amount agreed upon, and he received our money with a stiff, expressionless face. Then I headed off one way and my companions in a different direction.

I did not look for water to drink or to wash away the trip's turmoil, because someone I had just seen was probably dead—a flaming corpse. Otherwise, what was the significance of our taxi breaking down in the middle of a place dedicated only to death and refusing to move again till I had witnessed that tragic conflagration?

My throat was so dry that it was hard to swallow. I wiped away my tears as I started to search for buses heading to Najaf. When I found one, I boarded it and proceeded to mourn my brother with copious tears for the four-hour trip. Only minutes before sunset the bus arrived in the north terminal of Najaf, and I disembarked, almost a keening corpse.

I immediately heard a bus driver calling out, "One only! Heading out! Union Station!"

I ran to that bus, which was packed with passengers, and it departed as soon as I boarded—as if it actually had been waiting for me to arrive. The moment the bus left the entrance of the terminal, I noticed a soldier who looked just like my brother Iyas. He was also exiting the terminal, but on foot. I shouted loudly to the driver, "Stop! That's my brother! Please stop!"

The bus did stop, and I raced to open the door. I shouted as loudly as I could, "Iyas! Iyas! Iyas!"

The soldier turned when he heard me shout at him, stopped for a moment, and glanced toward me, but his face did not resemble my brother's. Then my disappointment fluttered around me. I felt intensely embarrassed too, closed the door calmly, and returned to my seat, taking refuge in my tears again.

The bus had started down the main thoroughfare after leaving the terminal when my eyes deceived me again. I saw another soldier standing on the sidewalk trying to hail a cab. Then I shouted at the driver again, "This is my brother! Let me out here!"

The bus stopped again, and after handing my fare to the man sitting beside me, I disembarked so hastily that I almost fell. I raced toward that soldier, who was climbing into a taxi, yelling, "Iyas! Iyas!"

The soldier stopped and turned to look at me, but his face did not resemble my brother's either. I stopped in my tracks, watching the young man leave me behind as he wondered why I was yelling. All the same, I steeled myself, wiped the tears from my cheek, and resolved to do what I must to return to my family before it became really dark. I pulled my bag from my shoulder and opened it to look for money, but found none.

I was in a tough situation. All I could think of now was to walk to our apartment, which was on the opposite side of the city. To reach it, I would need to keep a steady, brisk pace, first crossing the main thoroughfare between the terminal and the residential area and then proceeding to the Ansar neighborhood. After that I would take the streets that connected one district to the next.

Each time I met someone on the street, I would accost him and ask the name of the district we were in to judge how much farther I had to go on the route I saw in my mind. Those people answering my question would steal a look at my shoes and begin snickering.

By seven, I reached our apartment. My sister Layla opened the door for me. When she saw my eyes, which were swollen from weeping, and my pitiful condition, she asked me very anxiously, "What's the matter? Did something terrible happen?"

I nodded my head, trying to indicate to her that nothing had happened to me except that I'd witnessed an inexplicable death with my own eyes.

I left my shoes by the door after removing my socks too and placing them in my shoes. I dumped my bag on a chair and dragged myself to the bathroom. Then I turned on the shower and sat beneath it without removing my abaya. I continued to gaze at the dirt flowing from my abaya as it mixed with the water and ran down the drain with my tears.

Some minutes later my sister brought me a tunic, which I put on after I dried myself. I left my wet abaya hanging in the bathroom and emerged.

I asked my sister about Father, who had been gone for two days on an assignment for his job. She replied that he had telephoned to reassure my mother. She also informed me that my mother was asleep in her bed now and that our siblings were playing in their room. I summoned my courage and told her everything I had seen this extraordinary day. She began to blame me for my "stupid conduct," as she called it, and for my recklessness in going by myself to places I knew nothing about.

Before we finished our conversation, we agreed that this day's secret would not be shared with anyone else, no matter what. We would definitely *not* tell anyone else in our family. Then Layla asked me to put my ruined shoes and torn socks in a plastic bag and throw them in the rubbish bin before Mother woke up. Otherwise, I would be forced to explain to her how my shoes had become so worn out that the heel was ruined.

After throwing on another abaya, I went downstairs and tossed the shoes and socks in the trash bin. When I returned, I found that my sister had fixed us tea, triangular slices of cheese, and tasty *sumoon* rolls. So all of us children ate supper together while Mother continued to sleep soundly.

Immediately after supper I retired to my room. The moment I placed my head on my pillow, I fell asleep. *I saw people seated in groups in the courtyard of the Mahdi, who is the master of time, the Sahib al-Zaman (may God speed his relief), who according to the doctrines of Twelve-Imam Shi'ah is the twelfth and final imam and will "come to fill the earth with righteousness and justice after it was filled with tyranny and injustice." My mother sat there surrounded by my siblings, while I stood with Maysun watching all these people from whose faces fear had ebbed as the contentment that this sacred place afforded visitors left them.*

The odd thing was that none of these people were performing their prayers or carrying out the rituals of visitation or personal entreaty. Instead, they continued eating and drinking without observing the sanctity of this majestic place. More shocking still was that their loud voices violated the calm that must be observed in such locations.

My siblings were preoccupied, like the people around them, but a huge, extremely tall man with broad shoulders, a man whose face almost shone it was so white, who wore over each shoulder a white cloak that fell down to his feet, together with unusual clothing—wide light-colored trousers and high-top shoes—reminiscent of the Abbasid or Umayyad eras, and a turban, appeared from nowhere and began to approach these seated groups, whom he examined one by one. When I saw him approach me and Maysun, I asked very humbly, "My master and Lord, reassure me about my brother. Is he safe? My mother will die of grief for him."

He replied in a voice so sweet I almost faded away. "Do not worry. He will return. Tell your mother that. Tell her: he will return!"

He stood before me, lifted his hand, which seemed to be composed of photons of light, raised it to my face after contemplating my features briefly, and stroked my cheek a few times while repeating three times, "For celestial beauty."

Then he paused, regarded Maysun momentarily, and raised his index finger in the air before bringing it down gently on her forehead, where he drew three Xs. At that point, I woke, trembling all over.

The phone rang several times at dawn, so I roused myself then and dragged my body to answer it. The caller was my father. His voice sounded shaky, and he was speaking hastily and anxiously. He did not begin the conversation by asking how we were or reassuring himself about my mother's health as he did every time he called. Instead, he began by telling me, "Listen very carefully: Gather all your mother's medicines and the box of tissues. Put them in a bag near your mother's bed. Tell her to economize as best she can with the money she currently has until I return. Make sure there is an adequate supply of kerosene and butane in the apartment. Make sure all your siblings stay home today. Don't send them to school. Even you need to stay home today." Before he ended his message, as if he had remembered something extremely important, he added, "Before I forget: Don't open the door for anyone, regardless of how closely related to us they are. That's it! Stay safe! I will try to call you the next time I can!"

After quickly collecting my thoughts and rousing myself from my fright at all the orders he had given me, I blurted out, "What's happening?"

He replied, "God willing, I will explain when I come. That's it . . . Stay safe!" He hung up. The rasp in his voice emphasized the seriousness of what was descending on us. Despite all the mighty events that had befallen us during the Iran-Iraq War, my father had never been so anxious for our safety.

I went straight to my mother's room, even before I washed my face, and found her stirring in her sleep, as if she had been disturbed by the sound of our voices. When she sensed my presence, she opened her eyes and asked who had called. I told her and she frowned. To her, a call from my father meant he would be gone another day. When I relayed his message to her, while standing by her head, she sat up in bed, alarmed. She adjusted her position and then stood up to collect all her medicines in a sports bag that had been repurposed for this role a long time ago.

I went to the kitchen to check that the bottle of butane and the containers of kerosene were full. Then I returned to my room and attempted to fall asleep again but failed. So I took the copy of *al-Bayan wa-al-Tabyin* by al-Jahiz from the shelf and began to read it.

When I heard my mother calling me, I went to her. She asked me to eat breakfast with her. So I went to the bathroom, washed my face, and brushed my teeth till I was fully awake. I found she had risen and was preparing breakfast.

While we ate, my mother asked me about school, the professors, and the courses I was taking. She seemed less interested in my replies than in distracting herself from the worries my father's early and unexpected telephone call had caused.

My siblings woke one by one and were starting to prepare to leave for their schools when I informed them that Father had told me today was an unannounced holiday and that they were to stay home. Then each of them quickly and happily returned to bed and fell fast asleep once more.

By sunset, we began to hear many footsteps ascending and descending the stairs of our apartment building. I fell prey to anxiety and hastily locked the apartment's door with the key. Then I stood inside the door, listening to what was happening outside it. When the foot traffic had slackened a little, I heard a woman's voice, which I almost recognized, shout, "Saddam has fallen! The tyrant has fallen!"

I could scarcely comprehend what I had heard. The woman continued, as if she were a public herald who brought certain news: "People, Saddam has fallen. The Baath regime has fallen!"

I immediately ran to tell my family what I had heard. Then I stood in front of the TV seeking confirmation or denial of this claim. When the television proved of no use, since the station was simply broadcasting its normal programming, we all raced, together with my mother, to the windows to see what was happening in the street. Groups of men were taking to the streets. They were chanting "Death to Saddam and his cronies!" at the top of their voices. "Death to Saddam! Down with the Baath traitors!" Then they took off running in groups and as individuals toward the main thoroughfare, and other groups from the houses opposite our apartment complex, specifically from al-Amir District, crossed toward them and mingled with them to form a huge pedestrian procession that headed to the other districts.

For my part, I was astonished when I spotted the woman who had raised the first cry about the fall of Saddam because I recognized her immediately. This woman worked as a janitor in one of the governmental agencies. She had the hoarse voice of a chronic smoker. She was a distinctive figure who stood out in the crowd, for her occupation would normally not have required her to wear so much makeup or high-heeled shoes.

I focused my eyes on that woman, who continued to egg on young men with her chants to come join these processions and demonstrations. Eventually I saw her slowly separate herself from the crowds, pull a camera from beneath her abaya, and photograph them from different vantage points before calmly retreating to her apartment. This woman frightened me because she seemed more like a government spy than a revolutionary activist protesting the dictatorial regime.

Exactly at midnight, my father returned to us, wearing a dark winter cloak beneath which he was concealing his rifle. After he calmed down a little, bathed, and had something to eat, we learned that a revolution had occurred in Basra and spread to other governorates.

It could be attributed to the withdrawal of the Iraqi Army from Kuwait. Its soldiers had begun marching slowly back to the cities from which they had come. My father added in an anxious voice, "Let us pray God will deliver us from this evil, which will scorch the green twigs even before they dry."

We did not sleep that night, because expressions of joy at the fall of the dictator were not limited to cheering and drumming. Instead, most of the residents of our district and neighboring ones went on the roofs of their apartment buildings and houses to fire celebratory rounds into the air.

With the first rays of morning light, the violence began. Most of these mobs rushed to nearby government agencies like the Ministry of Education, the Ministry of Public Security, the schools, Najaf General Hospital, Saddam Teaching Hospital, and the Teachers Union building and began threatening the guards at those buildings, which the mobs then entered to steal anything and everything that they could lift, ranging from blood-pressure monitors and wall clocks to refrigerators and freezers, and it was all loaded into trucks and donkey carts.

After those buildings were stripped of appliances, the mobs set fire to them. Then it became routine to learn what was happening in the city by looking out the window or down from the balcony to see which neighboring buildings had plumes of smoke billowing from them and to watch people carry stuff away on their heads—things they had no idea how they would use. Their argument for taking these items was that they were entitled to them, since they were "the people's goods." Young men clad in civilian attire and black-and-red headcloths, holding rifles and ammo in their hands, manned checkpoints in the streets and prevented pedestrians from passing.

The situation rapidly deteriorated even further when these young men began to search for the homes of individuals who had worked in the security agencies and as policemen started killing them.

For three days we experienced this state of frightening, violent anarchy, which brought all daily life to a standstill as destruction and devastation advanced toward us from every direction. By the fourth day, electricity and telephone lines were completely cut throughout the city, and we became hostages in a prison surrounded by fires. We no longer knew whether we were safer at home or somewhere else.

Before noon on that fourth day, we heard a light rapping on our door, and Father asked us to stay just where we were while he went to see who it was. The visitor was a friend, a man approximately his age. They conversed in whispers. Then my father came to tell us we needed to leave our apartment and walk by foot to the mausoleum of Imam Muslim ibn 'Aqeel (peace upon him) in Kufa. Without any of us objecting or asking why we were leaving our apartment now, we all put on walking shoes and outdoor clothing and set off. I carried the sports bag with my mother's medicine, and my siblings all clutched small sacks filled with *sumoon* rolls, cakes, dates, and thermoses of water.

Once we were away from the apartment-complex district and on the main highway that linked Najaf with Kufa, we seemed to be part of a marathon for speed-walkers or a caravan of pilgrims returning from Mecca. Before we were a quarter of the way to the mausoleum, my mother's fatigue became obvious. She stopped and asked my father if she could sit on the sidewalk to rest. My father acquiesced, and we all sat down beside her, but the sound of explosions became very audible and made us leave that place quickly, hastening along with the groups that had begun to rush forward, oblivious to invalids, children, or the elderly.

My father shouted, "Hurry up! Go on ahead of us. Leave us! Your mother and I will follow you." We refused to heed his cry and continued to match our pace to theirs, or more accurately to my mother's steps. She would walk a short distance and then sit down, and we did too.

After we had walked nine and a half kilometers, we reached, by the skin of our teeth, the mausoleum of Muslim ibn 'Aqeel (peace upon him). Once we entered the shrine, we found it was swarming with people. By that point, Mother was unable to walk another step, so we left her with our father while we went to look for a place where we could spend the night.

My father approached a man who was sitting with his family in the shrine's covered portico and asked him if he would make space for us to join them there because my mother was an invalid who could not go anywhere else. The man looked at my mother first to ascertain that what my father said was true. Then he asked the members of his family to scoot closer together, in a narrower circle, to give us enough room to sit down.

We piled on top of each other there, after we placed our few possessions on the ground and spread beneath us a light cotton blanket that my father had been carrying. We survived that harsh night with its gloom and strangeness. We were not able, in its darkness, to make out the source of the reverberating sound of incoming artillery shells, because of the fatigue that had afflicted our bodies from all the walking.

We sat cross-legged on the ground after clearing enough space for our mother to lie down. We girls used our abayas as tents, into which our brothers crept to shelter. Toward sunrise, the sound of missiles, which had continued through the night, grew louder, and daybreak brought helicopters. Their trajectories split the sky and showered people with terror like a cloudburst of rain.

Throughout the night, our mother had searched our faces. Then we had smiled at her, trying to reassure her. But my brothers—like everyone else there—jumped up and began screaming in fright once a shell hit one of the tall minarets of the mausoleum. Then groups scattered wildly in every direction—we among them—after each man urged his family to leave this sanctuary and flee as quickly as possible.

We raced with others to some road we didn't recognize. It led us to an area with many orchards, but we seemed to have walked into a trap or a big ambush because the helicopters were flying over our heads, and the sound of exploding artillery shells almost deafened us as we searched futilely for a place to shelter. After he realized that everyone was exhausted from walking swiftly but aimlessly, it occurred to my father to seek shelter in the home of some of our relatives on the out-skirts of Najaf. We all agreed on this idea except for my mother, who could walk no farther. She sat down on the ground and said in a tired voice, "Leave me here and save yourselves."

My father became furious and shouted, "Have you gone mad? How could we leave you here? Get up and keep moving. Move. Otherwise, you'll die!"

Then his anger quickly abated when he looked at my mother and saw that she could scarcely breathe. We stood there, looking around for any way to take her where we wanted to go. Vehicles had disap-peared entirely from the roads. After about half an hour, a donkey cart appeared on the horizon, carrying a number of women and children. My father stopped it and asked the driver to take my mother and one of my sisters to a certain address. The man agreed in exchange for a substantial sum of money.

My mother climbed into the cart accompanied by one of my sis-ters, and I handed her the bag of medicine I had been carrying. Then the rest of us continued the remainder of the way on foot. Although we were exhausted, we walked briskly with long strides that mimicked our father's.

We reached our relatives' house at noon. It was small and contained three bedrooms. Two were on the ground floor, and the third was on the upper level. The family that lived here was very large, and most of them were guys, some my brothers' ages. The father was a small, cheerful elderly man. The mother was a tall, slender middle-aged woman who did not seem to welcome us. From the moment we greeted her as we entered the house, she pelted us with orders, as if we were her servants.

I and my sisters worked diligently to prepare the food that my father was forced to purchase every day. Then my mother helped the lady of the house prepare dough, and my sister baked the loaves in a clay oven.

Each day when we woke, one more variety of food would be missing from the menu. Red meat and chicken were the first to disappear. Then we stopped drinking tea. Finally, our meals consisted of bread and stewed fava beans or fried eggplant. Our nights were even worse than our days because we did not feel safe, comfortable, or linked to this house and its inhabitants.

The butane ran out and the kerosene was almost used up by the fifth day in this house that offered us only one bed, for my mother. The rest of us spread a single, old foul-smelling blanket on the floor and slept beneath it. My father slept with all the other guys in one room.

On that fifth day, the lady of the house woke me and my sisters in a frightening way and asked us to follow her to the kitchen. We trailed her there as if sleepwalking. She sat down on a wooden bench while we remained standing, watching what she did.

She picked up two empty bottles, one a cola bottle and the other an empty milk bottle, and poured a little kerosene into each. Then she twisted wool into a wick, which she cut in half. She put one wick in each bottle, sealed their tops with a piece of dough, and asked us to imitate what she had done. We did not succeed the first time, but after several tries we created a suitable number of bottles repurposed as kerosene lamps to light the house.

Although this seemed an excellent idea to economize the remaining amount of kerosene, in another respect it was very harmful to my mother's health on account of all the smoke the burning wicks produced. The moment those lamps were lit, smoke gushed from them and filled the entire room, and my mother, who was unable to bear that amount of smoke, began to suffer repeated coughing fits. Then the lady of the house was annoyed by my mother's coughs and criticized Mother loudly enough for her to hear. I grew furious at this woman whom we had never seen smile, not even in a phony way, since we had arrived at her house.

I wondered whether we could stand living with that woman for ten days, but the artillery fire was constant and airplanes circled overhead, leaving us no choice but to endure all this, albeit grudgingly.

On the morning of the tenth day, my father received news from a young man whose brother had just returned from Kuwait on foot. The gist of the news was that my brother Iyas had returned with a group of soldiers and would soon enter Najaf. The problem was that the Republican Guard, which had entered Najaf, Karbala, and the rest of the cities in the south, had begun patrolling them and arresting any soldier they saw. They would send these soldiers to Baghdad to be imprisoned or executed because the soldiers had refused to obey the orders given them to remain in Kuwait.

My father felt he had to leave that afternoon, accompanied by an elderly friend, for the city of al-Hirah, where they would stay in a hostel and watch for my brother's arrival. My father and that man returned with my brother the following day, after my brother had changed into civilian clothes. Because my brother showed signs of fatigue, suffering, and hunger on account of his long journey from Kuwait back to Najaf—a distance of 575 kilometers—my father exploited this weakness to my brother's benefit. Whenever they came to a checkpoint, my father would say that his son was very ill and was seeking treatment, since all the hospitals and clinics had been ransacked.

Once Iyas reached us, we all decided to return immediately to our apartment, no matter the consequences, especially since the streets had traffic on them again, however light. It was a long way to our district of the city, though, and my mother could not walk that far, especially after suffering asthma attacks during the night because of the smoky lamps.

For this reason, my father searched for a long time for a form of transport that would allow her to return to our apartment. All he could find was a handcart that belonged to a young man in the district. My mother and Iyas climbed onto it and the owner pushed it while we followed behind them for almost an entire day.

During this strange return trip, we encountered a man's body that had been abandoned by the side of the road, saw houses with all their walls demolished, and tried to avoid bumping into burnt debris of uncertain origin, since every sort of thing was mingled together.

When we neared our district, we found that the government agencies were ash-covered ruins. Destruction and devastation had affected houses, shops, and many markets as well. When we passed Maysun's house, we found the door ajar. A large portion of the wall had fallen, and the charred carcass of an automobile stood by the house's stoop. I started to race to see what had happened, but my father yelled at me not to. So I returned anxiously and rejoined my family's small caravan as we walked down the street, which was entirely empty of traffic. Our apartment building gazed down at us; its exterior walls were cracked.

The man pushing the handcart deposited my mother and brother at the door of the apartment building, which was entirely empty of inhabitants. We all were dragging our feet as we climbed the steps.

On the way there, we had been dreaming of falling asleep, but before we went to bed, my sisters and I swept up the broken glass from all of the apartment's broken windows. After my father rested his feet briefly, he began to fasten pieces of cardboard over the windows. Iyas fell fast asleep, even before eating or bathing.

The only food we found in our apartment were some dry *sumoon* rolls, which my brothers ate with such delight they might have been cake. There were also buckets we had filled with water before we'd fled.

After lighting some lamps and retiring to our rooms to sleep, we heard a light knocking on the door. My father rushed to open it after checking the voice of the person knocking. Even before this man greeted my father, we heard him say, "Abu Falah: save us. My family is dying of thirst. We've been without water for three days. For the sake of al-Husayn, give us a little water!"

My father hurried to the kitchen and brought him a pail filled with water, walking slowly. When he handed it to the man, the fellow accepted it incredulously. Approximately an hour later, he returned with the same bucket filled with dry dates, which was the only food we had for several days.

Even though the sound of artillery shelling continued, and we were frightened by the force of the explosions, we felt comfortable because at least we were home.

Chapter Nine

Although fatigue had overwhelmed my body, I was so worried about Maysun that I couldn't sleep. My previous bizarre dream about the twelfth imam tormented me after seeing her family's house so terribly destroyed. My eyes stared at the ceiling all night long, and despite repeated attempts, I failed to fall asleep.

As day broke on the horizon, I drew on my abaya and headed to her house. The street was totally empty of any movement. I did, however, notice a woman covered in an abaya in the house's yard, where she was trying to pick up trash. I raced toward her, hoping fervently she was Maysun. As I approached the house, however, the woman heard my footsteps and turned toward me. Then I discovered it was Maysun's older sister, not my friend.

I walked slowly toward her. Before I could ask what had happened, she took my hand and drew me toward three recently filled graves. She stopped there by those graves and began to speak hysterically. "These are their graves. This is my mother. This is Maysun. This is her nanny."

Then she fell to the ground and started to poke at the earth with a stick as she continued in the same dispirited tone. "We buried the corpses without washing them. We merely wrapped them in abayas.

Each one in her own abaya. Just imagine: Maysun's abaya was brand new. She had never used it. The cemetery is closed now. They said it will reopen in forty days. After these forty days, we will move the three bodies to our family plot in the cemetery.

"They won't be alone. My paternal aunt and grandmother will visit with them. Even my maternal aunt who died some months ago will. Most members of our family are in that cemetery. You know, I wasn't at home when the rocket hit our house and the neighboring ones. I had gone with my father and brother to close my father's shop in the Wilaya District. Once the shelling grew intense, we weren't able to return here and remained closeted in his shop till the shelling calmed down a little. We tried to call home, but the telephone lines had been cut. We returned to our house the way we had gone—on foot. When we returned, we discovered that my mother, my sister, and her nanny had been charred almost beyond recognition in my father's car as they tried to flee from the bombardment. That's my father's car by the gate; I mean, what's left of it. My father is very ill now. My brother has almost lost his mind. You know how attached he was to my mother. If we had stayed here with them, we would have been spared this sense of loss; we would have died with them and been at peace. You know: In the house next to ours, everyone inside was killed at the moment of the strike. Even their guests died with them. Eighteen corpses are buried in their garden. In the other house, the mother died, and the daughters lost limbs. You know Sitti Hana': her feet were cut off—as was her sister's arm."

She stood up and turned toward me, her face flooded with tears. Before she walked away, she asked, "Would you like to come inside?"

"No," I replied, choking even on these two letters.

"Then I'll head in." She walked away as if the earth were pulling her down into it.

I stood there, feeling annoyed by how bizarre dirt is, by how it can bury beneath its rough clumps even a spirit pulsing with life like

Maysun's. Our friendship would have lasted for many more years had that Strela-2 "eye" missile not dug a grave for her in the garden of her home.

I returned home after shedding all the tears I harbored. I found my father waiting for me on the sofa. When he saw me, he rose immediately. Finding my face covered with tears, he uttered three words before he sat back down with tears slipping down his cheeks. "Maysun. I knew!"

I went to my room and took out a piece of paper and a pen and composed my first elegy, which I called "Elegy for the Golden Downspout":

> I turned my face to the sky's creator;
> Then the blood of the hungry flowed out,
> and thus was created:
> Maysun Hasan Kamouneh.
> I was told their garden will embrace her body
> until deliverance,
> And that body parts were scattered
> Till the sand was filled with their nectar.
> And . . .
> Neither our watery trajectory
> Nor their painted odes
> Can erase the darkness of the amputees
> And . . .
> Between my blood and the weeping stone
> I flow.
> . . .
> Digging at the sky with earth's sharpened
> claws and talons.

This golden downspout is in the courtyard of the shrine of Imam Ali (peace upon him). When it rains, people collect this water, which they consider sacred because it is mixed with dust from the shrine's dome.

This poem was published in my first poetry collection, *'Cause I'm a Girl*, and ever since then I have always included an elegy for my incomparable friend in each of my poetry books. No other girl or woman has ever been able to take her place in my life. The most recent elegy I have written for her is "Before Maysun Was Martyred," which was published in my most recent collection:

> Before Maysun was martyred
> The sky was really blue,
> The streets were really wide,
> Women loitered on their stoops in the
>   afternoon,
> Crafting stories.
> While coffeehouses roared with men's
>   laughter!
> My father smiles and warns her:
> "Don't take Faleeha to the beauty salon.
> Turn your hair gold like the sun
> But let the girl's hair glow like the night!"
> She responds: "You have a difficult name.
> It doesn't pulse with the poetry of your spirit.
> If I were you, I'd change it."
> Then we would laugh!
>
> . . .
>
> My mother was the warmest of us:
> "Gather round a single platter so you don't
>   forget your emotions."
> My father says, "We cluster together like ants
>   around a lump of sugar."

After your passing, the world donned a robe
of dirt.
The wind of war swept the stoops of our
streets.
Women now wear their cares on their sleeves,
That are always black.
Back-alley coffee shops
Resound with phony news bulletins of
victory
Presented by a reporter who scoffs secretly at
the masses he addresses.
Men's voices in our neighborhood have
grown hoarse from smoking and
From imbibing their brimming cups of
defeat.
Your passing has turned my hair snow white,
Before I had only enjoyed a few years,
A preliminary stage,
Of slipping my spirit into your veins
To discover what blood flows through them.
Or whether the Lord drew from
Trees the rustling of their leaves
And from a cloud their soft-as-cotton feel
And dawn's first dew
To fashion you.
If you had tarried a little,
You would have seen
How some poets dedicate poetry collections
to me:
"Faleeha is a name the angels of poetry love,
and God adores it too."
My name has prevailed,

But you betrayed me by dying.
My mother has betrayed me by passing,
And my father has left us too.
All his wise advice fell on deaf ears.
We have eaten at numerous tables
Our fill of wars, blockades, injustice, poverty,
    separation, and exile.
And when I called out "My brother,"
The final sound fades away
As I gnaw my heart remorsefully.
Maysun, does it make sense
That a rocket fell on your house
And you dissolved so rapidly?
Is it comprehensible
That your only shroud was your abaya?
That your only grave was your garden?
If I curse one of them, will you return?
You must be satisfied with dancing in my
    memory.
Give me ten minutes
For me to sleep calmly;
Please:
Ten minutes, no more,
Because I'm very tired
From enumerating all the guiltless dead!

. . .

Something else kept my father awake that night: his worry that we did not have enough food in our home, because the dates his friend had brought him were about to run out. He was planning to tour the district and neighboring ones in hopes of finding someone selling food. He had scarcely left our apartment, though, when he rushed back and began calling me. When I went to him, he told me quickly, while having trouble catching his breath, "Go rouse your siblings and pack them into the pantry. I'm going to wake your mother."

I did not ask him why. Instead, I hastily herded my siblings to the empty pantry. When we entered it, our arms, hands, and shoulders collided as we crowded into this space, which lacked ventilation, since it was small and had no windows. When I closed the door behind us, we became a single mass of bodies. Once we were silent, we heard our father tell us, "If you smell a pleasant fragrance like an apple's, try not to inhale it." Then he left us to return momentarily with small moistened washcloths of different colors. Before he closed the door, he said, "Put one of these over your nostrils and breathe through it."

I shouted to him through the closed door, "What about Mother?"

He replied quickly, "I put her in the wardrobe."

I yelled again, through the wet washcloth, "You?"

"Never fear. I'll be fine."

I could hear my father's footsteps as he left. Then a lethal silence stole over the place. It was the type of calm that precedes the arrival of a storm. Soon we heard and felt the terrifying reverberation of a warning siren. Then fear spread through our bodies.

This time, the howl of the siren did not announce an air raid. It had a different sound and message—one I could not identify. My siblings started to lose their cool as they heard the repeated screams of unfamiliar sirens. They also began to experience a lack of oxygen in this tiny pantry, which was scarcely wider than its door. They were about to pass out, and their breathing was labored. I felt compelled to open the door, only to find the apartment enveloped in total darkness.

One of my siblings screamed with terror at this sight, and another wept. I walked out slowly, trying to find my way through the layers of this darkness. I wanted to discover what was happening. We could think of no reason why the bright light of day would suddenly turn to dark night, without any warning.

We heard the voice of Iyas, who had insisted on remaining asleep despite my father's repeated attempts to wake him. We heard him call out, after he woke to find darkness penetrating the room where he was sleeping: "It's Judgment Day! The hour has arrived. It's Resurrection Day!"

Weeping resounded everywhere. If this was Judgment Day, what should we do? Would we all die in a single flash? We started to bump into the furniture and objects around us. Then my father flung a few words to us like a life preserver in a raging sea. He was asking us to stay put till we heard the siren signal that the event had ended.

But we couldn't. We all raced in the direction of his voice and kept searching in total darkness for his body, trying to grasp hold of some scrap of his clothing. After a short search we found him, standing, enveloped in his white headcloth, his *kufiya*, by the door of the wardrobe in which our mother sat, coughing in a muffled way, since she held a damp washcloth over her mouth and nose. We all raced to him, and I glanced at the window on which my father's eyes were trained. I was frightened to see an enormous dark black cloud cover the horizon, apparently endless.

My father began to repeat, loud enough for us to hear, a single sentence, which he hoped would calm us, even though he sounded anxious. "Don't be afraid. It's not a chemical bomb."

Even so, we did not quiet down. To the contrary, that reassurance caused my brother to curse and revile the government. When my father yelled at him to hush, my brother left the room and returned to bed.

After waiting expectantly for a long time, the siren delivered the good news that the emergency had ended. Everyone else calmed down and sat on the floor near the wardrobe while I raced to the window, removed the cardboard from it, and scrutinized the size of that black cloud as it moved away over the horizon, and a flotilla of other black clouds of different sizes and shapes approached. I wondered what other surprises war still harbored for us now that the sky had rained down darkness.

The following day, residents of the apartment building began to return. When I heard our next-door neighbor collecting shards of broken glass, I seized the opportunity to ask her where those black clouds had come from. She told me, while gingerly picking up pieces of glass, that the clouds had come from Kuwaiti oil wells that had been set on fire.

With enormous effort, my father was able to acquire a few kilos of chickpea flour and some tea and sugar, and they saved us from going hungry. My mother prepared bread for us from the chickpea flour, and my sister made us tea. Then we all sat, as we used to, around one dinner mat. Even though the discs of chickpea bread differed in color, appearance, flavor, and taste from regular bread, we swallowed them because that was all we had to silence the pangs of hunger.

Once we had eaten our fill and before we left the dinner mat, my father asked my brother what he had experienced in Kuwait or Basra. Then my brother offered us his eyewitness testimony. We learned that his unit had received orders from on high to move from Basra to Kuwait under the cover of night. When his unit entered Kuwait City, they found that extraordinary numbers of the Iraqi Republican Guard troops had preceded them and were bivouacked in Kuwait City.

He said, "The Kuwaitis had not awakened yet. With the first rays of sunshine, they were shocked to open the doors of their homes and find us in their streets. The morning was very quiet. We heard no gunfire from anywhere in the city. That afternoon, some Kuwaitis emerged from their houses to buy bread from the few bakeries that were open. They were obviously astonished and surprised by what had happened. It's not an everyday thing to wake up and find soldiers from another country standing at the door of your house. It was normal to feel anxious.

"Speaking frankly, we did not understand what was happening either or why we had entered Kuwait with all these troops and heavy military weapons. We were simply obeying orders without asking any questions. Then members of the Republican Guard began to spread through the city and establish checkpoints to ensure security—as was announced—although I do not remember our experiencing any resistance from the Kuwaitis. After a few days, though, we started hearing reports that President Saddam Hussein had been deposed. So we hastily left Kuwait to avoid being killed and buried there once this news reached its inhabitants. We actually did ignore orders to remain where we were and returned on foot to Iraq."

My brother was silent for a time while he started to look around, as if incredulous to find himself surrounded by us. We did not ask him what he had witnessed on his way back to Iraq for fear of reviving pains he was doing his best to forget.

Time seemed dictated by a veteran director of horror films, someone who could control the day's timing as he saw fit, stopping a scene only to start another even darker and gloomier one.

Just when my brother had concluded his account, we heard heavy knocking on the door. One of my other brothers rose and answered the door. Then, without asking permission, three high-ranking armed officers burst in, speaking Tikrit-dialect Arabic. We girls ran with our mother to a bedroom to fetch our abayas. We then found everyone looking at the officer who was asking my father what had happened in this district. When he did not garner any information from my father, he asked the soldiers accompanying him to search the rooms for weapons. Before they started the search, my father informed them that he had a Kalashnikov rifle that dated back to the time he served in the People's Army. After a careful search of the apartment, that rifle is all they found.

As these three soldiers were starting to leave our apartment, we heard a loud, powerful voice, like a military call for backup, from the apartment above us. Then the departing officer hastily shouted back at us, "Everyone leave the apartment and go downstairs. Wait two meters away from the building's entry."

We all descended the steps quickly. My mother was the last resident of the building to emerge from it; everyone else had been given the same orders to descend and wait outside.

Immediately a large number of soldiers, who had been standing at the entrances of the various apartment buildings, entered our building, brandishing weapons. They rushed up the stairway so vigorously they almost made it shake.

In a few minutes, all of them emerged from the building. Each pair of men carried a large wooden box with its top broken open. When they placed these boxes on the ground, different types of ammunition, light weapons, and revolvers were visible.

A few minutes later, two young men, our neighbors' sons, were brought down in handcuffs and placed together with those boxes in an armored military truck parked by the entrance to the building. The rest of the soldiers climbed in, and it sped off.

Before the officer charged with searching our apartment climbed into another military vehicle, which was waiting for him, he walked over to the woman whom I had previously seen taking pictures of rebellious young men after she had exhorted them to participate in demonstrations against Saddam. She was now standing with other residents of our building, watching what was happening. He approached her, placed a hand on her head, and began to converse with her in a whisper as a proud smile adorned her face. He seemed to be praising her for the important information she had shared with him in order to spread peace and security among people.

The soldiers left the place, and everyone who had witnessed what had happened now realized the perils of living near this woman, who belonged to some political party—we did not know which.

We started to avoid speaking to her or encountering her, even by accident. The strange thing was that this woman advanced professionally after Saddam's government fell. In the blink of an eye, after working as a janitor in one of the government agencies, she became, overnight, the head of an entire archives and records department, even though she had earned only a literacy certificate, which qualified a person to be, at best, a messenger.

The next morning, helicopters hovered over the buildings of our residential community. They were tasked with dropping leaflets from the government asking people to immediately return any plundered appliances to the agencies from which they had been taken or to leave them in public squares for the army to collect and return to their previous locations. Anyone who failed to do so and kept an appliance belonging to the state would be subject to arrest and would be immediately taken to Baghdad to face imprisonment or execution.

After these leaflets rained down from the sky, littering the streets like paper raindrops, and reached the hands of people, who immediately picked them up and read them, those appliances and pieces of equipment appeared the next day, deposited at the public square and by the side of the road under cover of night.

That morning, when I looked down from the balcony, I saw an astonishing number of refrigerators, televisions, freezers, printers, table lamps, and chairs of various sizes and styles, as well as other office gadgets, piled up on top of each other. This was repeated for a number of days: people would slip quietly, by night, to leave their looted goods outdoors. Then soldiers would arrive with their rowdy clamor and military vehicles to carry those appliances back to the agencies from which they had been taken. This did not, however, mean that all those agencies recovered everything that had been taken from them. Instead, many of those agencies suffered from a lack of equipment for a long time. That was because many people refused to obey the orders conveyed by those menacing and threatening leaflets.

As a matter of fact, many people fell victim to their own stubbornness and disdain for the contents of those leaflets, despite the harsh language. In plain daylight, during raids searching for appliances, after the last scheduled collection of appliances set out on the street, many men—young and old alike—were arrested, within sight and hearing of everyone, because they had retained pieces of used furniture or an old freezer. We never heard what became of them.

We did not feel safe, not even after this fever of investigations by the armed forces for stolen appliances and weapons faded away, because subsequently we awoke to find ourselves belabored by loudspeakers calling on soldiers who had returned from Kuwait, deserted from other military units, or were home on leave to head to a hotel called al-Salam al-Siyahi to surrender themselves there to certain military units, from which they would be transferred to their original units. When citizens ignored these calls, despite the frequency with which they were repeated, since no one took them seriously and most former soldiers questioned the motivation for them and failed to obey this summons, these same helicopters returned and soared over our heads scattering different leaflets. These affirmed what we had heard from the loudspeakers and threatened that any man who failed to obey this command would be gunned down in front of his own residence.

We all felt trapped. It was no easy matter for us to make the terrifying decision to allow Iyas to turn himself in and to assure him that he would not be killed or tortured. On the other hand, if he stayed in our apartment, he risked arrest and death by a firing squad. Our home became a cesspool of anxiety. We could not focus and lacked the power to make a suitable decision, since there really wasn't one. All alternatives seemed likely to guarantee his certain death.

Iyas, though, clung to his refusal to turn himself in and insisted that he would stay in our apartment, even if that entailed his execution. So my father suggested he get his hair and beard cut military-style to prepare for any raid.

Within a few hours my father was also able, with help from some close friends, to provide my brother with an army uniform, boots, and beret. My father suggested Iyas use my father's military belt after it was shortened for him. My father also recommended that he wear this uniform during the day. Then, if a search team raided our apartment, my brother's excuse would be that he had returned that same day, on leave, from his unit in Basra. My father also asked him to refrain from mentioning the number of his military unit. That would tip them off that his unit had been posted to Kuwait.

As I've mentioned, during these days we lived on the set of a horror film, and its director kept transporting us rapidly from one scene to the next. We acted our parts perfectly without falling victim to the brutality and violence of those scenes. My brother had just put on his new uniform and started to try on the boots when some officers stormed into our apartment again. This time they weren't looking for stolen goods or weapons; they had come searching for AWOL soldiers.

Iyas kept his mouth shut, and my father spoke for him. He informed the officers that my brother was on leave and had just arrived from his unit in Basra. They did not believe him. They asked my brother the type of permit that he had received from the commanding officer of his unit to travel to Najaf. When my brother was not able to show them any official papers that established the truth of what my father had claimed, they wasted no time in pulling his arms behind his back and handcuffing him. They shoved him out of the apartment so forcefully that he almost fell on his face.

My mother began trembling from fear and then collapsed on the floor after seeing her son yanked from the apartment in this terrifying way after she had pleaded with the soldiers to leave him. My father rushed to her, trying to ascertain whether she was still alive while the whole apartment echoed with our screams.

The officer looked at my father, who was sitting on the floor and trying to revive my mother. Pointing his index finger at my mother, whose plight calmed his anger, the officer told my father, "If she hadn't fainted, you would be going with us too, along with your son!"

Then he strutted away, delighted with his booty, trailed by the soldiers who had accompanied him. I and one of my sisters raced to the window as tears covered our faces, and we saw Iyas shoved into an armored military vehicle parked in front of the building. My brother disappeared inside the vehicle, and it vanished rapidly. We had no news of my brother after that.

In a few days, the kerosene and butane in our home ran out. This, together with the cutoff of water, electricity, telephone, and health services, turned our city into a region totally isolated from the world. Most people were forced to use scraps of wood to cook whatever food they had—if "food" is the right word for what we ate. Since we lived on the second story of the building, my brothers brought scraps of wood and dry tree limbs they found in the streets to pile on the balcony.

Then, every day, my father would light a fire in two braziers. Once the fire died down to embers and the smoke subsided, my sisters and I, with advice from our mother, would make rounds of chickpea-flour bread and tea and fry some eggs my father was able to purchase secretly by night, after he heard that the owner of a shop in al-Amir District had started selling his wares for three times their original price.

Cooking food over a wood fire or charcoal took a lot of time and effort—including collecting the firewood, burning it down to embers, and preparing the chickpea dough. This effort was not limited to obtaining and preparing the food. It also included the task of cleaning the pots before using them—especially the frying pan and the teakettle. Because they sat in the fire, surrounded by it, their exteriors were entirely blackened.

All the same, we did not neglect to perform these tasks or feel bored with this continuous labor. How else would we have passed our long days at home when everything was closed and we had begun living a primitive, stagnant life?

Men in our district devised a way to provide water by selecting three or four men from the apartment building, in a rotation by apartment numbers, to fill tankers with water, after renting water tankers from the Water Bureau in Kufa; these were pumped full of water straight from the river. When those tankers arrived at our building, the men would distribute the water equally to all of us, since we all contributed to the cost of renting the tanker. Once we received our allocation of water, we would reserve some for bathing and washing dishes and clothes and place other amounts in pots to boil for drinking water.

Conditions continued like this for many weeks. When my father was asked to return to work, he, along with many other employees, was given the task of restoring and re-creating the office of the Department of Education. He had to arrive there early and stay late, especially because public transport had not been reestablished yet, and he was obliged to walk to work.

Once my father returned to his job, he became our first and last source for news of what was happening, in Najaf in particular, and in Iraq as a whole. Of course, he was especially interested in what had happened to the soldiers taken to al-Salam Hotel. Despite his many attempts to draw out his acquaintances and learn something, my father failed to obtain any information about my brother, or the fate of others like him, to calm my mother.

As part of the punishment handed out by the government after it had consolidated its power again, more than a hundred thousand Iraqis were slain. The marshes of southern Iraq were totally drained, and almost two million Iraqis fled to neighboring countries. Mass graves were subsequently found in many cities. Fifteen of these were discovered in the city of Hilla alone. The mausolea of the imams in Najaf and Karbala were destroyed, and those sacred mausolea and tombs remained closed for six months.

Yes, the insurrection failed, due to a lack of coordination and because it started as scattered demonstrations in reaction to the entry of the Iraqi Army into Kuwait. This rebellion—in which many young men died—failed, and the government's iron hand regained a choke-hold over the people. Most felt certain there would be no way to escape from this tyrannical rule, ever.

When the electrical grid was repaired and electrical current restored to homes, the first thing we saw on the television screen was the smiling face of President Saddam Hussein, who referred to the insurrection as "a page of treason and treachery" and called all the revolutionaries who had participated "hoodlums."

The return of health services, water, electricity, and telephone did not mean that life had returned to normal. The disappearance of many people was not a healthy indicator of what was referred to, metaphor-ically, in Najaf as "life."

Even when I entered my school on the first day and we were allowed to resume our studies, I found only a few other students. Most of the male and female janitors were working like busy bees cleaning the dirt and ashes from the large murals of the president. It was clear that they had started with this task, even before clearing out the debris left by fires and destruction, so they would not be charged with dereliction of duty as defined by newly implemented, unjust laws.

Within a few days, the enormity of the events we had experienced became clear. Many of our professors had disappeared, not to be heard from again for years. Some had left the country out of fear. Some had been killed. Others were MIA. Instructors were recruited to replace those who had disappeared, and we continued to attend lectures even though we had totally lost any belief in our futures. Our breasts were preoccupied by bitterness and by the brutal present.

Like a person who awakes to find she has lost her senses of taste and smell without prior warning, I found I had lost my interest for what was happening around me. No smile attracted me, and no tear consoled me. All I could do was to fashion a spirit of dent-proof stainless steel and to don it—a spirit capable of confronting events that were both unexpected and unavoidable.

One night when we had finished supper and were sitting in the living room watching TV, there was a continuous light rapping on the apartment door. My young brother eventually opened the door once my father asked him to do so. Then we saw an incredible sight.

It was my brother Iyas, who had returned to us, though not exactly safe and sound, after an absence of six months, each minute and second of which had been filled with regret and expectation. He entered our apartment with a body as thin as a dry twig, his hair disheveled, wearing tattered clothes, with long dirty fingernails, yellow teeth, and a face that suggested he had been infected with TB and jaundice.

He walked into the middle of the apartment and stood there, not knowing what to do. Everyone raced toward him, delighted, cheering his arrival. My mother hoisted herself up from the floor and tried to hug him. But he gestured for her not to, without saying a word, as if warning her that it was not safe to approach him. She calmly returned to where she had been sitting and proceeded to recite verses from the Qur'an, thanking God for His mercy to us and for bringing her son back safely.

Although he was disconcerted by my brother's strange behavior, my father quickly said, "Praise the Lord for your healthy return!"

Then my brother gave our father a look that suggested he was anything but "healthy." Because we Iraqis knew that only tears during those days served as the language of joy, we all began to weep in our joy at my brother's safe return.

Shaking a wounded foot that barely supported him, my brother sat down on a chair and removed the boot from his right foot, which stank so badly that it made everyone in the room nauseous.

Covering her nose with a hand, my mother shouted to him, "Take it off outside the apartment and throw it in the trash!"

My brother paused for a moment before unfastening his other boot and glanced at her askance. Then he removed it. My mother was infuriated by his rude behavior and rose to leave the room.

Suddenly my siblings' tears turned to laughter when one of my sisters commented merrily about the lethal force of that stench: "That boot died a long time ago!"

Iyas cast her a threatening look as he held up a boot and seemed ready to beat her with it. She was irritated and left the room too. Most of my siblings quickly followed her, as if fearful of my angry brother.

Before my father left to perform the prayer ritual to give thanks for his son's salvation, he merely said, "Compassionate God, we ask for Your kindness to us."

Once my brother had removed his boots, he sat for a long time where he was. Then he began to examine his toes that had nails so long they had torn his socks. When I saw him continue to examine those dirty nails, as if discovering them for the first time, I approached him calmly and took his hand. He obeyed me without objection, rose, and we walked together to the bathroom. I opened its door quickly, put him inside, and asked him to take off all his clothes except his underpants and sit down on the wooden bench.

He did that. Then I went to fetch plastic bags and began to place his clothes in the bags but was startled to find large numbers of black lice on them. I dropped them onto the floor and washed my hands repeatedly in the sink. I went to my room to look for a piece of white cloth. When I found one, I wrapped it tightly around my head. I brought a pair of scissors and returned to the bathroom to pick those clothes off the floor and put them in the plastic bags.

Then I called one of my other brothers and asked him to toss the bags in the trash bin outside. Next, I went to my father and asked him to lend me his clippers and razor. Taking them from him, I entered the bathroom.

I turned on both the hot and cold water to fall on my brother's head while he sat beneath the showerhead. My brother did not move. Instead, he remained lost in his alternative reality. I poured shampoo onto the loofah. Once the shampoo formed a lather, I brought that lather to my brother's body and began soaping him. My brother persisted in his sea of silence, even after I started clipping his matted hair with the scissors. Once I shortened those twisted hanks of hair, I shaved his head entirely with the razor. Then I turned my brother's face toward me, asked him not to move, and began shaving his beard and his mustache. After I had finished that, I sniffed a little, lifted his arms into the air, and shaved his armpits. Then I sat on the floor, gently drew his feet toward me, one at a time, and began to clip his toenails with the scissors.

When I sensed that my tunic and the cloth around my hair were getting wet, I removed the cloth and examined it carefully in the light to make sure there were no lice on it. Then I threw it in the little trash can in the bathroom and went to change my tunic. Once I returned, I knocked on the bathroom door to hand my brother clean clothes, a toothbrush, and toothpaste.

My brother left the bathroom with his appearance totally transformed, but he still preferred silence to words. He sat in the living room looking at the floor like someone gazing at a bottomless pit.

One of my sisters offered him some food, and he ate a little. From the way he ate, we assumed he had lost his appetite. Then he entered the bedroom to sleep. When we were sure he was asleep, one of my brothers "liberated" Iyas's boots and threw them in the trash bin down on the street.

Even though we understood how sacred a uniform is to a soldier, we were forced to discard his in the rubbish to prevent lice and infection from affecting us.

A week after my brother returned, relatives began to visit to congratulate us on his safe return. My mother was embarrassed by my brother's repeated refusals to meet people or even to emerge to greet them. During his fifteen-day leave, I never saw him undertake any project. He just continued sitting, staring silently at the wall of his room.

I could not take him to see a psychiatrist, because sending a person there implied a judgment by our society that he was "crazy." But I was unable to sit with my hands behind my back regarding what was happening to my brother. To learn what he was suffering, I had to encourage him to talk about it—first to diagnose it and then to help him treat it in some way.

I gently penetrated his lengthy curtain of silence when I brought a tray with several plates of food into his room. When he heard the door open and checked to see that I was the only person entering, he turned back to face the wall. But I did not hear any word from him banning me from entering. So, I came into the room, placed the tray between us, and sat down on the floor. I ladled bean broth onto the rice in a second dish and started to mix them together. When I had done that for a long time, my brother looked first at me and then at the tray with its plates of hot food. I pushed the tray a little closer toward him as if to invite him to eat.

I was overjoyed when I saw him lift the spoon and start to eat. Once I was certain that all the plates were empty, I lifted the tray and started to leave, feeling proud of myself for executing this taxing mission.

Before departing, I asked him, "Will you drink your tea here or in the living room?"

"Here," he replied, staring at the floor.

Leaving quickly, I assured him, "By the time you've washed your hands, the tea will be ready."

I returned to him with the tea tray, which also held some *kleicha* date pastries my mother had made to celebrate his safe return. He ate one and started to drink the tea calmly. Not too much later, he launched into the soliloquy he needed to make.

"They dragged me out of the truck and shoved me into the lobby of the hotel so forcefully that I fell on my face. When I stood up, another officer pushed me to the floor again. Then they demanded that I tell them my name, the address of my military unit, and my home address. They put me in a room packed with other soldiers like me, and we stayed there for two days, without anything to eat or drink. We peed on ourselves because they refused to let us leave that room.

"Two days later, large military transport vehicles came, and they packed us into them, with our hands still shackled. They took us to al-Radwaniya Prison Camp in Baghdad. They unpacked us there and placed us in a large *jamalawn* warehouse with a pitched roof. Before they released us from our handcuffs, the door of this warehouse opened, and swarms of soldiers of different ranks entered, like predatory locusts heading to fields to strip them bare. They carried scary whips.

"Those scourges began to lash whatever parts of our bodies they wished while we were powerless and could not even try to stay alive. We began to cluster together, seeking refuge in numbers. With nothing to shield us, screams of pain issued from our mouths every time the fiery lightning of the whips approached us.

"The more pain they inflicted on us, the more we retreated to the corners of the structure. When those corners grew crowded, we began to climb on top of each other until some of us reached the roof, forming a hill of living flesh. Those soldiers with whips thought this was hilarious!

"The summit of that mound was composed of us young soldiers, and at the base were the bodies of the older soldiers. As quickly as those whips flew, the mound grew higher until our heads were approaching the roof of this warehouse. We pressed down on bodies crammed together, and whenever the pain proved unbearable, we howled, and the snapping whips silenced us. They did not depart till their hands grew tired of beating us. Then they left us to collapse on top of each other, our spirits filled with revulsion.

"Next, many other soldiers came, dragged us to the ground, and shoved us into metal chicken coops. They began phony interrogations. They would not believe me when I swore that I had not set any fires, killed anyone, or stolen anything. They administered curses, blows, and torture to me. Once they tired of beating me with sticks and heavy whips, they imprisoned me in a cage barely big enough for two people, together with some old men. To tell the truth, I don't know whether they were old men or simply soldiers like me who had aged terribly on account of the torture. One of them had been scraping his skin with his fingernails till strips of it were peeling off. Another was coughing up blood. The third one we never saw regain consciousness.

"The plastic water mug passed from hand to hand and mouth to mouth until the brackish water in it was exhausted. They never washed that mug before bringing it to us. For nourishment, they provided us scraps of rotten food like those given to stray dogs.

"When we wanted the WC, a guard posted outside of it would count to ten in his commanding voice. If the person inside had not finished his business by then, the guard would kick the door with his foot and then enter to rain down blows on the person inside. Those were severe enough to cause him to fall to the ground there, rolling in filth.

"In al-Radwaniya Prison Camp, there were many ways to die. You either died from gastric diseases easily transmitted to you by other prisoners, from repeated bouts of torture, or from your fear of worse to come.

"The moment the first rays of light appeared in the sky, dozens of officers and guards would enter to select prisoners seemingly at random. They would lead them to the torture chambers, and then we would hear nothing but the sound of whips falling on bodies and the men screaming from pain.

"Many of us were killed by a firing squad, without any real or fair trial. I almost died of fright when a guard came and asked us to divide into two groups—one to his right and the other to his left. In the group to his right were soldiers who had returned from Kuwait and had not participated in any acts of destruction. I was one of them. The other group, to his left, included marauders and hoodlums, as he described them. I felt that I would certainly be executed at that moment. I recited the two *shahadas* in preparation for my death, but the officer looked at us and said: 'It seems that you guys are very lucky, because the benevolent commander Saddam Hussein—may God preserve him and watch over him—has issued an order pardoning you.' Then he turned to the other group and shouted to the soldiers around him: 'An eye for an eye!'

"I could not believe what my ears heard, and my eyes watched expectantly for the moment the huge prison-camp gate would open, even after they asked us to go to the 'warehouse' and sit there to wait till someone came to record our names and provide us with passes authorizing us to return to our cities.

"When the gate of the prison camp did open, I rushed like a madman onto streets that were totally unfamiliar to me. While I stood by the door of a small restaurant resting my feet, which were tired from running, the owner came outside and asked me to come in and offered me food and drink. He asked me what city I was from and then gave me the bus fare and asked me to visit the mausoleum of Imam Ali (peace upon him) on his behalf."

"Then we will go there tomorrow, you and I, and perform the ritual of visitation in his honor," I said to Iyas, wiping away tears with my hand. "Do you know his name?"

"Jaber. His name is Jaber," he replied, almost absentmindedly.

The following day, precisely at the time for the afternoon prayer, the two of us performed the ritual visitation in the courtyard of Imam Ali ibn Abi Talib (peace upon him) on behalf of Jaber, a lineal descendant of Adam and Eve.

My brother cloaked himself with silence once more and continued to report to his military unit, unable to forget the various forms of bitter torture he had endured or how he had satisfied his hunger with fear for many months and sated his thirst with tears and how he could only await his uncertain future, one that might leap at him at any moment from the lips of a guard who did not know the meaning of "mercy."

My brother did not again discuss the torture he had endured until two years later when he told this story to his wife during their honeymoon.

Is it merely coincidental that, on the first day of February 2021, the day I finished writing this chapter about my brother, I woke, terrified, from a strange dream about vomiting my bitterness, and that before I could catch my breath, one of my sisters contacted me on WhatsApp to inform me that Iyas had just taken his last breath in Al Sadr Teaching Hospital in Najaf after having trouble breathing? He fell victim to the lack of oxygen canisters in that hospital during the coronavirus pandemic.

Chapter Ten

I've long wondered about the United Nations' decision to punish Iraq's invasion of Kuwait. Would it have been possible to sanction Saddam Hussein in a way that did not terrify the Iraqi people and starve them with a vile economic blockade that lasted for thirteen years? The Iraqi Army could not have entered Kuwaiti territory without orders from their commander.

Although I don't know the details of international laws and their enforcement, like the rest of the Iraqi people, I was harmed by the sanctions against Iraq in UN Security Council resolution 661, which was issued on August 6, 1990.

It is extremely natural for someone who has acted impolitely and improperly to be sanctioned, but it is unjust for this penalty, whatever it may be, to extend to even one additional person. We even find, cited in Islamic law, verses from the Qur'an stipulating this. For example, God Almighty in the Holy Qur'an (52:21) says: "Each person is responsible for his deeds." He also says (6:164): "Every soul is responsible for its own actions; no soul should bear the burden of another." In other words, punishment should be applied solely to the perpetrator of a crime. This rule does not seem to be applied to rulers of countries and to heads of states. The moment a ruler breaks an internationally recognized law or infringes on the rights of another people, his people are punished—not just him.

The important point is that we were subjected to an economic blockade that resulted in our suffering pitiful hunger, deprivation, and exposure to various maladies as a result of the major lack of medicines in our hospitals and clinics. Within the boundaries of Iraq, we lived like caged prisoners and were denied contact with the outside world.

During those lean years, the Iraqi economy deteriorated noticeably. Most male government employees left their jobs because of the sharp decline in the value of their salaries. Each government employee received a *monthly* salary of three thousand dinars, or the equivalent of two and a half US dollars.

You can imagine the disastrous condition of a government employee, especially one who had a family to support and care for, who had to pay daily expenses, the rent for apartments, and water and electricity bills. Most professors, research assistants, and bureaucrats quit their posts to pursue one of two paths: leaving Iraq for other countries like Jordan and Syria; or embracing some trade like selling cigarettes on the street, driving a taxi, working in a bakery, or setting aside a room in their home as a small shop offering daily necessities.

Women teachers began to practice other professions inside their homes—like repairing used clothes, knitting garments with wool salvaged from discarded garments, and *riyafa*, which is taking torn abayas and men's cloaks and embroidering them, or mending ragged rugs and carpets—in addition to their classroom instruction.

I personally witnessed what happened to three elderly professors who had earned advanced degrees and taught me various subjects at the university. These professors left the university to practice different trades, saying they were entering the free market. In fact, they were selling household wares in the souks. The financial need afflicting professors also affected students. Most male students left their schools, universities, and institutes to join the swarm of day laborers as unemployment strangled society, especially after many factories closed, laying off their employees.

The level of the health services provided to us free of charge in public hospitals and people's clinics deteriorated substantially after thousands of physicians left the country, and medicines and medical supplies disappeared from these facilities. A patient being treated in a hospital was forced to buy large quantities of any medical supplies or medicines he needed from private pharmacies. A million and a half children died due to lack of proper medical treatment.

Hospitals were also no longer safe places for a woman to deliver a baby for lack of proper ways to care for her or her newborn. Therefore, many pregnant women resorted to delivering their child in the home of a licensed midwife, and as a result, many women died during childbirth. In our district alone, eight women lost their lives in childbirth when assisted only by a licensed midwife.

With this serious deterioration of Iraqi infrastructure, bribery and nepotism increased among employees of the state. Signs of poverty were apparent at most economic levels. You did not need to look very far to find light blankets transformed by a tailor's skill into a man's jacket or cloak, worn to ward off the winter cold. It was not possible for an ordinary family to afford clothes, shoes, bags, or school supplies for their children, who handed down garments and shoes from one child to the next till these were worn out.

I remember once running into a neighbor on my way home from school who was so delighted that she could scarcely stand still. After greeting me, she told me with tremendous joy: "Something miraculous happened to me today! I found a treasure in our house. I was worried about how to find the money to buy new shoes for my daughter, whose current shoes are totally worn out. Her older sister wears a much larger size because she is twelve and my younger daughter is eight—as you know. I was about to ask her to skip school because there was no way she could attend class barefoot. But as I began to clean the pantry today,

I found an old wooden box there. When I opened it, I discovered that it was filled with all my older daughter's cast-off shoes! Even though she had worn them, they look new and are in different styles and colors, praise the Lord!"

When I repeated "Praise the Lord," I had to restrain myself from bursting into tears. I left her and continued on my way, remarking to myself, "How pathetic! We consider finding used shoes a miracle!"

During those bitter years, new occupations unknown in Iraq previously were devised. People made money by selling blood instead of donating it to invalids who needed it. Each time I accompanied my mother to the hospital, I found a queue of young men with pale faces sitting on the benches by the hospital's fence, waiting for someone to ask what his blood type was.

Frequently in markets and along many streets, you saw women who sold medicine and different types of medical supplies. A medicine you didn't find in the hospital or a private pharmacy, you would see sold by women vendors on the sidewalks at exorbitant prices.

A market once granted a person a form of relaxation; now entering a souk and strolling through it was more like torture, because your eye would see attractive things, but your hand could not touch them—they cost too much. Vendors began to sort and display their wares in a way that made a buyer afraid to ask the price, which wasn't fixed—not to mention the psychological harm that a person who dared to ask the price of something might suffer from the shabby way he was treated.

For example, a fishmonger would isolate excellent large fish in special locations and call out: "Food for men who repair tires!" The point was that unless you worked in a garage, you would not have enough money to eat them, since a single kilo of this type of fish cost twenty thousand Iraqi dinars. A government employee would need to save his salary for six months to buy a pound of that fish.

Fruits had disappeared entirely from the markets. The only ones remaining were a type of dried date called *khalal* and melons, and prices for them varied, almost daily. That was because the Ministry of Commerce no longer supervised the prices of goods displayed in those markets.

I remember one day I was searching for a little pure honey to help my mother suppress her asthma attacks. When a man sold me a spoonful of that honey for a thousand Iraqi dinars, he boasted about his skill in diagnosing diseases. He said a rich man had come to him with a daughter who had a large ulcer on her right breast. The man said doctors had advised him to excise it to keep her condition from deteriorating. The man had come to this vendor because his daughter was afraid of the operation. When the vendor had learned the location and depth of the ulcer, he had prepared a salve for her and asked her to rub it on the ulcer three days in a row while she continued cleaning that ulcer. He had also advised her not to wear a bra during that treatment.

"They took that remedy from me, gave me my asking price, and departed. Three days later the man returned by himself, his face beaming with joy. He thanked me profusely for curing his daughter. The ulcer had dwindled away totally, and no trace of it remained. Out of appreciation for me, he presented me with two large red apples. Imagine: two apples! I held each one in a hand! I will never forget that night. When I brought those apples home with me, my wife and I relished eating them. I can still remember their taste!"

I could not blame this herbalist for his great delight over two apples, because fruit, and especially apples, had become very hard to find. If you did find them, they cost as much as jewels in those days. This is a situation I would not wish, even for a moment, on anyone living today.

During that period when merchants competed fiercely and greed infected them, the black market began to provide them with limitless profits; with lightning speed, they were able to display obscene amounts of wealth. Their houses extended skyward and expanded in all directions till the names of streets became blurred in the minds of residents, who referred to a district by the wealthy merchants who lived there.

Saddam Hussein's sole preoccupation over a period of five years seemed to be building presidential palaces in most of Iraq's cities. Their number was rumored to have reached one thousand. Two hundred were in Baghdad, and one hundred sixty were constructed on the right bank of the Tigris River in Tikrit. Engraved into the marble or alabaster over their portals was Qur'an verse 3:26, in which God says to Himself, "You grant power to those You will and remove it from those You will." These palaces were given names like the Palace of Peace and the Palace of Prayerful Prostration. Every visit by Saddam Hussein to inspect the stages of construction for one of his palaces was carried on TV.

I remember that during one of those inspection visits, the man in charge of that particular palace complained to Saddam Hussein that date-palm shoots brought from Basra and al-Fao to plant at this palace could not tolerate the different soil in Baghdad and that most of them had immediately died once they were planted. So Saddam Hussein suggested that a crew transplant to that palace a group of full-grown palms with clusters of dates growing on them along with enough dirt from al-Fao to receive them.

Saddam Hussein also objected occasionally to the way staircases were built—that the grade was too steep. He frequently asked project engineers and contractors to replace those steps so that he could climb more easily to the upper stories when he reached an advanced age, because he aspired to immortality like many previous kings, sultans, and mighty rulers.

Expensive stone statues of President Saddam Hussein continued to proliferate in Baghdad. On every national holiday, and especially on his birthday, which occurred on April 28, Iraqis were obliged to celebrate publicly in the main streets and squares as children, wearing shirts emblazoned with a color portrait of the president, performed dances and sang patriotic anthems while carrying bouquets of artificial flowers of various colors. Public agencies and schools were also beauti-fully decorated for these festivities, and all the expenses for them were covered by the employees and workers in the agencies and the teachers and pupils in those schools.

Ordinary people experienced brutal lives as they endured the scourge of abject, relentless, crushing poverty, having been deserted by their government, which had inflicted these woes upon them. One day, I was performing the rituals of visitation at the shrine of Imam Ali ibn Abi Talib (peace upon him) with one of my fellow students and noticed the color of the abaya of a woman who was also performing the visitation. It had been worn so often that its black had turned totally blue. We waited for this woman to complete the rituals and then approached her. When my classmate asked about her economic situation, the woman told us she was a widow who was raising her two orphans by selling harmala (African rue) and henna every day near the saint's tomb. She said that this was the only abaya she had.

My classmate immediately asked her to wait there while we rushed to the office of the Islamic Charitable Society—after covering most of our faces with our abayas, leaving only a single eye visible. We entered the office and found some men standing on both sides of a turbaned gentleman who sat at a simple desk. We greeted the men in a barely audible whisper. When the man wearing the turban noticed us, he gestured for us to come forward, and the men stepped aside to make room for us. We approached the desk, and when he asked why we had come to him, my classmate immediately said, "Noble Shaykh, I come today to inform Your Honor of the condition of an impoverished widow who is raising her orphaned children. Her abaya is worn out, but she cannot afford to buy another one. If you do not believe me, you can send one of your assistants to find her and speak with her to ascertain the truth of what I am saying. I would like a few dinars to buy her another abaya, even a used one."

The man, who had been leaning on his elbows on the desk, adjusted his position and said loudly and rather shrilly, "There is no money in the treasury that I can hand out for this reason. There are many women like her. I do not have the authority to distribute money for such cases."

My classmate interrupted him and asked angrily, "Isn't an abaya a necessary symbol of piety and chastity for a woman? If so, shouldn't this symbol be a necessity for her? If you do not have any money to distribute in such circumstances, may I borrow from you enough money to buy this woman a used abaya better than the one she is wearing now? I promise I will return to your office tomorrow. I am from a prominent family and live in al-Amir District. I belong to the household of so-and-so."

My classmate mentioned the name of her family to reassure him about her ability to repay the money she wanted to borrow. Once he sensed that she was telling the truth, he loaned her the money and handed her a receipt to sign. He asked her to return the sum to his house, which turned out to be near her home—just one street away.

We left the office and then went with the woman, who was waiting for us outside the shrine, to a store that sold used abayas in the Grand Souk. We purchased one, which seemed to be in excellent condition and her size. The woman thanked us and departed.

I met my classmate two days later so she could recount what had happened when she returned the money. "I went to the home of the turbaned *shaykh*. When I knocked on the door, I heard a woman's voice ask who was there. I told her my name and why I had come. She asked me to wait till she had asked permission from the inhabitants to allow me to enter. She returned a few minutes later, opened the door, and led me to the kitchen, where I sat down to wait for the man, as she instructed me.

"All the furnishings in the house were extraordinarily fancy, and even the woman who had opened the door for me, and who by her conduct seemed to be the housekeeper, wore fine imported garments that looked very expensive.

"The *shaykh* descended from the upper story of the house, and I greeted him, and he returned my greeting. Then he asked me to hand the money to the woman who had opened the door for me. I did. She accepted the money from me, but without offering me so much as a glass of water.

"Before I left, I asked the *shaykh* to give me a receipt. Then he told me, 'I attest that your debt is paid in full.'

"So I said goodbye and quickly left. All this happened without anyone even trying to look the other person in the eye. The transaction between us seemed to be purely mechanical and unrelated to the Islamic religion, which is based on the excellent treatment of other people and on displaying good character."

My wealthy classmate launched into a lengthy and astonished discussion of what she had seen in the home of that turbaned *shaykh*—the furnishings and things she said were beyond description. My reaction was negative, because it seemed that poor folks like us could only hope for assistance from God.

As those years passed, we forgot why the embargo had been imposed on us and no longer dreamt of a day when we might be relieved of its sanctions. We were sure that all the international promises made to us were fraudulent. The most we could hope for was to stay alive. We began selling pieces of furniture we did not need. Then we sold our extra containers and plates. Next, we sold our used clothes at super-cheap prices. When the sale of those items netted only enough to buy some food, we decided to sell our main pieces of furniture in the apartment. Most households dispensed with all electrical appliances except for a television and a refrigerator, and women and girls had to wash their family's clothes by hand after electric washing machines were sold. And by no means was there any stability during those thirteen lean years, not even with the Oil-for-Food Programme that was proposed by the United Nations in 1991 and accepted by Iraq in 1996. Even then, many restrictions controlled the quantity of oil the country could export and that only at a greatly discounted price.

The food-ration card distributed monthly to citizens at no charge was restricted during the first year to flour, rice, sugar, tea, cooking oil, soap, bleach, Zahi Mentho-Lyptus tablets, milk for adults, milk for babies, Cerelac infant cereal, lentils, broad beans, chickpeas, tomato paste, salt, triangles of processed cheese, razor blades, Amber toothpaste, and chicken. Supplies of these soon started to decrease, with chicken being the first to disappear. It was only available once a year, during Ramadan, and limited to one frozen chicken per family. Then baby milk and cleansers disappeared, together with things like razor blades. Excellent commodities that had been on sale in the markets were soon replaced by inferior goods, most of which were unfit for human consumption, because both importers and vendors began to adulterate these items. In lieu of black jasmine tea with its fine aroma, some vendors and corrupt merchants dyed sawdust black with clothing dye, dried it, and sold it as tea. For this reason, some families bought excellent brands of tea at exorbitant prices and drank tea only once a week or reserved it for guests. Other families added boiling water to tea several times and continued drinking that brew till it finally lost its flavor and color.

Flour was sold after being adulterated with white dirt, fine sand, or lime. Women suffered a lot as did owners of bakeries when trying to clean this flour, knead it, and bake it. This tainted flour was responsible for many illnesses. Even the falafel sandwiches we ate at the university suddenly cost much more, and it was hard to afford them every day. Someone who normally would have ridden a bus to work or school now had to choose between going without lunch or walking.

When red meat disappeared from the markets or became exorbitantly expensive, women became adept at making vegetarian food daily.

Instead of making skillet kebab with beef or lamb, they would prepare a type of kebab consisting of a mixture of vegetables instead. Green squash was peeled and finely chopped. Then finely cut celery leaves, shredded onion, flour, and salt were mixed with the chopped squash. This "dough" was kneaded and fried in oil. No other flavorings or spices were added, if only because they were not widely available. Meat or chicken stews were replaced by "air" stew. This dish was prepared by frying an onion in a little oil till it browned, and then adding water and salt. It was poured over cubes or dry discs of bread.

The vegetable that achieved the greatest renown during the embargo was the eggplant, dubbed the "Monster of the Skillet." It appeared at all meals of the day. It was served fried for breakfast. At noon we ate it as a stew with tomato paste. At supper we ate it grilled. If we wanted to buy pickles, we looked first for pickled eggplant. Eggplant also appeared as an appetizer that we called *badhijaniya*, and some women, including my mother, became experts at making eggplant jam.

As a direct result of the unjust embargo, like everyone else with a middle-class income, my father eventually sold all our electrical appliances and furniture, leaving us with only the gas range, refrigerator, television, and air conditioner, an indispensable appliance during the blazing summer.

Naturally our first major sale of furniture was the set of sofa and chairs that had furnished our parlor. We replaced these as seating for our guests with foam pallets covered with colorful sheets of a cotton-polyester-blend fabric. Those pallets were set out when guests visited and put away as soon as they left, to preserve them for as long as possible.

Although my father had retained his job at the Department of Education, he failed to find any other employment, and so my brother Iyas was forced—despite the harms and woes he had suffered from war—to reenlist in the Iraqi Army in order to retain his monthly salary.

I was obliged to search for another job to provide whatever assistance—no matter how small—to my family and myself, because my monthly salary would buy nothing more than a serving of fried eggs.

I also continued to attend some of the special events sponsored by the local Writers and Artists General Union in Najaf. My attendance depended on having enough money for the bus fare there and back to the meeting in Khan al-Makhdar.

I did, however, experience some harassment from young men who belonged to the local union at that time. They accused me of being a dilettante and of not being a member of the national General Union of Iraqi Authors and Writers. They claimed that unless a person belonged to that organization, they should not be considered a literary figure, no matter how profound their knowledge of Arabic culture.

Because one condition for membership in the union was being a published author and having published a number of poems in several generally recognized newspapers and magazines, and because this would be the first book I published, meeting this condition was not an easy step for me, especially since I did not belong to a family with a history of publishing to provide me with useful advice. Nor did I have a girlfriend who could encourage me to embark on this adventure in such a challenging arena. Most important of all, I did not have the chunk of change I would need to publish such a collection.

All the same, the moment I proposed this plan to a professor at a session of the union, he rose from his chair and introduced me to the proprietor of the publishing house al-Nifaq, which was located in Najaf. This publisher was also a member of the union and a friend of this professor. So the three of us sat down together after the session to discuss my proposed poetry book. We talked about the name of the book, the number of pages, the type of paper it would be printed on, the number of sections it would have, the cover design, the typeface used for the title, and the quantity to be printed. We also addressed details of the publishing process and the distribution of the book in Najaf and beyond. We did not, however, discuss the most important point of all: the amount I would need to pay the publisher. Because this would be my first book and no one in my city or outside it knew me as an author, I was obliged to underwrite the cost of its publication.

That same year, two of my sisters married, and my brother became engaged. Several young men offered to marry me but rejected my one condition, which was that I be allowed to continue my studies until I earned a doctorate.

Apparently, my engagement was destined, in the womb of the Unknown, to occur during a period of mourning. One day an acquaintance of my mother's died, and I accompanied her to his wake, during which a woman saw me and asked me to help her clean the house. So I did that chore diligently. A week later, that woman came with her husband to arrange my engagement to one of her sons. My father had some doubts about this proposal, because we did not know this family well, and my mother left the decision to me. I repeated the condition that I be allowed to complete my studies after the wedding.

I really hoped they would not agree to this precondition, but they did. Then my engagement was officially announced two weeks after their visit. His family visited us again to present me a betrothal gift, which consisted of earrings, a simple necklace, and a ring, all pure 21-karat gold. That young man had saved up for several years to buy these.

In Iraq, a bride is expected to preserve this jewelry to adorn herself on joyous occasions like weddings, circumcisions, or birthdays. She tries hard to avoid selling them, except in emergencies when she has no alternative. Frankly, my pressing emergency situation was the publication of my first poetry collection, and I was forced to take that gold and sell it, unbeknownst to my family, and fork over that money to the owner of the publishing house.

This period also brought other important events, some of which changed the course of history, like the discovery in the Austrian Alps of the mummy Ötzi, which was believed to be the oldest human mummy; the choice of Berlin as the capital of a unified Germany; the appearance of a solar eclipse viewed by twenty million people in Hawaii, Mexico, Colombia, and the western United States; the European Cup victory by Manchester United after it defeated Barcelona with a score of 2 to 1; and the release of the video game *Sonic the Hedgehog*.

Publication of my poetry collection was officially approved by the Ministry of Information in Baghdad on the first day of the seventh month of 1991. The title was *'Cause I'm a Girl*. The cover was also printed in Baghdad. The designer used a red drawing of a girl, showing only her hair, all of one eye, and a bit of the other.

At the end of the week, the proprietor of the publishing house called me to say that he had put the finishing touches on my book and sent it to the printers. In his next phone call, he told me when he would receive copies I might want to distribute to my friends and acquaintances. When I heard that, I experienced moments of euphoria unlike any I could have imagined as I visualized the size of my first book of poetry, the font and size of the type used to print my name on the cover, the manner in which the publisher would present the first copy to me, and how I would leaf through its pages. I experienced those moments in a continuing dream in which I alternated between dozing off inside its velvety folds and awakening to the splendor of its actual existence.

Then the moment really arrived when I received the call summoning me to collect some copies. I went to the office, which was located on al-Sadiq Street in the Wilaya District, but I do not recall the details of how I made my way there. Those events remain vague and uncertain. Time stopped. What is engraved in my mind about that day is the moment I set eyes on the pile of books that were placed on the table like a Valentine's Day bouquet waiting for me. The only part I heard of the speech the man made when he handed that pile to me was the expression: "A thousand congratulations!"

I will not be lying if I write that everything around me in that room suddenly changed into some fluid flux in which many colors fused together to become light. I sensed then that I was standing on unsteady ground that might propel me into uncharted territory—a place located somewhere between reality and the imagination.

The moment I received the bundle, I headed back to the bus stop, uncertain how to travel while I was carrying such a load, even as I experienced what it meant to walk on clouds, because the rowdy calls of passersby were transmuted to a sweet whisper, and the roar of the vehicles became dreamy, romantic music.

When I climbed aboard the bus that would take me home, I surveyed the other passengers only to find that their countenances were amazingly good-looking and their clothes extraordinarily chic. The driver resembled no one more than a pianist, and when my hand held out the fare to him, he bowed his head delicately. As he accepted the money from me, his smile was astounding. Once I reached my neighborhood, I felt that everyone I encountered deserved a kiss and a hug from me, as if each new person I saw was my newly found true love.

My father was the first person to receive a copy of this poetry collection and was delighted, especially after he read the inscription: "To my father, I love you, despite everything." What I was referencing with the last two words was the war and its repercussions, which had frequently kept my father away from us and preoccupied him, depriving us of his attention.

He asked me for a second copy that he would present to the Public Instruction Library where he worked. So I gave him another one.

Every member of my family shared in my delight, even those who were not interested in poetry or literature. By the end of the day, after I had sated myself reading my poems to myself in my room, I placed my book on my pillow beside my head, and we took a nap together.

My father continued to take his copy with him to work for many days, carrying it around so carefully that anyone who saw him would think he had received a celestial gift. He showed it to all his friends and colleagues at work, saying, "I am the father of this poet. I am Abu Faleeha Hassan."

In keeping with this publishing house's protocols when a new book was released, its owner thought it appropriate to organize a small book-signing party. He picked a date and contacted me to ask whether that day would be convenient. I agreed to it. For my part, I invited two of my colleagues who had read my book and liked it.

At 5:00 p.m. on the appointed day, I went to the headquarters of that publishing house, which consisted of three large book-filled rooms and a large hall reserved for receptions. This building in Wilaya was also located on a street lined with specialty bookstores and bookshops.

I could not believe my eyes when I entered the hall and found it filled with a large audience of men. The moment the head of the publishing house caught sight of me, he came to greet me and then introduced me to the people there as "the poet Faleeha Hassan." Then he asked me to sit in the chair reserved for the guest of honor.

The hall was packed with people, all men, and extra chairs had to be brought in to accommodate everyone. Even then, there were not enough chairs, and some men had to stand throughout the event. My two girlfriends and I were the only women present, and they were accompanied by their brothers.

The master of ceremonies for this session began by welcoming the audience and thanking them for having taken the trouble to attend and for their support of young poets, especially for young women poets. Truth be told, these hordes of men had not come to support me. Instead, their goal in attending was to find out what kind of girl had been insolent enough to defy convention and thrust herself among them—trying to make a name for herself in this entirely male poetry scene.

I read some poems that I myself had selected for this event. First I read two rather long poems. Then I read some very short poems. One of these was "My Hope":

> I hoped to come to you,
> But our streets are red,
> And I have only a white dress!

Another was "Full Disclosure":

> My worry is vaster than this earth.
> To expel it from my chest,
> I need more earth than the earth.

A third poem was "Question":

> As I climb the stairs of my house,
> I ask, from deep inside me,
> "You're so steep, how can anyone walk up
> you?"

The fourth poem was "Thief":

> The sea stole my tears;
> That's why it's become so vast.

When I finished reading, members of the audience attacked me with their questions, observations, and comments, like hungry eagles swooping in on a single prey. In the blink of an eye, they all seemed to have become professional critics who had discovered in these poems an easily swallowed morsel to shred. They attacked me for lacking a poetic soul and criticized the book for containing too many very short poems—what they called "flicker poems."

I responded nonchalantly to their vapid yelps by quoting the tenth-century thinker al-Niffari: "The wider the range of vision becomes, the narrower its expression should be."

When they heard me reply in this calm way, especially since they did not like my reference to a Sufi philosopher, voices emerged even louder from throats grown hoarse from anger. My publisher, the master of ceremonies, tried in various ways to calm the group and did not remain a neutral party in this heated debate, which became an unfair battle. As moderator he did his best not to alienate any guest, no matter how committed to his own view or how devoid of respect for fair play he was in this debate, and without regard to how illogical or extemporaneous a critique might seem.

I was astonished both at the number of different viewpoints presented and the fact that they had all been prepared in advance, for each man to repeat like a parrot. None of these remarks was inspired by reading my poetry. I knew that because my book had not yet been released in bookstores, even though a few copies had reached the hands of some readers. It would have been impossible for everyone in this large crowd of men to have read it—especially since the point of this gathering was to introduce my book and to encourage the audience to purchase it.

I believe it is unfair to judge a book only by its cover or title without exploring the ideas it expresses in the commonwealth of words printed on its pages and reject the dictum that says it is easier to talk about a book you have not read. In any case, I was truly infuriated by the unruly conduct of a Najaf poet—one considered to be important—who arrived late, headed straight to the table where my book was displayed in a pleasing and harmonious way, yanked out a copy vigorously, and, even before opening it, raised it high in his hand and began shouting, "This collection is an insult to poetry and to the entire city of Najaf." Then he threw my book back down on the table and left the hall as quickly as he had entered. No one present volunteered to reply to this poet or to refute his opinion, even though this man had appointed himself the ultimate arbiter of poetic taste. The expressions on the faces in the audience indicated that they supported this chauvinistic opinion, inspired by the fact that I, the author, was a woman. As the discussion turned into a screaming and shouting match and became totally incomprehensible, a poet who had come all the way from Baghdad asked the moderator whether he might comment.

The moderator granted him permission and asked the audience to quiet down so the visitor's remarks could be heard. Then this visitor greeted members of the audience and congratulated the publishing house for sponsoring this gathering in these extraordinary conditions.

"I do not know why we still believe the maxim that says 'Our local musician can't sing.' If this poetry collection had come to us from outside Iraq and been written by a woman poet who wasn't Iraqi, we would have honored and feted her. But because this book was produced by a local poet, we refuse to celebrate her in an appropriate way. Speaking for myself, I support the poet Faleeha Hassan. I shake her by both hands and wish her a glittering success."

Once the poet had made this comment, I felt a truce had been established between me and all these rowdy knights. So I regained a little poise. That lasted till most of them had left the hall, and I stayed behind to speak with a group of people numbering no more than the fingers on one hand. They actually wanted to obtain a copy of my book, and the heated opinions had whetted their appetite for it.

Although I had heard an extraordinary quantity of the hatred and ire vented, I returned home with the pride of a victor who had realized a huge success. Exactly two months later, I received another call from the publishing house. The proprietor informed me that the thousand copies of the first printing had sold out. He wanted me to come to receive my royalties and told me that *'Cause I'm a Girl* was the first book of verse by a woman to be published in the city of Najaf. By publishing it, I had become a pioneer.

Not surprisingly, the eyes and tongues of jealous people began to aim sharp arrows at me, and their poisons splattered me almost every day. This phenomenon upset a young poet enough that he took the initiative to visit me at my university and tell me that my name was being bandied about over cups of tea in almost every coffeehouse and literary club in the city.

My renown spread throughout all of Iraq, and I began to receive invitations to poetry festivals and literary meetings, and even to help organize them. I endeavored to accept most of them. Shortly thereafter, poets in other cities began to associate Najaf with me. Through my many publications and my participation in these events, I became a feature of the creative firmament of Iraq.

Eventually, even ordinary people began to recognize me on the street, greet me respectfully, and sometimes even recite one of my short poems. I remember one day when I was preparing to board a bus, I heard a surprised passenger tell his friend loud enough for me to hear: "Look, it's *'Cause I'm a Girl!*" I smiled shyly then and boarded that bus.

Of all the awkward and yet beautiful situations that occurred, I recall what happened when I was invited to the Mirbad Festival in Basra. It was my first invitation to this festival, which almost all Iraqi and Arab poets dream of attending. The moment I entered the hall, took one of the seats reserved for participants, and adjusted my posture, two young men ran toward me. One had a television camera on his shoulder and the other was helping aim it toward the audience. They were accompanied by a beautiful TV presenter with a microphone.

After I had fidgeted several times where I sat, I noticed that the cameraman had his camera trained on me as if he were taking pictures of me in different poses. I felt flattered, and the smile that appeared on my lips was inspired by both pride and embarrassment. For a few moments I felt that I was a well-known poet and that this was why the television crew was trying to transmit my image to all of Iraq.

While I was enjoying this delightful sensation, the TV presenter calmly approached me, holding her microphone out toward me. When the man seated beside me moved to make room for her, she leaned toward me to whisper, "My dear, could you please move a little the other way? We are trying to get some shots of the singer Adeeba, who is sitting behind you."

Her request chastened me, and I felt embarrassed. I squeezed my body to the far side of my seat while my eyes were trained on the floor as I attempted to flee from the camera lens, which was edging closer to the singer behind me.

Even if you did become an esteemed poet with a special literary status that was acknowledged by your family, acquaintances, and people you encountered, you were still forced to endure choking hunger on account of the bitter embargo and were denied the simple pleasures of life. And if you wished to find some relief, you were forced to search for it. Otherwise, your only refuge was in a dream, which might drag you to destruction as you fell into the snares of thorny reality.

Since I spent all my time among books, I found the courage one day to drop by one of the stationery shops located near the university. Some of these offered typing and printing services to students for their theses and dissertations. I asked the proprietor of this shop whether he would offer me computer keyboarding lessons. The man agreed and said that in addition to this gig, he worked as a math instructor in middle schools.

He suggested I come there immediately after I attended my lectures. So I began to frequent that shop and, within a week, felt at home at a computer keyboard after learning its secrets. I was overjoyed by this success and started to look for ways to gain back the sum of money I had expended on these lessons.

Luck came to my aid one day when I was passing by that shop on my way home. I saw and heard the extremely angry proprietor curse and swear at someone over the phone. I hastened my pace then, but before I had gone far, heard him race after me and ask me to stop for a few moments. I did. Then he asked me quickly if I could type a twenty-page research paper that same day. I said I could but that I did not have a computer at home.

He suggested I take one of the old computers and a disk from the shop. The research paper was handwritten, and he asked me to type it. Once I did that, I could save it to the disk and bring that to him.

I was overjoyed by this proposal but refused to take the old computer without paying for it. So I suggested to the shop owner that I keep the computer and pay for it in installments. He agreed to this plan, especially since the computer was an old one he had repaired repeatedly.

I hailed a taxi, and the shop owner helped me place the components of the computer inside it. Across the street from our apartment building, the driver helped me set the computer on the sidewalk. Then I paid him, and he drove off.

When a young man waiting for the bus saw me, he hurried to help by carrying the heavier part of the computer. I carried the lighter parts, and we walked across the street slowly. Once we reached the door of our building, he placed the computer on the ground. I thanked him profusely for his help and he left. I then called my brothers, who carried it carefully to our apartment, where we set it in my room. I reassembled it there.

I was overjoyed when I found, in our pantry, a small round table that had become discolored over the years. All the same, it was the right size to hold the computer. My mother brought a white plastic chair from her room to complete my office.

I did not go to bed that night until I had typed the research paper and saved it to the disk, which I delivered to the shopkeeper the next morning before I went to class. He checked the typed paper on his personal computer and was incredulous when he found that everything was right—even the footnotes.

He thanked me, put his hand in the till, and brought out some cash to give me. I thanked him and suggested he put back some as part of my payment for the machine. He refused and asked me to enjoy these first fruits of my new endeavor. Before I left, he stopped me and gave me a large manuscript and the same disk.

He said, "We have three weeks to complete this. What do you think?"

I took the project from him and said, "God willing."

I spent some of that money to buy sweets to celebrate my first contract with my family. I split the rest of the money equally between my mother and father.

After eight months of continuous and persistent work as a typist, I bought a new computer to replace that old machine, which I had been obliged to have repaired almost every month.

Next, I bought a real desk for my new computer and a wooden chair, even if these were secondhand. These were a lot better than the wobbly table and the plastic chair, which had lost one of its legs after I used it for two months. Then I'd substituted a pile of bricks for the missing leg.

I gradually became self-supporting; with the money I earned from this job, I supplied some of my family's needs. I gave my monthly academic salary to my father each month to add to other money to pay for my mother's treatment. I felt proud when my siblings asked me to buy them something they wanted or school supplies. Even when my sisters married, I made a major contribution to the expenses of their weddings.

But none of this implied that—given the bitter circumstances of the embargo—we could set aside any money for the future. What our right hand received, our left hand paid out, with the speed of light, for necessities.

Most of these research papers, master's theses, and doctoral dissertations were produced by students enrolled at different universities, and each time I began to type a thesis or dissertation, I imagined that it was my own work and that I was the student who would, in a few days, defend it before a committee appointed for this purpose.

With the passing days, I acquired a critical sense that allowed me to distinguish the degree of competence, or the defects, of the theses and research papers that were delivered to me to type on the computer.

Month by month, various forms of poverty, want, illness, hunger, and ignorance affected most people, and yet, even so, some were still subservient to the image that had been created for Saddam Hussein. I read in a newspaper an interview with an artist who had drawn a portrait of President Saddam Hussein in his own blood. He said of that painting: "I draw my blood each morning. I am proud to have painted a picture of the leader, may God preserve and watch over him, with my own blood."

Once, Iraqi television covered a visit the president paid to one of the impoverished areas of Baghdad. While Saddam Hussein was exploring this region, an individual, who was in the prime of his life but whom hunger and deprivation made look middle-aged, appeared from the vast crowds of people gathered around the president's motorcade. His hair was disheveled, and he wore a shabby striped dishdasha, the original color of which one could hardly guess because that garment had been worn so often. He asked the president to do him the honor of visiting his modest home.

When the president accepted this invitation, entered, and sat down on a chair his bodyguards brought in, and after that impoverished man's family surrounded the president, the man asked Saddam Hussein to permit him to reveal a personal aspiration. The president agreed to hear this ambition, and the man said blissfully: "Your Honor, President Saddam Hussein, may God preserve and guard you, my wish is to have a life-sized statue made of you from pure gold and for this statue to be sent into space in a spaceship that orbits the earth. Then all the satellites of both hostile and friendly nations will notice it."

Saddam laughed conceitedly, like a war hero, and replied, patting the man on the back, "It's devotion like your love for me that enrages our enemies!"

While attempting to cover his legs with his tattered dishdasha, the man replied, "You are the glory of the Arab people and of the world."

Even though Iraqis were divided between those who secretly opposed Saddam Hussein and those who supported him privately and publicly, fear united everyone. The longer the embargo continued and the less confident people felt, the more impossible it became to discuss the condition of the country without exposing oneself to the risk of imprisonment or execution.

One of my father's friends, an elderly work colleague, disappeared one day. We did not see him again for three years. By then, he had aged even more and become diabetic. When he made contact, my father asked why he had disappeared for so long. The man told him he had been incarcerated in a dismal prison as a result of a trap set for him by a colleague to get rid of him.

My father's friend explained, "While I sat with one of our colleagues in a coffeehouse, drinking tea and playing dominoes like the other men there, my workmate suddenly asked me in a loud voice, as if he wanted everyone in the coffeehouse to hear, 'Can a single individual represent an entire society?'

"I had immediately replied, 'No. No one individual can represent an entire society, no matter how large or small it is.'"

The other man had then stood up and, as if he had expected that response, proclaimed in a loud voice, "That means you do not accept that President Saddam Hussein—may God preserve him and keep him—represents Iraq. He is a single individual, and Iraq is society—isn't that so?"

"Before I could say yes or no, several men jumped me and dragged me out to a waiting truck. They took me straight to Abu Ghraib prison in Baghdad.

"I remained there for three years and was cleared only a few days ago. Then, although I was found innocent of any crime or dishonorable conduct, I could not reclaim my previous employment. Now, with the help of relatives and acquaintances, I am trying to find a job."

We poor people were left to our own devices, held prisoners by this embargo, while our government and wealthy people became richer and more avaricious at every moment.

Chapter Eleven

In 1993 I completed my studies for my BA. After receiving this degree, I was transferred out of the elementary schools to work, also as a teacher, in one of the most important secondary schools in Najaf: the Latakia Secondary School for Girls, a school reserved for girls with exceptional intelligence or who belonged to wealthy families.

Despite this school's standing and its superiority to other schools, it was situated in a questionable location. On its right was Najaf General Hospital, and to its left stood Najaf's main courthouse. For this reason, it was quite common to witness troubling scenes outside the school—like coffins carrying the deceased from the gate of the hospital, escorted by wailing women; or shackled prisoners being taken from police vans and escorted into the courthouse. On more than one occasion I saw a prisoner escape from his guards and disappear into the crowds.

The mood in my classroom was often roiled by the sound of screams from the hospital or a gunshot from the courthouse. Even so, I loved working in this school because many teachers I had studied with in middle school and at the Teacher Training Institute were now my fellow teachers. I also progressively strengthened my bond with my students and gradually acquired their confidence. Then I began to serve as a repository for their secrets.

When I returned to teaching, all my excuses for postponing my marriage dissolved, and I was obliged to take this fateful step, which I had long dreaded.

Truth be told, the life of a traditional Middle Eastern girl is very difficult. No sooner does she emerge from childhood and develop a mature allegiance to her natal family than she is extracted from that family by the nearly obligatory law of marriage. She leaves all her own family's rules, to which she has grown accustomed, and goes to serve another family, whom she has barely met and whose customs and daily routines she lacks any knowledge of.

I experienced this frightening move after becoming engaged to someone about whom I knew nothing. Even though my parents had asked if he was a good fellow and everyone had praised him as a person of excellent morals, his true nature was revealed to me only after I married him.

My marriage was scheduled for the seventh month, and I resigned myself to that with a total lack of enthusiasm. Because I could not bear to have anyone's fingers groom my face but my own, I did not go to a beauty salon and sought a natural look with nothing artificial. I did not want to look like other brides with their tinted faces covered with so much powder they were scary to look at.

I also dressed myself in a white bride's dress, which, unlike most other girls, I had never dreamt I would wear. When the bridegroom saw me descending the stairs without an abaya, he refused to escort me the rest of the way unless I donned an abaya and covered my head.

I rejected his mandate, hoping with all my heart that he would be stubborn and that the marriage would not be completed. But his older brother acted as a mediator between us and persuaded him to give in and ascend the staircase and escort me from my apartment while all the neighbors watched. They crowded the steps to see me leave along with the other people who were participating in the celebratory procession.

I did not feel anything whatsoever as I descended the steps beside that stranger. I allowed what happened after the bridal procession to proceed any old way and did not exercise my mind thinking about it. I advanced forward with him, oblivious to his anger, which was unprovoked and inappropriate. The only possible explanation for it was a man's unsuccessful attempt to impose his male dominance over a woman. For his part, he walked beside me, speaking angrily about my stubbornness, my refusal to wear an abaya, and my bad conduct, which he described as "silly."

When we entered his home to the clamor of the crowd there, he escorted me to the bedroom and left me there. When a long time had passed, I began to remove my wedding dress and calmly placed it in the wardrobe. I put on a new white dress and started to look in my handbag for something to pass the time. All I found were two poetry collections. The first was *The Sea's Blood Is Blue* by Shakir al-'Ashur, and the second was *Blood Beats Against the Windows* by Mamduh Adwan. Without feeling thirsty or hungry, I read through both books eagerly and then fell fast asleep.

The next morning, I woke to the sound of someone chewing. When I stretched and tried to sit up in bed to search for the source of this sound, I was alarmed because my hand touched an odd-feeling surface of something round. When I sat up straight, I found that a soccer ball had been sleeping beside me in the bed.

Meanwhile my husband was greedily devouring his breakfast. When he realized I was awake, he turned his face toward me and asked, with a mouth filled with food, "Are you hungry?"

Looking at the food that was almost slipping from both sides of his mouth, I replied, "Not that hungry!"

He ignored my response and turned his attention to the plates of food, finishing off anything left on them. Meanwhile, I exited the bedroom modestly, carrying a white towel in my right hand and toothpaste and a toothbrush in the other.

Seeing a woman of the family quickly exit from the bathroom, I realized where it was and took her place there, keeping in mind the number of other women in the household who might have to wait till I was finished before they sought out the bathroom. I washed my face and brushed my teeth quickly, as if in a race against time.

When I returned to my room, I found that my new husband had changed his clothes to fresh ones. Before he sat down on the bed, he told me sharply, "I want you to know that my allegiance to two things in life—my mother and soccer—is paramount. You posed, as a precondition for marriage, completion of your higher education. My condition for you to continue life with me is that you should not upset my mother and not interfere with my athletic life."

I did not think he was serious about what he said about soccer, because he was not a famous player. If he had been, I would have heard of him, because we Iraqis know what all the current members of the national team look like and remember even the names of those who have retired. The soccer player currently sharing a room with me with the title of husband was not one of them.

Before he completed this tirade, without bothering to introduce himself, his mother pushed the door open and joined us, without asking our permission. Even before greeting me, she headed to her son, hugged him, and began to shower his face with kisses, as if she had not seen him in ages. Once she finished kissing him, she looked at me and said in a tone that was more a command than a request, "Get yourself ready to go out. The women want to greet you outside."

Then she left the room, departing with the empty food tray. My spouse did not tarry; he departed behind his mother. Then my sister immediately entered and planted two kisses on my cheeks. When she noticed the soccer ball resting in the bed, she whispered in my ear, "How many goals did your husband's team score yesterday?"

Her silly jest embarrassed me, and to stop her from tormenting me any further with such vile talk, I told her, "Nothing happened, and I feel hungry."

She replied that this was totally normal and to be expected. "Doubtless like any other bride, you felt embarrassed about eating in your new husband's presence. I brought some *kleicha* pastries, and my thermos. We'll eat breakfast together."

Then she left the room quickly before returning with breakfast for the two of us. Personally, I would have preferred for her to wait to visit me on another occasion. I needed some time to forget the disgusting image of my husband wolfing down his food.

This household seemed to differ completely from ours, and not merely in the number of males. Their mother was domineering and not at all the way she had presented herself when she came to seek my engagement to her son. The husband was totally absent. All of her nine sons sided with her in everything she said. They could not disagree with her even when she was clearly wrong. Her only daughter, because of all the pampering she had received, could not distinguish between doing something wrong when she thought it was right or even between truth and error, no matter how self-evident they were.

I felt that a negative power lurked in this household and that it might communicate itself to me. For me to survive unscathed, I would need to set myself rules and try to apply them. As a matter of fact, some of these rules did benefit me, and I attributed the failure of most of them to problems in implementation, not to any design flaws.

One of these rules was not to start a conversation with any person in this household. I left that to them. This aspirational goal or rule was applicable to everyone, including my husband, naturally. As a result of my application of this rule and my long periods of silence, I spared myself any error in the name a conceited person preferred.

Any conversation between me and my husband concerned a victory or loss of a local soccer team in the youth league, where he served as a trainer. If his team won, my husband entered our bedroom that night carrying a box of sweets. After he had changed out of his athletic gear and bathed, he would climb into bed and begin devouring those sweets while boasting of the potential of his athletic team, the goals they had scored, and the most important player on the team. Once he had gobbled down all the contents of the box, he would fall sound asleep. If his team lost a match, he would enter the room as if invading it and remove his athletic shoes while cursing everyone who had played, casting his glance around the room, his body reeking of BO and the dirt of the playing field, while searching for something onto which he could vent his anger. When he did not find what he was looking for, he left to bathe, and I did not see him again till midnight.

My only refuge was reading novels, which I gradually began to substitute for my reality. Clipping vignettes from my daily life to post in my imagination was unsatisfactory, because the result was a doubly terrible scene, one I was forced to endure twice. It might then become a lengthy, obsessive fixation that haunted me for the next half a day. I would relive it as a nightmare that contained even more painful details. Using instead material from novels I read allowed me to protect myself from those around me.

The first quarrel that erupted between me and my husband was about how I arranged our clothes in the wardrobe. I kept it closed, and systematically put his athletic socks in the lowest drawer together with his other sports clothes while placing his other garments in the top drawer. He considered this a personal assault and a slam against him— while I thought I had merely arranged clothes in a wardrobe. When he began shouting, cursing, and swearing, I kept still. I escaped inside my head and searched for a love poem lodged in my memory. Once I had clasped it and focused entirely on it, I withdrew from his tantrum to the quiet of the bed. I lay down on it and closed my eyes, imagining that the poet was whispering the words of this poem to me.

When I woke from my brief nap, I found that the large mirror that had hung on the wall had been smashed to smithereens too small for a hand to pick up. So I left the room to search for a small soft broom and two plastic trash bags.

When I returned to my room, I swept up the fragments of glass and placed the largest piece of glass on the floor. Once I was certain that there were no more shards of glass left in the room, I walked outside to toss everything in the dumpster while his family looked on dumbfounded. Meanwhile, my husband was searching for gauze and a bandage for his wounded hand.

My second rule was to repay a small kindness with a larger one, and to disregard an unkind act, no matter how huge it was.

My third rule was to remember that true joy does not come from what other people do but from inside. Whenever I felt sad, I reached deep inside myself and extracted something to make me feel some past joy, even if only for a moment.

The fourth rule was to keep in mind that nothing lasts forever, no matter how long it seems to, and that however long it was delayed, I would enjoy some future bliss.

Although I had not wished to become pregnant until nine months after my marriage, I soon discovered that I was. Then, because in this household I only occupied a single, small room barely big enough to hold the most basic bedroom furniture, I was obliged, at my father's suggestion, to empty my room in my family's apartment by selling off my computer, the computer desk, and desk chair. I spent some of that money buying baby clothes and retained the balance for the delivery. During my pregnancy, I experienced the true meaning of this adage: "Hell is the absence of logic."

After my first seven days of marriage, my mother-in-law, or "aunt," as I was obliged to call her according to the usage observed in Iraq, shed the skin she had worn when she came to ask for my hand in marriage to her son.

But her true character was only laid bare once I resumed work at my school after the summer holiday, which lasts for three months in Iraq. When I returned home, I was flabbergasted to find that the lock on the door of my room had been broken and that the room's contents— whether clothing or personal effects—had been rifled through as if they had been searched by a team of police officers or security officials.

When I rushed to my "aunt" and asked incredulously what had happened to my room, she brazenly claimed that they had used up all the cold water in the refrigerator and had needed to get some more from the mini fridge my father had given me as a wedding present. As I grew ever more furious and asked her why anyone had searched through my clothes and personal effects, she screamed in my face, as if wanting to make sure everyone heard her, that these items did not belong to me, because her son had purchased them for me.

I calmed down, made no reply to her, returned to my room, and closed its door behind me, leaving the room just as it was until my husband returned that evening. But the moment he saw everything scattered around the room, he vented his anger on me. When I explained what had happened, he attributed my unwillingness to tidy everything to my laziness. Instead of discussing what his mother had done, he went out and bought a new lock, which he installed on the door.

But the battle did not end there, because the lock was broken repeatedly, whenever my "aunt" or her daughter wanted something from my room during my absence. As a result of their raids, I lost a lot of my clothes, jewelry, and personal purchases, including a cassette tape I had recorded of Abdel Halim Hafez.

Then matters escalated to the point that I would enter the apartment and find that the small TV, which I had bought with my own money, had been taken from our bedroom and placed in their living room. When I tried to reclaim it, I was accused of being selfish. I had just picked it up when I felt an urge to destroy it in front of all of their eyes as my "aunt" showered curses on me. I managed to control my nerves, though, if only because I did not want them to crow about my loss of the machine.

Her repeated intrusions into my room robbed me of any sense of security, and I felt that I could no longer trust anyone—my husband least of all. Whenever I discussed what was happening with my own mother and father, they advised me to adorn myself with patience for my "aunt" and to respect her. They said that every marriage, at the beginning, has some frustrations that must be ignored for the marriage to flourish and succeed. As these phrases kept being repeated, I began to feel it was pointless to discuss with them what was happening to me. Their mindset could provide no real solution to my problem.

Meanwhile, that woman's incendiary behavior reached incredible levels. Whenever I scrubbed the floor tiles of the apartment after sweeping and cleaning them, she would burn a piece of old plastic hose pipe and rub it over the tiles that I had just cleaned. Once she was sure the tiles were dirty, she would leave them until she sensed it was about time for one of her children to return from work. When one of them entered the apartment, he would find her hastening to fetch the cleaning equipment. She would demonstrate her concentration on sweeping and scrubbing, as she repeated audibly, "Filthy women only know how to read and write!" Whoever had just entered would trust her words without trying to find out what had actually happened.

Once I was pregnant, I began to feel hungrier than usual. But when I returned home from the school, I would find there was no food whatsoever in the house, even though my husband and I contributed to the household budget!

My "aunt" would wait till my husband returned from work at six and then call me to prepare food for him. Otherwise, she ignored my existence as if I were invisible. When this situation was repeated several times, I was forced to buy prepared food at the school shop.

If, as on Fridays, the weekly holiday for schools in Iraq, I did not happen to go to the school, I would go to the market to buy something to quiet my hunger, but she would then dispatch one of her sons to follow me and find out what I was doing. When I visited my mother and told her what had happened, she started to prepare types of food that could be stored and preserved for several days—like *kleicha*, and sweets made with date syrup, sesame, chickpeas, and peanuts, and a dry milk syrup pudding and give them to me. But not even my mother's presents were safe from the hands of my "aunt" and her daughter; they disappeared completely from my room the very next day.

A number of my "aunt's" nine sons lived with their wives and children in different districts. Whenever she realized there was nothing to be gained from quarreling with me, she would rush off to visit one of her sons—but not before she had taken care to store the household provisions of rice, sugar, and cooking oil with a trusted neighbor. She would also remove from the cooker the lighters for its four burners. She would take with her the regulator for the gas and carefully conceal the bottle of gas in her room. Only then would she leave.

One effort my husband did make to lessen the intensity of these quarrels was to purchase an Aladdin kerosene heater and then ask me to prepare food on it. He placed it in the corridor leading to our room. Whenever I prepared food for us on it, I needed to watch the rice cook and set it aside and then cook the stew next.

One day while I was cooking, I felt a need to go to the bathroom. I quickly turned down the fire of the heater and left after placing the kettle of stew on it. When I returned, I saw my "aunt" scuttling back into her room. I feared some mischief, but promptly forgot the matter when I found the kettle was still closed as it had been, cooking on the heater.

When my husband returned in the evening, I brought dishes, spoons, the ladle, and the tray from the kitchen and offered him the food, steaming hot, the way he liked it. He put a spoon in the lentil soup and poured that broth over the rice, mixing them together, and brought some to his mouth, but before he chewed anything, he spat it quickly on the ground, raging and storming. I was amazed by his behavior and tried some for myself. It was too salty to eat. I was furious and told him that his mother had done this. He did not believe me and left the apartment. He did not return till 1:00 a.m. I ate the rice, plain, and dumped the lentils down the drain in the kitchen.

The months of pregnancy were difficult for me, especially since this was my first experience of it. Worst of all was not being able to assume that people would believe what I told them. My "aunt," who had experienced pregnancy and delivery multiple times, knew full well the pressing need a pregnant woman has to relieve herself, especially during the final months. That woman, when my husband was out of the apartment on a two-day work assignment, locked the door to the toilet and put the key in her pocket.

For this reason, despite my shyness, I went repeatedly to the neighbors' to use their toilet, alleging that the walls of the toilet in my husband's residence were being painted. I had to avoid drinking any water or other liquids during the evening so as not to disturb the neighbors' sleep.

I actually believed this excuse I used with the neighbors till I saw my "aunt" give the key to the toilet to a son so he could pee.

I shook my head with disbelief and raced to my room. With breakneck speed I put on some clothes and my abaya and raced outside. I was really lucky to spot a taxi, which I hailed at once and headed to my school, begging God to grant my bladder the strength to retain the liquids that had collected inside it all night long.

Once I reached the school, I pounded on the door repeatedly. When the school guard opened it for me, I raced inside without even greeting him. He was surprised that I had come so early and disapproved of the strange way I had treated him. I also sensed that his questioning looks followed me as I fled toward the administrative section. I threw my bag and abaya on the floor and entered the teachers-only toilet, where I broke down in sobs.

At the end of that day, I went to visit my family and told my mother what had happened. She exploded with anger and had to use her nebulizer several times to be able to breathe again. Then I regretted coming and weighing her down with my problems. I swore to myself that if her condition improved that day, before I left, and she did not need to go to the hospital, I would not share with her what I was suffering. My life, difficult though it was, was not more valuable than my mother's.

She finally was able to catch her breath and calm down. I was totally delighted by this and forgot what I had been complaining about. Before I left her, she suggested to me that I might speak calmly to my husband and suggest that we leave his family's residence and rent a place of our own.

After my husband returned from his work assignment, I told him what had happened to me. He did not believe me, since the toilet door was now open. Thus, yet another time, my "aunt's" crude cunning defeated the truth.

The following day, at a calm, peaceful moment, I suggested to my husband that we should leave this apartment and rent one of our own. Even before I had finished my sentence, he exploded with anger and began to talk in a loud voice, describing what I had said to him as disrespect for his parents. He said God would punish me with an evil outcome for this suggestion and that my final resting place would be the fires of hell. I was amazed by his statement, which seemed to imply that I had defiled something sacred.

I would have liked to prolong my discussion with him, but when I sensed that someone was listening to our conversation from the other side of our door, even though it was loud enough to hear without eavesdropping, I fell silent to avoid giving my "aunt" and her children something else to gloat about. Just as the war and the events that followed it should not have been allowed to turn me into an evil caricature of myself, I would not permit this man, who claimed to be my husband, to degrade my life with his petty, pious slogans, which he had memorized without even beginning to understand what they meant.

For this reason, I did not raise this topic with him again to avoid appearing to him to be Satan's handmaiden who had come to live in this blessed household to cause divisions between the parents and their children and convert the tranquility of this "pure" household into an inferno.

Because I wasn't in a good mood during my first pregnancy, I was able to go to the writers union only twice. The first time, I attended an innovative session on the visual arts presented by some young artists and painters. I was really happy when one of them came up to me to express his admiration for my work. When our conversation progressed, I asked whether he would be willing to draw a portrait of me in charcoal, and he immediately agreed. He informed me that he would be honored to be the first to draw a portrait of the poet Faleeha Hassan. He asked me to bring him a photo the next week to use as his inspiration.

I told him, though, to wait a moment while I searched my pocketbook for one. And just as I expected, I found a picture that had been taken recently. I handed it to him. He took it, promising that he would work hard all the next week on my portrait.

When I went to the union the following week, I found my portrait waiting for me. When I asked the young painter what I owed him, he refused to accept any payment at all. From his point of view, it was impossible to place a price on art. I thanked him for his present. After that session, I stopped by a bookstore located near the union and bought a frame with glass for that portrait.

When I entered my room, I hung the portrait over the bed beside a large portrait of my husband, assuming that this was my private room, which I had every right to decorate as I saw fit. But I was wrong about this too. The moment my husband returned from his job, his eyes fell on that portrait, and he said incredulously, "Aren't you ashamed by what you've done? Where did you find the nerve and audacity to hang your portrait on the wall? Suppose one of my friends wants to enter my room. Would I invite him in, only for him to find your portrait on the wall? Or should I apologize that I cannot entertain him here because of this portrait?"

I replied calmly, "First of all, you have told your brothers not to enter this room. How, then, would you begin entertaining friends here? Secondly, what is wrong in having a picture hung in a corner where only the two of us will see it?"

He did not reply to either of my questions. Instead, he screamed in my face, "How long did you sit in front of this respected painter so he could finish this portrait?"

I was shocked by his question and replied, "I loaned him a snapshot, and he converted it into a portrait."

He grew even angrier and said, "So you hand out your photos to every Tom, Dick, and Harry?"

At this moment, I realized it was pointless to pursue this conversation. In his bogus debate he had only one weapon, which was to scream. From his point of view, this sufficed to demonstrate his virility to the people eavesdropping on our conversation.

Then I stole a fleeting glance at the portrait, smiled, and lay down in my bed. When I looked up at the ceiling, I sensed that it was undulating like a tranquil river. Once I closed my eyes, I saw a small boat on the horizon. The Iraqi musician Kadim Al Sahir was in that boat, which gradually approached me, and the musician invited me to join him on board. I accepted his invitation, and after we drew away from the bluff, Kadim Al Sahir began to serenade me, in his touching voice, with one of his beautiful songs.

When I woke the next morning, I still felt the joy of my dream and was rather hungry. Before I left for work, I prepared breakfast for both of us and brought it to our room. We ate breakfast together as usual, even though my husband was always put off by the slow way I ate.

Once I had finished work, I returned home only to find that the glass of the frame had been smashed and my portrait had been torn to pieces and dumped in the trash can in our room. I felt such deep anger and sorrow that the food I had eaten at school rose inside me and I vomited into the washbasin sink. Then I returned to my room, where I sat to wait for my husband's return, without even changing my clothes. When he entered the room and sat down on the bed, I carried the trash can to him and asked in a voice dripping with rage, "Why?"

He replied in his loudest voice, "Don't you understand the enormity of your error? How dare you compare yourself to me? I know full well that the reason you hung your picture in the room is that you can't stand for me to be the only person who has a picture in this room. You refuse to acknowledge that I am *the man*, and you are only a woman. Just go to my parents' room and see if you find a portrait there of anyone but my father. Just my father! Do you understand?"

I left him to his delirious rant, picked up my bag, drew on my abaya, and headed to the front door. But he suddenly stopped screaming, raced to pull the abaya from my head, and closed the door. I considered leaving the apartment without an abaya then, but such an action would have reflected poorly on the way my family had raised me. So I abandoned that idea and returned to my room, where I plunged into a profound silence.

Ever since I had first felt the fetus stirring inside me, I hadn't wondered about its sex, because the feeling of an embryo stirring inside the mother is itself a miracle that should not be ruined by some attempt to learn whether it is male or female.

What was important was that my husband, once the labor pains intensified and I asked him to take me to the hospital, did help me and carried the bag of baby clothes. I walked slowly toward the door of the apartment, having trouble keeping on my feet because I was in such pain. I began to bite on my finger while I attempted to keep from screaming and waking the people asleep in our apartment.

When my "aunt" heard us leaving, she caught up with us at the door and shouted after my husband, who had left me balancing myself against the wall while he rushed off to hail a taxi. She screamed at him, "If your wife delivers a girl, don't bring her back here!" Then she returned to the apartment and closed the door behind her.

I felt that my "aunt" was finally offering me an opportunity for relief and showing me a way to escape from her prison. I thanked God mightily for what was swimming inside me, because all indications suggested she was female.

My firstborn was, in fact, a girl. Two years later I gave birth to another baby girl. Four years later, the third girl followed in succession. Then my "aunt" broke ties with me totally. She only visited us again on the day I gave birth to my only son, in 2002, when she entered my home in my absence. She lifted the sleeping newborn from his cradle and placed around his neck a necklace she had made of different denominations of Iraqi banknotes.

Once my husband heard his mother's statement ("If your wife delivers a girl, don't bring her back here!") and when the newborn actually was female, he felt very distressed, even as I rejoiced. The lack of joy he felt at the birth of his first child was attributable primarily to his expulsion from his family's home. He was being banished from his mother's paradise, inside which he had lived for his entire life, and he lacked any stratagem for returning to his "homeland."

He had no choice but to obey his mother's expressed desire, even if it was bonkers, because what a mother says in our country is a sword that descends on the necks of all her children. He was obliged to take me to my family's apartment once I was discharged from the maternity ward and leave me and my daughter there while he returned to his family's home. After searching nonstop for a rental apartment, he came to tell me he had leased a suitable apartment not far from my family's home. He described it in one brief sentence: "The building consists of a small block next to another block of comparable size and structure."

I was really delighted by my husband's initiative; I would finally have my own private home, where I could live a tranquil life free of problems and vexations. I summoned all my strength and picked up my daughter. Then I said goodbye to my family and departed.

The taxi's entire route was over paved roads to the Adala District, which was recently developed and almost uninhabited. I thought it was a really good sign when the taxi stopped in front of a large newly built house, which no one had lived in before. I would have liked to ask my husband why he had referred to this large house as a small block. But my husband, once we had climbed out of the taxi, quickly took my bag and headed toward a small house cheek by jowl with the large one. It had two small doors made of rusty copper, or at least that's what a person seeing them might think.

"It's a dump!" I exclaimed in astonishment when I saw my husband head to one of the doors to open it.

He replied, "I chose the house on the right because it has a front garden."

I was not pleased by this house but had no other choice. In this wreck, I found a secure refuge that would at the very least keep me far removed from the maelstrom of problems my mother-in-law, I mean my "aunt," created.

We both cleaned the house and arranged the bedroom, to which he had moved the furniture from his family's house before I arrived. Even before nightfall the kitchen was ready to use, and although I was exhausted, I was able to prepare soup and green beans.

Because I was enjoying maternity leave from school, I was not obliged to wake especially early, since my daughter kept me awake all night. I woke at ten and put on my plastic sandals, which stayed by the door to the room, and headed to the WC, which was a freestanding building in the center of the garden, near the outside door to the house.

I opened the door to the toilet, preparing to enter, when I was shocked to find a black creature with many legs, much larger than a man's hand, floating on the surface of the water in the toilet. When I looked closely at it, I saw that it was a giant black arachnid unlike any I had ever seen before.

A shudder spread through my body when I saw it floating there. I closed the door gently. Then I pulled myself together and raced for the large plastic basin in the bathroom. I quickly filled it with water from the tap, lifted it with difficulty, and carried it slowly to the WC's door, which I opened quietly so the hairy thing wouldn't notice me and attack—or slip out toward the house. If it did, I would not be able to deal with it the way I wanted.

I clenched my teeth in disgust when I saw that hairy thing floating on the nasty water and felt I would throw up. Steeling my nerves, I closed my eyes and raised the basin. I emptied the water on the creature all at once and heard the splashing sound of the water as it struck the black body. When I opened my eyes and did not see the creature anymore, I searched the WC thoroughly to be sure there wasn't another similar beast there. Then I closed the door to the WC, returned the empty plastic basin to its place, and began to vomit.

That afternoon my husband returned from work. While we ate lunch and drank tea together, I told him what had happened that morning and how I hadn't felt comfortable entering the WC till after one o'clock for fear another creature like the one I had seen would appear. He interrupted me as he rose and started to pad toward the bed for a nap, saying, "These creatures are common in the summer."

I was surprised that he didn't ask for details about what had happened and hadn't even troubled himself to inquire how I had gotten rid of this intruder or whether it had been a venomous spider or a large black scorpion.

At sunset, I tried to forget what had happened and sat enjoying the calm of this place. The quiet seemed novel and beautiful. In fact, it brought a whiff of freedom, which was something I had lost when I married. I thoroughly enjoyed the idea that I was in control of my day, could sit wherever I wished, fall asleep and wake up whenever I wanted, and eat and drink whatever I fancied without anyone criticizing me. The only threat to this beautiful reverie was a premonition that another wretched creature might appear, forcing me to yet again spend countless blazing summer minutes searching the whole house for cracks and crevices—places vermin and small noxious creatures might lurk. Since I had not found any such problematic apertures, the toilet topped my current list of possible dangers.

I brought a plastic chair out of the kitchen and sat in the courtyard by the door of the bedroom, leaving it slightly ajar so I could hear my daughter, who slept during the day and, like other nursing infants, stayed up all night. The sun set gradually till I could no longer see it and disappeared beyond the horizon, leaving only its golden rays, which dissolved with amazing elegance into night's pitch-black cloak. This sight was so beautiful that it scared me, and I rose from the chair like a sleepwalker and found the light switch. I flicked it on and glanced at the lamp at the top of the wall as its light flooded the whole house. I turned to go back to where I had been sitting, but a rustling sound reached my ears. Alarmed, I twirled completely around, toward the sound. With feet firmly planted on the ground, I opened my mouth and my heart rate shot up. Then a shudder of fear rippled through me, filling my entire body, as my gaze fell on a procession of large yellow scorpions emerging from a hole that had been covered by a pile of sand and bricks left over from repairs to the wall. I wanted to flee as far as possible from the line of scorpions, each of which seemed fastened by an invisible thread to the arachnid behind it.

But I couldn't; my feet seemed glued to the ground. The sight of the open bedroom door alerted me to the great danger that could strike my sleeping baby should these scorpions change direction and crawl in there.

I gained control of myself, summoned my reserves, and raced to the bedroom, from which I emerged with a long wool shawl wrapped around my head. I was also now wearing a long tunic that reached to my feet, which I had covered with wool socks and plastic shoes without heels. I gently shut the bedroom door behind me and checked to be sure it was securely closed. Then I ran to the other side of the house to fetch a heavy wooden-handled mattock, which the landlord had used to plant a garden. I had trouble carrying it because it was heavy but nonetheless ran with it toward the procession of scorpions, which were slipping around and creeping off to cover large areas of the wall. With all my might, I struck the first scorpion. Without even checking whether it was dead, I felled the next one with an even more powerful blow. The more scorpions I knocked off the wall, the more daring I grew at confronting them as they scattered in different directions. Some even went into attack mode, raising their tails high and exposing the venom-filled glandular sacs at the end.

All the same, I forgot my fear and followed them. I examined the bodies of scorpions felled by my blows, which were so fierce they threatened to bring the wall down too. After a skirmish that lasted for half an hour, the ground of the garden was littered with the bodies of dead scorpions, which began to glisten in the gold light of the lamp. I stood, leaning on the mattock, listening for any rustling sound from these dying bodies. I breathed a sigh of relief once I felt confident these golden, venomous blobs could not move—had totally lost the ability to move. I allowed the mattock to slide to the ground and headed to the faucet. I turned it on and filled my palm with water to wash my face. Then I went to the kitchen to fetch a metal container filled with kerosene and a box of matches. I placed these beside the water tap and used a broom to sweep all the dead scorpions into a pile, poured kerosene on it, lit a match, and held it near the pile. Finally, I sat back down in my chair to watch the golden bodies glow ever more incandescently as they burned.

Once the golden color of these flames faded and gradually turned to ash, I began to remove my protective outer garments, one at a time. I quietly opened the door to the bedroom and entered. I really wished I could take a cold bath then, but my daughter was stirring. I hastened to the baby, checked her clothing, and found it was wet.

My husband returned at ten that evening. After eating his supper, he watched a soccer match on television. He didn't notice the smoky smell permeating the whole house. I wondered about this man, who seemed to have inherited his mother's listlessness. Ignoring his indifference, I said, "Do you know there are scorpions in this house!"

He was intently following the match, but replied, "Ah . . . That means we didn't rent the house with the large black viper. That's good!" Then he leapt from his chair in delight, celebrating a goal that the team he supported had scored.

After we completed the lease on this house, we moved to another house that was new and fancy, a residence no one had lived in before. Once we moved to that new house, my nights spent wakefully watching for caravans of spiders and scorpions were over.

We lived in this new house for a number of years, but our delight in its relative calm and tranquility evaporated when, in 2003, a large section of the wall fell, shattering its windows as a result of violent, repeated aftershocks from a type of ground artillery known locally as mortars. These were used by various militias in an attempt to bombard, dislodge, and exterminate American snipers who sheltered behind the Agricultural Bank on the street opposite ours. This state of affairs forced me to leave this house after I had invested in rebuilding it. Then we moved elsewhere in the same area.

While the economic embargo lasted, as its years multiplied, life became increasingly difficult and complicated for most Iraqis. I, personally, had to endure this difficult life and pay all the household expenses, without assistance from anyone, while I depended on my primary occupation as a teacher in the secondary school and my secondary occupation, which was typing university dissertations and theses—especially after my husband lost his job but did not trouble himself to search for or even consider finding another job. To the contrary, he considered what I contributed to the household's expense to be my duty, one to be fulfilled without any grumbling—not even for a moment.

I suddenly sensed that I had become a man—the man responsible for my family. I needed to feed and clothe the members of this family, provide shelter for them, raise the young in a proper manner, and create a healthy climate suitable for their lives. I forgot totally that I was a woman.

For his part, my husband developed extraordinary, ingenious abilities to create problems merely by entering the house. I was the one who attempted to alleviate these problems as best I could.

When he objected to staying home till I returned from work and started yelling as loudly as he could that his manhood would not permit him to work as my servant and my nanny, I solved this problem by paying one of my sisters every month to care for my children while I was at work. My sister agreed to this but stipulated that I bring them to my family's apartment.

That meant I had to wake each day at six to prepare whatever food we had for lunch and then fix breakfast for myself and my children, leaving my husband sound asleep. Then I would walk my children to my family's residence and leave them there. Once my school day ended, I retraced my steps and walked them home.

My husband frequently woke drowsily when we entered the house at noon, and I do not remember a time while I served as a teacher, regardless of the heat, cold, rain, thunder, dust storms, or even sandstorms, that I did not make these two trips a day with my children.

The chasm between me and my husband gradually increased. He had lost his status as a husband and any respect accruing to him as a spouse. He simply became someone who excelled at causing problems.

If one day he entered the house and did not find a ready-made occasion for a quarrel, he would look at the shoes lined up by the door and object that they were not arranged properly. Although he continued to create such problems, I was no longer able to escape my daily tragedies by reading or daydreaming. Instead, I would retreat to sleep.

Whenever my husband opened his mouth to create new problems, I would take my children to bed with me and fall asleep surrounded by them. Once I closed my eyes, I felt I was a child their age and started to enjoy childhood games popular back then, games like blindman's bluff, hopscotch, or playing house.

We would all get wrapped up in the details of our game until we saw my husband approach and try to upset us or force us to quit our game—or he would topple whatever toys we were playing with. Then we would all attack him, throwing pieces of brick, pebbles, or stones we had gathered from the street, and he would flee.

To tell the truth, I garnered some satisfaction from those dreams. It was as if I really were a child combatting the tyranny to which she was exposed. I would wake feeling healed and sensing that I had stockpiled all the calm I needed for the next five or six minutes while I remembered who I was, where I was, and the names of the children currently sharing the bed with me.

In 2003, American president George W. Bush decided to "liberate" Iraq from the regime of Saddam Hussein. The inferno of that liberation, however, afflicted innocent people as well as that regime. Before Baghdad fell, when George W. Bush sent us many rockets as presents during the opening days of April 2003—so approximately three weeks earlier—an important battle called the Battle of Najaf occurred in the Sea of Najaf. It lasted for just one week. The People's Army was deployed there, alone, with rudimentary weapons, to confront the American ground forces supported by overwhelming air power. As a result, most of the members of the Iraqi People's Army died as martyrs or were wounded.

Although my father was elderly and suffered from chronic diabetes, which had caused him to lose one eye and suffer a damaged foot, he was sent to join this battle. The moment I heard from my mother, during a visit to her, that he had been gone for five days, sent to participate in that unfair battle of totally incomparable forces, I felt terrified for my father's safety.

So I came early the next morning, left my children in my family's apartment, and returned again to a war front, alleging that I was going on a school visit even though that school was actually closed.

This time, the war front was not in some unfamiliar territory. It was in my own city, on streets I knew. All I had to do was take a taxi to the beginning of the Wilaya District. Then I walked down totally deserted streets for approximately half an hour, moving from one street to the next until I reached al-Tusi Street, where I could see scattered groups of Iraqi soldiers who had mounted the rudimentary weapons on hotels, restaurants, and apartment buildings, which were partially or totally destroyed. Some members of the People's Army were sticking their heads out of the shattered windows of those buildings. When I saw the head of a man in one of those high windows, a man who resembled my father, I called out loudly, "Daddy! Daddy! Daddy!"

When he heard me, he called back just as loudly, "Who is your father?"

"Hassan Dakhel."

He answered, as if speaking into some device, "He's not with us. He's in the forward sectors, near the sea."

When I heard the man refer to forward positions, I felt I was as good as dead. Even though I did not hear any shots, everything I encountered in the ruins through which I was advancing caused me to tremble and to pray to God to help me find my father alive.

I ran as fast as I could, ignoring the eyes of the soldiers watching me. They certainly thought me a crazed woman racing in her abaya through those ruins in search of some quixotic goal. Once I reached the second section of the city and advanced beyond Tel al-Hawish, while wanting to cross to the road leading to Bahr al-Najaf, I saw a man approximately my father's age, or slightly older, seated on an otherwise vacant sheet of aluminum. He was trying to prepare tea on a wood fire he had lit.

I approached and greeted him. Then I asked him about my father. He smiled at my unusual presence and said my father was there: in that tall building. He said he would fetch him if I would just stay put. I did not believe the man but felt obliged to remain where I was and see what would happen. When my wait had lasted more than fifteen minutes, I began to believe my hunch that I could not trust this strange man who had forced me to wait there alone.

A question sprang to my mind: How could an army or part of one be concealed within these skeletons of buildings? My patience was exhausted, and I was turning to continue my search when someone shouted behind me, "Here's Daddy!"

I could not believe my ears when I heard my father's voice, and my heart nearly stopped beating when I saw him standing before me.

He also seemed incredulous to see me there. "Has something bad happened to your mother? Why have you come here? How did you know how to find me?"

"Mom is very ill. I am here because I want you to return with me. I learned from everyone I encountered about this battle. Everyone is talking about it. The sound of the artillery shells and the airplanes keeps us awake all night."

My father replied angrily, "Instead of coming here, you should have taken your mother to the hospital. I don't know when you have ever done something so rash. This war is no joke. Who led you to believe that my commanders will give me permission to abandon them in this fierce battle?"

I also sounded angry when I snapped: "I swear by God Almighty that I will not budge! I will remain here no matter what!"

My father's anger intensified, and he screamed in my face, "Stay here, then! I'm leaving. Don't talk with that man."

I took a deep breath and thanked God that my father was still alive.

After minutes of waiting that seemed to last forever, my father returned with his bag and his rifle. He limped along beside me. This time his ankle would twist when he tried to climb the stairs as we navigated between the tall buildings.

We walked along together as quickly as we could. Once we reached the end of the thoroughfare and entered the first street of the city, we saw a car parked there. My father approached the driver, who was waiting for someone. He greeted the driver and asked if it would be possible to convey us to the Imarat residential district.

The man agreed, but on the condition that the man he was waiting for join us. His passenger was on his way to Kufa. We all climbed into the taxi. Even though it passed deserted streets and houses that had been evacuated by their inhabitants, I felt a boundless happiness because I was sitting beside my father, my shoulder was touching his, and both of us were alive.

When I began to repent the lies I had told him, I leaned toward him to apologize, but he replied, with his eyes focused somewhere in the distance, "Don't apologize. I lied to them and told them your mother had died—so they would let me come home with you. I know you have no one to help you should the worst happen. Don't tell your mother what I have said, because she will think my words are an ill omen. You know her very well."

I naturally would not tell my mother anything. Unfortunately, the expression *veritas norma sua est*—"truth sets its own standard"—is rarely applicable, at least not during a war. Wars occasionally require very convincing, massive lies if we are to escape death, even if only temporarily.

◆ ◆ ◆

The American legions advanced toward Karbala while American airplanes started destroying bridges linking cities with their suburbs. One of the first people killed in these raids was my mother's paternal aunt, who was martyred in al-Meshkhab. She had been heading to the market to shop. When the bridge there was bombed, it was cut in two, and she was killed before she could reach the end of that bridge. Her son had to search one full day to find her head among the body parts of other victims. Her body, which was enshrouded by her abaya, was caught on one of the wooden arches of the bridge.

This terrifying news reached my mother by telephone. She exploded in tears at the loss of her affectionate aunt and this terrifying manner of death. That same day a rumor spread widely among the residents of our district that the US Air Force had picked targets for bombings that would soon begin. The first of these was the Building of Iraqi Security, headquarters of the Baath Party.

This rumor came to me from one of our neighbors who worked in the courthouse. Since all of those buildings were located near the Imarat residential district and I had moved in with my family, bringing my children with me, I suggested then that they should come back to stay with us in al-'Adala District until this crisis ended.

They were hesitant to accept my invitation, since they knew full well the problems my husband would make should they spend even one night. But I pleaded with them, and my sister's fear of the sound of the airplanes finally caused them to yield. They returned with me to my house that afternoon.

We walked toward my house, each one chatting with the person beside her about news heard and rumors being spread. When we reached the house, my husband opened the door. His displeasure was apparent on his face when he saw my family standing beside me. But when he saw how displeased I was about his hesitation, he was able to rise to the occasion and welcome my family, who all recognized what a phony welcome this was.

The moment the sun set, I saw my husband open the door and leave the house. I trailed after him to learn why he was leaving in such a strange way, and he told me, after he closed the door behind us, he was going to spend the night with one of his friends, without even bidding goodbye to my father.

I felt upset but attempted to gloss over his irresponsible conduct with my family, because it was clearly improper for a man to leave his guests. But my family soon forgot the matter when the military aircraft flew overhead, fully covering the sky for a time, and we began to hear the roar and reverberation of their engines as if this were a marathon for the heaviest type of elephant.

With every burst of gunfire, the earth shook beneath our feet. We began to move from one room to another, trying futilely to find protection from their walls. Despite many attempts, we were not able to flee from the house.

These aircraft did not strafe any of the targets we had heard about. Instead, they pounded the Governorate Building of Najaf, which was located near the Adala District. When the bombardment quieted down a little, as streaks of dawn appeared in the sky after a night filled with my sister's screams, which we heard every time a bomb exploded, she opened the house door, raced to the street, and returned to our apartment, shouting, "God damn your husband and anyone who ever visits him again!"

The members of my family followed her back to their apartment. They insisted that I accompany them, and I did. My husband did not turn up at my family's flat till that evening, when he came to inform me that our neighbor, who had predicted what the targets of the American bombardment would be, had died of a heart attack triggered by her fear of the planes' bombardment the previous night.

When the bombing lasted several nights and struck a number of buildings near the Imarat residential district, my father insisted on taking us to a house that belonged to some of his relatives, far from the city, near al-Qadisiyah.

We gathered all the things we would need and departed, but my husband refused to come with us. Since there was a lack of potable water, we drew water from the river and boiled it. Even so, many people there were afflicted by intestinal ailments transmitted by the contaminated water.

My children all contracted chicken pox. When I was able to obtain some medical supplies for them from one of my father's relatives, who worked as a physician's assistant in a people's clinic in that district, I isolated them in a small room and began to care for them and supervise their recovery. At once, my thoughts wandered through the events we were experiencing, and I saw my life pass in scenes quickly before my eyes, as if I were watching cinematic clips that kept rerunning the same scenes, but filmed in different locations.

I would almost have sunk into those details and their sufferings had it not been for the sound of a huge commotion. I woke from my stupor, stood up, and looked out the window, which overlooked the street, where I saw all the men and women who had been out on the street racing toward their homes, almost stumbling. The children running behind them were screaming, "Americans! The Americans are coming!" Everyone quickly entered his own house and locked the door behind him. The ensuing silence was terrifying.

After a length of time I could not judge, our ears were struck by tremendous sounds that almost deafened us. My sick children woke, crying.

Although I was alarmed by those sounds, which I thought were advancing toward us, I turned my attention to my children, even as

I kept my hands over my ears. Even so, I saw all those huge tanks, heavy artillery guns, giant Humvees, and heavily armed soldiers with scary weapons pass before my astonished eyes down the asphalt street, parallel to the house where I was sheltering, separated from them by only a few meters.

Chapter Twelve

A week before the Battle of Najaf, on March 20, 2003, the coalition forces—the military forces of the United States, Great Britain, Australia, and some other allies—entered Iraq to combat Iraqi government troops. This offensive has been called names like the "Second Gulf War," the "Iraq War," the "Iraq Liberation War," the "Liberation of Iraq," and the "Shock and Awe Campaign."

Saddam Hussein was arrested December 14, 2003, in a campaign called "Operation Red Dawn," after a search that lasted for eight months. After his trial, he was hanged at dawn on the first day of Eid al-Adha; in other words, Saturday, December 30, 2006. Many satellite channels broadcast highlights of the execution. His death marked the end of the Baath Party, which had ruled Iraq for more than thirty-five years.

Iraqis were divided into more than one group about that execution. Some were incredulous about these fast-breaking developments and could not wrap their minds around the end of his rule, even after watching his trial, which was broadcast on the different satellite channels. Other Iraqis viewed Saddam Hussein as a nationalist hero who defended the Occupied Lands in Palestine. They thought he did not deserve to be executed and especially not during a religious holiday.

A third group, most Iraqis, regarded Saddam Hussein as a tyrannical dictator who deserved this punishment for his many evil deeds.

In that year, the economic sanctions on Iraq were also lifted, and in only a few months, the salary of an Iraqi employee increased noticeably, according to his length of service. Various features of democracy also appeared: people voted in real elections, which had disappeared totally during the Baath Party's rule. Now government was determined by a competition between multiple political parties.

The individual Iraqi acquired the ability to express his opinions and to state them frankly. On the other hand, many manifestations of violence spoiled that individual Iraqi's ability to practice this democracy.

The most significant manifestations of violence were booby-trapped vehicles, which killed hundreds of innocent people; not a day passed without our witnessing or hearing about the explosion of one or more of those vehicles in areas crowded with people. These explosions extended throughout Iraq, and some hundred thousand Iraqis fell victim to them, mostly civilians.

Improvised explosive devices (IEDs) also played a brutal role in killing innocent people. In the fifth month of 2007 alone, approximately 2,080 IEDs killed or wounded thousands of Iraqis of various ages across the country.

As a manifestation of democracy, Sayyid Muqtada al-Sadr mobilized his followers in demonstrations and peaceful marches to demand that coalition forces leave Najaf, in particular, but also all of Iraq. He was one of the Shi'i leaders of Iraq and derived his authority from his father, Muhammad ibn Muhammad Sadiq al-Sadr, who was an exemplary symbol of Shi'i opposition and struggle in the time of Saddam Hussein.

He had rebelled against the ruling party in that era. He was also the first imam to lead prayer in Najaf after Saddam Hussein forbade that. He had voiced his opposition to the Baath Party in many sermons he delivered at Friday prayers. Hundreds of worshippers packed the mosque in Kufa back then, and many groups of men delivered their prayers by the tombs of the imams near the mosque. After praying, these worshippers quickly moved into the streets around the mosque. That so enraged members of the ruling party that they ordered him assassinated in 1999. He was killed together with two sons: Mu'ammal and Mustafa, who was almost fifty-five. They were returning to their home in the Hanana District of Najaf when a Kia vehicle pursued them. When Muhammad ibn Muhammad Sadiq al-Sadr crashed into a tree, some attackers climbed out of the unmarked car and fired a number of bullets at the sayyid and his two sons. One son died immediately, and the other died later in a hospital from injuries he had suffered. The wounded sayyid was transported to a hospital, where he was slain by a bullet to his head.

When news of his slaying reached his aides, supporters, and followers, they began to attack Iraqi Security Forces, police stations, and Baath Party offices in a rebellion referred to as Sadr's Rebellion of 1999. Thereafter, Sayyid Muhammad Sadiq al-Sadr was referred to by many sobriquets, including the Blissful Martyr, Friday's Inspiration, the White Lion, and the Friday Martyr.

When Spanish and Salvadoran forces fired on demonstrators from the Sadrist movement, killing 160 of them, Sayyid Muqtada al-Sadr called on the Mahdi Army, which was the military wing of the Sadrist movement, to attack with missiles and mortars the military base in Najaf called Andalus, where the Spanish forces were headquartered.

Soon, the Second Battle of Najaf was announced on April 4, 2004. It lasted until August of the same year. The Mahdi Army was headquartered in the center of the Old City of Najaf—which was referred to as al-Wilaya District, home to the shrine of Imam Ali (peace upon him), the Valley of Peace, and the Region of the Revolution of al-'Ishrin— while Sayyid Muqtada al-Sadr sheltered in the mosque of Kufa.

In addition to the death and devastation this battle brought, many buildings, houses, and streets were destroyed. Substantial damage was sustained by the dome and minaret of the shrine of Imam Ali (peace upon him), and major destruction affected the cemetery known as the Valley of Peace.

I did not go to the battlefront during this war. Instead, the battlefront came to me.

One morning I opened the door of my house, preparing to go to work, and set off as usual, carrying my young son under my abaya while my three daughters walked beside me. The totally empty street made for a stifling sight. I felt, as we proceeded along it, a frightening calm, as if something was about to happen.

The regular route I took each morning to my family's home, where I left my children, did not seem the same that day. The only people on the street were armed young men wearing civilian clothing. But each of them identified his affiliation by a piece of green cloth, which precisely resembled the line that distinguishes a sayyid on the tombs of the imams. In Iraq we call it *'ilach*. These young men were hurrying to find places to set up mortar launchers they carried on their shoulders.

Their presence made me nervous but did not frighten me, because they were heading in one direction and I was going the other way. As for my daughters, whenever an armed youth passed by them, they would cling to my abaya, almost making me trip on it and fall.

My daughters forgot their fear the moment they set foot in my family's apartment, where they ran off to play with the dolls. For his part, my son was sound asleep and continued sleeping when I put him in his bed there.

I set off for my school once I checked whether my father had left for his job. The fact that he had gone to work meant that no sudden work stoppage had been announced for the day.

No sooner had I entered the classroom and begun a lesson about Arabic grammar than we heard from every direction the sound of mortars and explosive projectiles. Each bomb shook our classroom when it exploded, and the students began to scream.

Because I felt responsible for those students, who were trembling with fear and had begun to shelter in the corners of the room and under the chairs, I steeled myself and asked them, in a voice that betrayed no hint of fear, to stay clear of the windows and, if possible, to remain calm, since screaming did not help in such situations and would only make matters worse.

My words, though, had no effect and our situation deteriorated when we heard footsteps on the stairs and then the thump of a body falling there. The distraught students assumed that someone had entered the school and taken control of it. This meant that I had to summon even more courage to determine the source of these sounds. I opened the door of the classroom and went down the stairs to find a teacher stretched out on one of the wide steps after fainting there.

I returned once more to my classroom and asked some of the students to assist me. We were able to carry that pregnant teacher down to the teachers' room. Praise the Lord, she did not miscarry.

The principal quickly contacted the students' guardians and asked them to come immediately to take charge of their girls. In only about two hours, all the pupils had left the school, along with the teachers and the principal. Unlike the rest of them, who had been picked up by spouses and siblings, I crossed the street as usual and stood there waiting for a taxi or bus to come, but there was no sign of any traffic. In fact, all the shops on the street had closed when their proprietors heard the explosions. Even the hospital and the courthouse were totally empty.

It was terrifying to stand on the deserted street. At such a moment, the motion of a drape behind a closed window was enough to frighten you; you would think someone was observing you from behind that window.

I realized that hoping to find transport was an impossible dream and decided to proceed home on foot. At that moment, a young man emerged from nowhere and approached. He began harassing me, using phrases laden with sexual innuendos. I felt more than upset but did not know whether to speak harshly to him or ignore him.

In our country, rejection of a harasser is not attributed to a woman's strength of personality or rights but is interpreted as naughtiness and shows that this woman has not been brought up well. Words spoken by a molester have frequently been compared to a dog's barks. When a dog barks at you, you don't bark back at him. In a confrontation with a molester, a woman should keep quiet. A molester, however, interprets the silence of a woman and her lack of reaction to his actions as compliance, in keeping with the saying "Silence is a sign of acceptance." So he continues his actions.

The moment I moved away, that young man became even more aggressive. He reached his hand out toward me, attempting to seize mine. Then I screamed at him as loudly as I could, "Have you no shame? Get away from me! Be on your way."

He looked angry and replied hostilely, "Do you think you're Sophia Loren? You're just some Black woman!"

I grew even angrier at his crudeness and shouted in his face, "Black! White! Leave me alone, or you'll regret the consequences!"

Mocking my words, he replied, "What will you do to me, whore? I can bury you so deep no one will ever find you!"

I was enraged when I heard him call me a whore. I moved right in front of him and told him, looking him straight in the face, "I'm not a whore. The woman who didn't raise you properly—she's the whore!"

I was about to slap him, but at that moment a large bus arrived at the speed of lightning and stopped behind me. It seemed to have emerged from the earth, splitting it open.

When the youth saw the door of the bus open and the driver call for me to climb aboard, he fled. I boarded that bus, recognizing its driver, while fiery anger flamed within me after hearing such vile language.

The moment I reached our apartment, I raced to my children, rounding them up, and bundled them out of the apartment without greeting or speaking to anyone. I sped with my children down the street, which was still filled with armed young men. When I approached our street, one of them was starting to set up an artillery gun there, in front of a building that was still under construction.

The moment he placed it, the young militant began to load it. I raced as fast as I could and encouraged my daughters to run to our house and enter it before the mortar was fired, profiting from the time it took to fire this type of weapon.

We actually reached the house a moment before the shot was fired. We all began pounding on the door of the house in turns. It did not occur to me then that the key was in my handbag, which hung from my shoulder. All the same the door wasn't opened until after the mortar was fired, stirring up a sandstorm around it. As its dusty circle quickly spread across the ground, my daughters began weeping loudly while they pounded on the door. Finally my husband opened it, rubbing the sleep from his eyes.

He asked with astonishment, "What's the matter with you? Is the world on fire that you pound on the door like this?"

After I got my daughters inside, I retorted, "The world is on fire! Don't you hear?"

In fact, once we were inside our house, artillery fire started flying over our heads. We stayed inside the bedroom unless one of us needed to use the toilet or prepare some food.

There was more to fear from those projectiles at night; so we slept by day and stayed up all night. The only night I dozed off, I saw my grandmother in a dream. She was racing down a long street, fleeing, carrying on her head a bundle wrapped in cloth. When I asked her in amazement why she was fleeing, she told me, as she continued running, "They have struck our tombs and leveled them to the ground. So I'm carrying this bundle of your grandfather's bones to bury somewhere else."

After we were stuck in our house for days, we began to feel hungry. We had exhausted our food supply, which was meant to last only a couple of days because we had never imagined that a new war would flare up this quickly.

Although my purse was filled with the cash from my salary, which had been adjusted upward in a very satisfactory way, I could not provide food for my children once all the shops and markets were closed by a curfew.

We resorted to eating the jujubes that hung from the branches of the towering buckthorn tree in our garden. Whenever the shelling let up a little, I would slip into the garden and use a plastic basket to collect all the jujube fruit that had fallen to the ground. After I cleaned them thoroughly, we would consume one whenever we felt hungry. Eating too many jujubes, though, can cause diarrhea in some kids, and after my children ate more jujubes than usual, they all suffered from diarrhea. Then I had to go to my family to fetch medicine after discovering we had none in our house.

I scurried to my family, and my mother gave me the bottle of diarrhea medicine she kept in the refrigerator. She also put into a plastic sack a kilo of rice and of lentils, a bottle of oil, two small tins of tomato paste, and a little sugar and tea. I thanked her and quickly returned home while armed men watched.

This flareup ended in seven days, but for stability to settle over my city took more time than that. Even when it arrived, we felt cautious and circumspect. When the fire of war flares up, even if it suddenly subsides, that does not mean it has been extinguished—not even if it lies dormant for a long time. Instead, it means that any airborne spark can cause it to flare up again. So we definitely did not feel secure or settled.

I customarily visited the shrine of Imam Ali (peace upon him) every week and was quite distressed when the entrance to this mausoleum and its holy courtyard was closed. That place had become for me something like the Wailing Wall, where I would lodge my complaints, bemoaning the pains that tormented me the moment I entered our house.

I longed for my place of supplication because it was the only location where I felt truly safe. One night I lay in bed with tears of longing misting my eyes and asked God to return to me the reassuring moments that had been forcibly stolen from my days.

No sooner had I fallen asleep than I heard a powerful voice that silenced spirits even before ears heard it. The roar in my ears said: "Come visit me next Monday. My mausoleum will be open on that day!"

When I woke the next day, I was filled with an inner vitality and power I had never experienced before. When Monday arrived, after I completed my school day, I took a taxi to al-Wilaya station. From there I walked like an impassioned lover to the shrine, with tears flowing from my eyes, as I recited to myself all the prayers and short *surahs* of the Qur'an I knew by heart.

The familiar roadways and streets had changed a lot since many buildings there had been destroyed. When I approached one of the coffeehouses frequented by men who come from distant cities and villages to bury a relative, I found that it had been converted into a public court where people had been executed—as I heard from street sweepers conversing with each other. They were busy cleaning the streets of dried blood and ashes, even as the smell of death still emanated from that place.

Hurrying past, I entered the Grand Souk, where I found that most of its shops had been broken into and looted. I also saw numerous large white placards on destroyed goldsmiths' shops. Written on these in large black or red letters was: **A TRUST FROM GOD AND HIS MESSENGER.** Portions of the roof of the market had been damaged where it had been struck by various projectiles. A few proprietors of shoe and clothing stores were cleaning and restocking their shops.

I walked through this place with some other supplicants whose faces reflected none of the normal glow of a visit to this shrine. They all seemed to be walking cautiously, preoccupied by the danger they were in while taking the only rugged route open to visit the imam after all other approaches had been closed off with barbed wire. With almost every step I took, I stumbled on some hole or debris.

The sight of blood mixing with water as it flowed over the pavement of the holy shrine as I entered saddened me. I saw a number of young men with bandaged heads trying to clean it using hoses with water from the cistern that stood at the center of the holy courtyard.

I could tell from the expressions of other visitors that they were wondering about the source of all this blood. I found an answer to this question only when I saw that one of the covered porches of the holy courtyard had been transformed into a clinic where wounded people were treated. A placard hanging over it said: **MEDICAL UNIT OF THE MAHDI ARMY.**

I drew part of my abaya over my face and approached the door of this covered porch, where I saw that some women were busy tidying the area and cleaning it. This looked exactly like a ward in a hospital, but without any beds. Lest anyone notice me, I hurried to the holy shrine. Before I entered the sacred mausoleum, I was confronted by the lofty minaret with its golden gleam. Some of its gold tiles had fallen when a projectile hit it. In the holy courtyard there were many pits from mortars in the pavement. Despite the evidence of violence, the moment I approached the golden screen behind which lay the body of the imam (peace upon him), I felt that my spirit had returned to me again.

I rid myself totally of my sorrow, anxiety, and fear by completing all the rituals and prayers of a visit to this shrine, and I had only gone a few steps to head home when I heard a familiar voice call out my name from behind me. I looked back and found our neighbor, the seamstress, whom we had once lived near in the region of al-Madina Street.

I greeted her warmly, and she kissed me on the cheek. Then we strolled off together through the holy courtyard. As we walked, she asked me for news of my family and about me. So I reassured her that everyone was well. When I asked her how her husband and children were, she replied that her children were fine but that her husband was disabled and could not walk. When I asked her why, she told me in detail, as we walked toward the minibus station.

"You know that I married Abu Najah when he was living with his widowed older brother, who had no living children, in the same house on al-Madina Street. You know as well that my husband and his brother owned a shop where they sold rice and wheat together in the Khan al-Makhdar District. One morning when fighting had flared up between the Mahdi Army and coalition forces, my brother-in-law departed for the shop, even though my husband had advised him to stay home. He left our house despite his brother's warnings. Moments after he left, we heard a loud, reverberating sound as a mortar hit the street. My husband opened the door and went into the street, where he found that his brother had been hit by that projectile.

"The bombardment grew more intense as the combatants exchanged fire, and my husband still had not returned home. I did not feel that I could just stay and watch from the house. So my older son, Najah, and I raced down the same street my husband and his brother had taken. Halfway down the street, we found my husband lying on the ground with his hand embracing his brother's head, which was wrapped with his kerchief.

"I was panic-stricken by the horror of this sight and began to scream and slap my head. When some young combatants saw us, they came to us. Once they determined who I was and that my husband was still alive, they carried him off in a stretcher, still clasping his brother's head, and brought him to our house.

"My son set off with some combatants to search for his uncle's body. When they found it, they brought it to our house as well. With help from those young men, we were able to connect my brother-in-law's head to his body, which lay on his customary bed.

"Surgery was performed on my wounded husband in our house, with rudimentary medical implements, by a medical doctor who was a volunteer in the Mahdi Army. When the doctor completed that operation, he informed us that if my husband recovered, he would never be able to walk again, because that doctor had removed shrapnel lodged in his spine. Now he actually can't walk and uses a wheelchair to get around.

"We buried my brother-in-law the next morning in our family's burial site in Wadi al-Salam Cemetery, after we were able to find an undertaker from our district.

"My two sons are fine now, but they grew up fast and matured early. They took their father's and their uncle's places before they were really ready—without experiencing the normal stages of development, if you catch my drift."

When we reached the station, before each of us boarded a separate bus that would take us to our part of the city, I said a warm goodbye to this fine, stalwart woman and wished her peace of mind and long-lasting comfort. Then I boarded my bus, still reflecting on the details and bizarre nature of what had happened to her family.

That year, there were important events in my life as a writer. Once my reputation as a poet and a literary figure of note spread through Iraq's cities, I was invited to appear at multiple literary festivals and conferences. Professor Abd al-Hadi al-Fartousi, now the president of the writers union of Najaf, asked me to allow myself to be nominated to the union's board of directors once the union was able to reclaim its building from the people who had seized control of it. I accepted his invitation and became the first woman director of the union.

I functioned as the public relations officer on the board with Professor al-Fartousi as president and the poet Hamudi al-Salami as vice president. The other directors were the poets Sa'd Sahib and Hussein Nasir Jabr, who was the treasurer. This organization continued its work until 2010. I, however, had to resign due to urgent circumstances beyond my control.

One day I was returning from the union with a group of writers who included Professor al-Fartousi. At that time, I asked whether he would write an essay about my poems, especially given that numerous critics who were not from Najaf had published such essays in newspapers and magazines.

He replied that he was not a critic. I told him that he possessed the necessary critical gift and the required skills. The goal was simply to increase readership of works of literary criticism, whether translated or originally written in Arabic. In fact, a month after this conversation, al-Fartousi wrote an essay about a poem I had recently published. Then he continued to write about my poems as I published them.

Once Professor al-Fartousi wrote these essays, writers in Najaf began to consider my works favorably and also wrote essays they published in newspapers and journals, following the example of writers and critics around the world.

An essay published by the poet and translator Hussein Nasir Jabr produced a similar effect. After he presented a program about translation for the union, I suggested to him that he might translate some of my poems into English. Although he was hesitant at first, he eventually agreed. Some days later he came to give me those English-language translations of my poems, which he then placed in the journal *Gilgamesh*, which was published in Baghdad. After this, several Iraqi translators translated my poems and published them in journals and anthologies of poetry both inside and outside of Iraq.

After I published some other collections of poetry, people wrote even more about them, and major Iraqi critics wrote excellent and important essays concerning them. The Iraqi critic Yasin Alnasayyir wrote a very important essay entitled "Read Poet Faleeha Hassan." In it he said: "In this short collection of poems I feel that for the first time I am reading mythological events displayed in a museum. We live these moments and then leave them, but our shadows remain there with them. This poet does not merely draw on mythology; she creates a new Iraqi mythology."

All this important criticism and these essays made me feel significant and made up for some of the pressures imposed upon my life while I lived with a man with whom I had forced myself to cohabitate through all the years of our marriage, even though I never succeeded in understanding him.

My seat on the board of directors, however, did not please all of the writers in Najaf. In fact, most of them went public with their enmity and hatred for me. Then a number of writers began to boycott the union's literary evenings and festivals. Since I was responsible for public relations, I suggested to the board of directors that we visit some of those union members who had been absent for a long time and discuss with them the reasons for their boycott. Everyone agreed with my suggestion, and the first of these visits was to one of the writers who worked for the magazine *al-Sihha*.

We visited him at his place of work, and because I had not met him before, the moment I entered his office with the other members of the board and greeted him, he whispered something to one of his friends who had accompanied us on that visit. The other man smiled broadly as he gazed at my face.

When we were all heading to the bus stop, one of my writer friends told me, "Mr. So-and-so was amazed to see you. He told me: 'I thought Faleeha Hassan was white—not Black!'"

At the time, this comment delighted me. I did not take offense at it until I heard it many more times as a common epithet for me from the mouths of writers whom I had falsely believed were my friends. I did not find any relief from this episode until I wrote a poem about it.

Because finishing my master's degree and doctorate was a lifetime dream that I had nourished since I became a teacher, I endured a bitter and rough life to achieve it. In 2004, when my service in secondary schools had reached the required stage to enroll in a master's program, I submitted the necessary papers for study in the College of Education for Women.

Once I submitted this documentation, I had to begin preparing for the examination. I set aside time to study daily after I finished my day's work at the school. Thus, after I cleaned the house, washed the dishes, prepared my lesson plan for the next day's instruction, and took a nap, I would wake to resume studying for an examination, which everyone, including Napoleon Bonaparte, feared. He had reportedly said: "I'd rather be on the battlefield than in an examination hall."

Because I was afraid of disturbing the sleep of those who shared the bedroom with me if I turned on the lamp, made some unintentional movement, flipped the pages of a book, or dropped a pencil on the floor, I decided to surrender the only bedroom to them and study in the kitchen.

Keep in mind that, in our previous home, once we had rebuilt the wall that had been destroyed by a stray projectile and had replaced the glass in all the windows, we were told by the landlady's family that we had to move out of the house we lived in, the house in which we had endured Najaf's second war, because the landlady, who had been living outside of Iraq with her husband, had suddenly decided to return to her homeland.

Then we moved out of that house and rented another one, which was fifty square meters and laid out in a somewhat eccentric manner. This house had two sections. One was a very lengthy room. The second, which was exactly parallel to the first, consisted of a bath and a WC that shared a wall. Beside them stood a separate kitchen.

Because we in Iraq used Butagaz canisters for cooking, I could not use the gas heater to warm myself in the kitchen—for fear of inadvertently causing a fire while I slept. I would study all night long, wrapped in my blanket. Once I caught sight of the first rays of morning and heard the call to prayer, I would rise, perform the dawn prayer, and cook the food for both lunch and breakfast at the same time.

At seven thirty, I would be waiting for the bus that would take me to my school, after sending my two older daughters to their primary school, which was inside the same residential community as my family's apartment. I would send my youngest daughter to her daycare and deliver my baby son to my sister.

During the afternoon preceding the examination, I looked for a black ballpoint pen to use in answering the questions on the exam, as was required, but didn't find one, because, without my noticing this, all my ballpoint pens had run out of ink. Then I was forced to leave my children alone in the house, after I locked the door to the kitchen and the door to the house, while I raced to buy a pen from the store at the end of our street.

This store was a room at the front of a house. The proprietor was a diminutive, disabled man who could not move his feet. His wife would bring him out each morning and set him in the chair and then go back inside to perform household chores. Customers who wanted to buy something from the shop had to search for it themselves. If they found what they wanted, they would give the money to the proprietor and depart.

This is what I did, after I greeted the man in his seat and he welcomed me. When I asked him for a ballpoint pen, he told me he kept all the pens on a shelf attached to the side of the fridge.

I hurried inside to fetch that pen. I was in such a rush and so preoccupied by the examination that I did not notice a fan with rusty blades on the floor ventilating the fridge's compressor. Because the cover had been removed from the fan, the tail of my abaya caught in its blades, which might have pulled me toward it if the man had not shouted to warn me.

I yanked hard on my abaya, and the fan fell over onto its face even as its blades continued to rotate. When the woman heard the man's cry, she rushed to us. Once she caught sight of the fan, as she chewed and gnawed on the tip of her abaya, she quickly pulled the fan's cord from the outlet in the wall, which stopped the blades.

I pulled the end of my abaya from it, feeling tense and nervous, trying to fathom how this had happened. But then I remembered I had left my children alone in the house. I took the pen after paying for it and rushed out as the woman and her husband continued apologizing to me. I prayed to God that no one would see me on the street and notice my torn abaya. Once I was home again, I put the torn abaya in the wardrobe and shed few tears for it because I was so anxious about the career-deciding examination that would determine my admission to a master's program.

At dawn on the appointed day, I reviewed some important points after I performed the dawn prayer and fixed food for our lunch and breakfast as usual. For breakfast I drank some tea. Then I got dressed and prepared to leave but did not find my abaya with my clothes in the usual place. I searched futilely for it everywhere. Someone seemed to have deliberately hidden it from me. I woke my husband, who had told me to leave the children with him today, that he would take them to their schools and to my family.

I glared angrily at him as if to demand: How can I go to my examination without an abaya? Continuing to search for the abaya, I ran to the bathroom, where I found it totally immersed in water in the basin. I could not believe my eyes. I was incredulous when I saw that but rushed to pull it out of the basin and wring it dry forcefully with my hands. I threw it on, raced back to the bedroom to fetch my handbag, and went out to the street.

It was almost seven thirty. All I could do was run to the end of the street to search for a taxi. Finally, a driver saw me and stopped. I climbed in without even telling him my destination. After starting his engine, the driver asked where I was going, and I told him the College of Education for Women in al-Amir District.

When I arrived there, it was about five to eight or perhaps a bit earlier. I ran to the examination room on the second floor. Once I reached its open door, the head proctor prevented me from entering, since the exam had begun five minutes earlier. I could not bear to listen to the stream of admonitions that poured from that lady's mouth. So I left her in midsentence and hastened to the ground floor.

I ran to the other wing of the college, heading for the office of the dean of the faculty, but when I entered that building, I found the dean's office was closed. I hastened then to the assistant dean's office, without even asking the secretary's permission to enter. Before I greeted him, I recounted to him briefly what had happened to me as tears flowed from my eyes.

The assistant dean pulled a sheet of paper from the drawer of his desk and wrote a note on it. He handed it to me and said, "Give this to the proctor."

I returned to the examination room as swiftly as I had left it. When I handed the paper to the head proctor, she nodded her head resentfully as she read it. Without even uttering a syllable, she gestured for me to enter with a wave of her hand. She shoved that note into the pile of papers on her desk and then handed me the sheet of questions and the exam booklet.

I quickly hung my abaya on the wooden door of the hall and returned to sit in the chair that bore the number assigned to me. Then it was a race with time as I answered the questions. The easiest one was writing out the first *surah* of the Qur'an with all the diacritical marks, including all the tittles.

I was the last woman taking the exam to enter that hall. I was also the last to leave it.

After I finished, I handed my exam booklet to one of the proctors and then returned to my seat to sit there. I felt a chill run through my body, since my clothing had been dampened by my wet abaya. I had felt cold the whole time.

Once the proctors left the room, I took that abaya from the door and found it was still damp. It had even left a puddle of water beneath it on the floor. I grasped then the reason for the strange looks the proctor had given me when I started to leave.

I walked home, not feeling in any hurry to return to my house. A day that I had begun by running could only end with slow and measured steps. I walked along as if sauntering through a garden, allowing the hot rays of the sun to stroke my abaya and dry it. At that moment, I experienced the day's great compassion for me.

Months later I learned that I had passed the exam and been accepted into the master's program. I stopped teaching once I obtained permission to continue receiving my full salary for three years. In fact, at the end of 2006, I did receive my master's degree in Arabic language and literature, magna cum laude, after spending years studying in my kitchen.

Chapter Thirteen

Fulfillment of my mother's prophecy that my twin siblings would be the death of her came in 2005. In that year, on August 31, my twin brothers, Falah and Sabah, went to Baghdad with millions of other visitors to commemorate the martyrdom of Imam Musa al-Kadhim (peace upon him). A number of citizens of Baghdad erected tents and pavilions on the Bridge of the Imams and nearby to provide food and water to assist visitors expected from other Iraqi cities that were predominantly Shi'i.

A terrorist group, though, first fired a number of mortars at districts of Baghdad like al-Kadhimiya, killing and injuring many people. At the same time, a rumor circulated that a terrorist with an explosive belt would blow himself up after slipping in among visitors on the bridge.

The pilgrims crowded together and many threw themselves off the bridge into the Tigris River. The crush of visitors also suffocated many of them. Other pilgrims were crushed by the ambulances and police cars that had been stationed on the bridge to protect them.

Residents of al-Kadhimiya recovered the bodies of those who had drowned in the river. One man who helped pull drowning victims from the river was the heroic diver Othman al-Obeidi, who witnesses report rescued 388 individuals before drowning himself from exhaustion and fatigue.

Madinat al-Sadr received the bodies of those whose next of kin were unknown, and these were first buried there. Then Sayyid Muqtada al-Sadr purchased a tract of land in Wadi al-Salam Cemetery, and those corpses were reburied there.

My brothers were among those pilgrims and were unable to contact us, because they had lost all their possessions, including their mobile phones, in that crush of people on the bridge. Therefore, my mother, on seeing broadcast coverage on the satellite channels, believed that my brothers had died. She broke down completely when she watched all those bodies being dragged from the river, imagining that her sons were certainly among them.

I was visiting my family when my mother suffered palpitations as she stared at those corpses on TV and searched for my brothers' faces. Pain gradually rose inside her, and she began vomiting liquid of a strange color. She did not stop until a doctor administered some medicine both orally and intravenously in the emergency room. By the next day, my mother's condition had stabilized a little, but I was very anxious when I saw that a portion of her tongue had turned blue when she opened her mouth while attempting to swallow her medicine, which I was administering with a spoon.

I left my sister and father with her and went to speak to the physician. He told me my mother was in more critical condition than she seemed. All he could do was stop her bouts of vomiting—nothing more. The X-rays from that morning showed a tear in her gallbladder, and there was no way the physician could perform any surgery to reconnect her gallbladder. That was because of her medical history and because tests showed that her heart muscle was impaired and appeared to be abnormally small. I left the physician's office and tried to act normal with my mother and those around her, but I felt the bitterness of another loss assailing me.

My father also sensed that my mother was dying and asked her to return home, but she was terrified, and nothing would reassure her except the presence of the doctor near her—a physician who could save her when she needed him. For this reason, my father agreed to her decision, and my mother remained in the hospital for several days, during which all our acquaintances, relatives, and friends visited her.

My two brothers eventually returned safely from Baghdad and told her everything that had happened to them on the Bridge of the Imams, but even so, her condition did not improve. Her body seemed to be gradually withering.

One of those nights, I dreamt that my mother had placed a beautiful girl around six years old on her shoulders and was heading to the cemetery. My dream scared me, and I wept a lot, because I was certain that her end was near.

I went to her the next morning instead of to school. Then I found my father, brothers, and sisters surrounding my mother on every side, weeping. When she saw me enter, she asked me to bring my children so she could say goodbye to them. She also asked me to make her some of the chicken soup she loved. I raced out of the room, but her tired voice followed me again. I heard her ask me to bring the visitors' book. So I did.

My husband accompanied me this time to visit my mother. I informed him that I would spend the day with her. So he took our children home after she had the chance to speak to them.

One of my sisters and I spent the night with my mother in the hospital room. My father sat outside the room as he had done since she'd entered the hospital. When my sister started to feel sleepy, my mother asked me to recite the prayer known as the Adeela. Then I placed my hand on her forehead and began to recite this prayer to her while I wept silently:

> *In the name of God, the Compassionate,*
> *the Merciful, God bore witness that He is the*
> *only god (as did the angels and those who possess*

wisdom) and that He is the Almighty and All-Wise and that God's religion is Islam. I, a weak, sinful, rebellious, needy, destitute, humble servant, testify that He is my benefactor, creator, sustainer, patron. There is no god but He, the possessor of bounties, favors, blessings, generosity. He is eternally Almighty, everlastingly sapient, one and immortal, hearing, seeing, willing, discriminating, and ever aware.

He has incorporated us into the ummah of the supreme Prophet, the dearest friend of God, the superlative being, the most pious person: Muhammad (God's blessings and peace on him and his descendants). We heeded him, believing what he revealed and in the Holy Qur'an that You revealed through him. We believed in his successor, Ali, who was appointed by the Prophet on the day of Ghader, identifying him with these clear words: "This is Ali."

I testify to the existence of pious imams and righteous successors after [Muhammad] the chosen messenger. These are Ali, who vanquished the infidels, his eldest son, Hasan ibn Ali, and Hasan's brother Husayn, the grandson of the messenger of God; obedience to them is in keeping with God's will. They were succeeded by Ali, Muhammad al-Baqir, Ja'far al-Sadiq, Musa al-Kadhim, Ali al-Riza, Muhammad al-Taqi, Ali al-Naqi, Hasan al-Askari, and the Mahdi, our appointed savior, a clear argument and the established successor, whose continued existence guarantees the existence of the world, whose blessings provide people with their daily bread, whose presence stabilizes heaven and earth. Through him, God will fill the earth with equity and justice after it was overwhelmed by tyranny and oppression.

My God, I have accepted Islam as my religion, the Qur'an as my book, the Ka'ba as my central axis, Ali as a friend of God and Imam as well as al-Hasan, al-Husayn, Ali ibn al-Husayn, Muhammad ibn Ali, Ja'far ibn Muhammad, Musa ibn Ja'far, Ali ibn Musa, Muhammad ibn Ali, Ali ibn Muhammad, al-Hasan ibn Ali, and al-Hujjat ibn al-Hasan (God's blessings on them as imams). My God, I have accepted them as imams. You are capable of everything.

As I recited this prayer, my mother was serene, and seemed to find the most solace in the prayer's closing:

I bear witness that death is certain, interrogation in the grave is certain, raising the dead is certain, the bridge over hell is certain, the trial is certain, judgment is certain, the Book is true, paradise is real, and that hell is real. The hour of resurrection is certain, and God will raise the dead from their graves.

God, I hope to receive Your favor, Your generosity and mercy so that I may enter paradise, where my conduct does not assure my entrance, for I was not obedient enough to merit Your bliss. But I did believe in Your unicity and Your justice. I depend instead on Your favor and generosity thanks to my Prophet, his offspring, and Your special friends.

She gradually abandoned herself to sleep. Once I had finished reciting this prayer, my mother snored audibly once and never woke again.

Weeping, I roused my sister. When she observed what had happened, she started slapping her face and head fiercely while wailing, "Why did I fall asleep? Why didn't I bid her farewell?"

The other women in that ward were frightened. One screamed, "I see the angel of death approaching!" Then she died.

Another woman, whose daughter was with her, asked the daughter to remove her from that ward. The girl quickly took her mother outside to the garden, where she died.

Yet another gestured to me and said in a barely audible voice, "Recite Qur'an for me." So I ran and placed the visitors' book by her head. Then I quit the room, which resounded with the cries of women slapping themselves while they crowded around my mother's body.

My twin brothers were the first to perform the funeral prayer over the pure shrouded body of my mother in her coffin, in the garden of the hospital, before they took her to the corpse-washing station.

Not much muscle was required to lift that coffin from the ground. My father and brothers and one other man carried it and placed it on top of a taxi to take it to the corpse-washing station. We girls hired another vehicle that followed the taxi bearing the corpse.

The corpse-washing station's door panels, on which time's fingers had carved deep grooves, were open wide. The place stank from a mixture of camphor and dry leaves of the buckthorn tree and the stench of dead bodies. Even its beige wall did not tempt people entering to stand there and contemplate it, not even for a few moments.

We walked down a concrete hallway toward two rooms. The room on the right was reserved for men and that on the left for women. They carried her into the room where women's bodies were washed. Spiders had spun pale webs there, and fine dirt covered the black stone of its window ledge as well. A loofah sponge lay beside a bar of soap.

Once the men carrying the coffin entered the corpse-washing building, with us girls trailing behind them, a woman of about sixty approached us. She seemed old to us but still retained the energy to perform her job with few breaks. She welcomed us with the expression of a person accustomed to dealing with death and told the men, "Place her here."

They did. After putting the coffin on the floor, they opened it and lifted my mother's body from inside. They placed my mother's body on a solid hexagonal concrete counter that was two meters long and three meters wide. It was situated near an oval basin with a water tap at its head. Its other end was a drain to catch the water from the corpse-washing.

We tearful women were anxious to see what this woman would do with our mother's body. The old woman entered the room and stood in the walkway between the counter and the basin. Once she was certain that all the men had left, she removed my mother's garments, one at a time, setting them on the edge of the counter. Then she fetched a little water and a bar of laurel soap and began to wash my mother's hair, which glowed like a constellation of stars in the night sky. As the water poured over it, it began to glisten. Next, she mixed a little camphor, the fragrance of which haunted the entire place, with water and poured that liquid all over my mother's body while murmuring appropriate *surahs* from the Qur'an.

After that, she pulled my mother's hair back and fastened it with a white cloth cord. Then she placed my mother's head inside a bag of white cloth, which she fastened tight. Next she dressed my mother in a white sleeveless blouse that reached below her navel—after she allowed her interlaced fingers to press on my mother's belly to make sure there was nothing left inside it.

She wrapped a cord of the same fabric around the belly. Then the woman dressed her in a third piece of fabric from the belly to the feet. Finally, she clad the entire body in its shroud.

Throughout these procedures she murmured many prayers. Another woman, who had been waiting outside this room and watching her skillful movements, helped her carry the body to the coffin and place it deftly inside.

Then the corpse-washer asked the men, who had been waiting outside, to enter and take away the corpse. Some of our relatives picked up the coffin after covering it with a clean black abaya. They carried it through the courtyard of Imam Ali (peace upon him) in preparation for the soul's passage to another life.

My father was not able to last more than two years without my mother. During that time, he suffered many strokes, and his vision became so weak that he almost went blind from weeping so often for my mother. He would visit me almost every day and discuss with me his exceptional relationship with my mother—as if I had not witnessed that pure loving bond myself.

In the tenth month of 2007, he rejoined my mother after a heart attack left him hospitalized. Once the physician had examined my father, he asked us to purchase a syringe, from a pharmacy outside the hospital, to shrink the clot, because the hospital did not have any.

Although that syringe was expensive—about 150,000 rials—we all pitched in with what money we had and handed it to my brother, who raced to buy it. By the time he returned with it to the hospital, he found that my father had departed to his final resting place.

I was unable to attend my father's wake the way I had attended my mother's, because the moment his corpse passed by in the street where I was waiting to bid him a final adieu, the earth turned and shook under my feet, and I fainted. When I came to, several days later, I was at home. I examined what I was wearing and found I was dressed in black. Then I realized that what I had experienced had not been a nightmare but my bitter reality.

I resumed my normal life but with sorrow and pain following me everywhere. When I felt it necessary to change the circumstances of my life, I thought of switching my work assignment from secondary teaching to university instruction. I had a right to request this change, since I had completed my master's degree.

To make this request, I was obliged to go to Baghdad, which during this period was the most dangerous city in the world. Many murders occurred there daily, and you might be killed because of your sectarian identity or die either after being kidnapped or from explosive belts and IEDs. All the same, I risked the trip.

The minibus I boarded that morning set off, with several other passengers aboard, and I thought I would arrive at the Ministry of Education and Instruction early. Our bus did not stop until we reached al-Hilla, the city between Najaf and Baghdad, when our driver climbed down to greet another driver he knew and to ask why there was such an enormous crush of buses there.

When he hurried back to us, he started the engine and turned around. The passengers did not protest when they learned that this congestion had resulted from the discovery of a booby-trapped bus in the region.

We waited two whole hours until specialists from the armed forces were able to dismantle that old white vehicle. They shackled the arms of the young man who had been driving it backward and beat him severely.

Then one of the soldiers quickly placed a sack of thick black cloth over the youth's head and shoved him into a military vehicle parked nearby.

Everyone was upset, including our driver. No sooner had he started backing up his vehicle than some American soldiers almost killed all of us with their bullets. Without realizing it, he had been nearing their military convoy, which was also located there.

All the passengers' mouths released a single scream: "Watch out!"

He came to a dead stop there and turned to look behind him. Then he saw the mouth of the machine guns aimed at us. The blood stopped circulating in my veins, and my nerves were only able to reclaim their previous calm when I saw the hand of an American soldier gesture for our vehicle to pass.

After this long delay, our bus had to speed faster so that the passengers would be able to complete whatever mission they had come to Baghdad, the City of Peace, to perform.

When we approached the city's outskirts, though, we were stopped by a military vehicle. The soldiers demanded that we climb out, and we were subjected to a barrage of questions: Where do you come from? Which districts of Baghdad are you going to? What is the reason for your visit? Do you have any weapons with you? What is your occupation?

That was not our last checkpoint. Every time our vehicle went a short distance, we were forced to stop for a second, third, and fourth military inspection.

Despite the delay caused by all these mandatory stops, I did not feel truly nervous until our bus sped up and passed a flaming oil tanker. A body near it was enveloped in fire even as it waved futilely to passersby: "Stop! Save me!"

I reached the Ministry of Education and Instruction at 2:00 p.m. When I asked for the official in charge of transfers between secondary and university education, I was told that he was in a meeting and that I would need to return the next day if I wished to see him.

My only option was to depart. I left the office upset and descended the building's many steps. I felt devastated that I had not been able to accomplish the task for which I had suffered so much, putting myself in grave danger.

I paused beside a middle-aged man whose dishdasha smelled of tea. I put out my hand to flag down a taxi that was passing. Two young men on a motorcycle stopped in front of me, and one of them shouted at me, "What's your identity?"

My hand froze in the air, and I started to tremble when I heard that gruff voice demand to see my ID. But I was shocked when I heard the man standing beside me shout at me as if scolding me: "Why have you come now? What do you want from me? Didn't I inform them that I would be late today? Come on, come on: I'll see you across the street. Come, let's be quick about it!"

Then he dragged me by my hand and began racing me across the street as my feet almost tripped over the end of my abaya, which the wind had begun to wrap around my legs and then unfurl. Once we reached the end of the street, which was blocked off with many large, thick concrete barriers, he spoke to me in a quiet, affectionate voice this time: "From here, bend down a bit and go through this opening, run quickly, and don't stop till you're on the far side of the river. I'm going to return to work now and leave you in God's care and custody."

I wasn't conscious of myself and simply raced to the far side of the bridge. There, I mingled with some people waiting for taxis. All I remember after that was shoving my body among the women as I climbed onto a bus that returned me to the Alawi terminal, which was almost deserted this suffocating afternoon. I exerted all the energy I possessed to search for minibuses departing for Najaf. I found only two, and they were empty. Two tall women were standing beside one and pleading with the driver to start at once so they would arrive in Najaf before sunset.

The driver, though, would not consent to depart for Najaf until the bus was filled with passengers, even if that meant he had to sleep over in the terminal.

When one of the women spotted me, she approached and greeted me in a mournful voice. Then the three of us headed to another driver. When the other woman spoke to him, he agreed to depart from the terminal right then if we paid him double the normal fare. We accepted his terms reluctantly.

Before we boarded the bus, that woman lifted from the ground a medium-sized wooden box like those used to transport fruit and vegetables, intending to carry it on board with her. The driver, who feared that box contained an IED or part of a weapon, refused to let her, unless she opened the box to show him what it contained.

Before the woman opened the box, she thrust her hand into her pocketbook and pulled out a set of papers with government stamps and many different signatures. Weeping, she showed these to the driver and said, "The head of my only brother is in this box. That was all we found of him after the explosion. We are taking it to Najaf for burial in the cemetery."

The driver opened the box to verify that there was nothing else in it. The moment the bus left the terminal, the two women sank into a profound slumber. I did not; my eyes were fixed, all the way to Najaf, on that box. I was wondering what had happened to the rest of his body, forgetting all the dangers I had encountered. The least of them had been the attempt to kidnap me.

My husband's sense that I had become too independent, as if I had no one to support me in life, caused him to tyrannize me even more, and the problems he caused without any pretext multiplied. I would feel lucky if a day passed when he did not cause me trouble.

My worst days were those when my husband discovered that I had published an essay in some newspaper or magazine or when I had been interviewed or had published a poem or short story in a journal. On such occasions he would spew provocatively derisive comments at me. If I tried to reply, my entire day would become a nonstop quarrel that would end only when he grew tired of talking and shouting. Then he would leave the house or go to bed. If I remained silent and ignored his derision and ridicule, he would go wild and begin to wreck the electrical appliances I had bought for the house.

Once I realized that living with him was impossible, I asked him to divorce me. He seemed incredulous when he heard me and turned into a predatory wolf.

I felt obliged to visit his two older brothers, visiting each in his own home. I told them about the daily problems that had occurred from the day I married their brother to the present. They did not believe me. One asked to accompany me to my house and discuss these problems with my husband, thinking he might find some solution for us.

My husband, however, flew into a rage while his brother was there. Once he realized how weak his arguments sounded to his brother, he started to curse and swear at me. He did not stop there; he took down the sword that was hanging on the wall and began to threaten that he would slice off my head if I didn't keep quiet. Then his brother suggested that I should give my husband twenty million Iraqi dinars and leave my children with him in exchange for his agreement to divorce me. I did not accept that ridiculous suggestion. Even if I had been able to hand over that much money to him, how could I surrender my children to an individual as irresponsible as my husband?

The other brother suggested that I leave my husband's house and come to live with his wife and children in their house. I rejected that idea totally, for what would be my status if I lived with my brother-in-law and his family?

When our discussion of a divorce reached a dead end, even after I discussed it with my brothers, who offered me no support, I had to postpone execution of this project till a future time and continued to endure daily scorching in that endless inferno.

One day a journalist interviewed me and published it in a local newspaper. He asked me to come, the afternoon of the day that interview was published, to the directorate of the University of Kufa to receive my copy of that interview. He told me he would meet me after a conference he was attending there, since that would be near the Adala District, where we lived. Because—as usual—my husband wasn't home that afternoon, I took the children with me and walked to that building.

When the conference concluded and the journalist left the building, he handed me the newspaper and started talking with my children and kidding around with them. When I suddenly looked behind me, I found my husband sitting on the ground, dressed in athletic clothes. He was pretending to be tying the laces of his trainers.

I was startled to see this, and when one of the children noticed him, she began to shout to him, "Papa, Papa!"

He raced off to join some athletes who were waiting for him and left with them, ignoring his daughter. All the way back to the house, I tried to forget what had happened, reflecting on the details of the interview that had been published. The moment I entered the house and started to close the door, I felt a strong shove that almost knocked me to the ground.

Then my husband entered the house, screaming, "What were you doing with that man?"

"I got a copy of a newspaper that carried an interview with me."

He shot back with the same angry timbre of voice, "Do you want me to believe you walked all that distance for a newspaper? There's definitely something going on between you two!"

I could not keep myself from shouting back at him this time: "Are you crazy? How can you insult my honor this way? You're insane!"

When he heard the word "crazy," he raised his hand and slapped my face. The ring he wore on one finger cut my cheek, which started to bleed. When he tried to hit me again, I left the house after using the foulest language to characterize him, forgetting that the children were with him.

I hailed a taxi and headed to my brother's house. The moment he saw what had happened to me and I recounted to him the course of events, he suggested that we go to the police station together, where I lodged a complaint against my husband. The officer, however, did not take my complaint seriously. He considered it a family quarrel between a husband and his wife—nothing more. Therefore, I went to the hospital to have my bleeding cheek bandaged and to have a medical report written about the assault so that I could submit it as evidence when I applied for a divorce.

The nurse in her medical report described it as merely a superficial wound that had not required stitches and that would heal in a few days. Then she bandaged it with a piece of cotton soaked in blue iodine and walked off. Her report did not help me, but the moment I returned to my brother's house, I found that my husband had brought the children there, after learning I had gone to him. He had left them there with a message that he would kill me the next time he laid eyes on me because I had dared to complain to the police about him.

My brother's only suggestion was for me to return to my husband. When I refused, he asked me with some embarrassment that I go to my sister's house because—as he alleged—he wanted to live in peace. I bowed to his request and took my children to my sister's house. She was also less than delighted to see us.

Since I was determined to file for a divorce, I was obliged to fetch my papers from my house—things like my ID, certificate of citizenship, and marriage license. So I put off going to work and went to my house at a time when my husband typically wasn't there because he was playing soccer. I took my two oldest daughters so they could help me collect the clothing we would need while living at my sister's.

There actually was no one home when we entered the house, and I quickly placed all the papers and cash I needed in my handbag. Then I put our clothes in a large suitcase. We were on the verge of leaving the bedroom peacefully when we heard my husband's footsteps as he entered the house. My daughters were alarmed, but I asked them to be calm, because no matter how excited or angry he was, he was still their father and would not harm them.

When he entered the bedroom, though, and saw us standing beside a suitcase, he began to roar and foam at the mouth. "How could you dare lodge a complaint against me with the police? If you think you will live after what you have done, you are dreaming."

The girls' alarm and fear were increased by these words, and they began to weep loudly, but he ignored them and sped from the room after locking its door behind him. He shouted at the top of his lungs, "I'll burn you alive! Your corpse will be charred before you leave here. With this simple lighter I will end your life, and your poetry won't be able to save you."

I was torn between believing his threat to set the bedroom ablaze and searching for a way to calm my daughters, whose tears and screams were making a bad situation worse.

Should I say I was lucky that day, or should I say that my two daughters brought me luck? When my husband left with sparks flying from his eyes to search for some propane or oil we used in the little generator when the electricity was off, he did not find any. So he was obliged to go borrow some from a friend's house. Meanwhile I managed to break the lock on the door with multiple forceful blows from the sword I had hidden from my husband on top of the wardrobe, after he had threatened to kill me with it on an earlier occasion.

We fled quickly to the street, hailed a taxi, and returned to my sister's house. There we all calmed down, and I contacted the headmistress of my daughters' school and asked her to excuse them from attending for a week, alleging they were ill.

On the morning of the next day, I went to my school, where I claimed to all my fellow teachers who asked about the wound on my cheek that I had fallen on something sharp on the stairs. They might almost have believed me if they had not seen my angry husband asking for me at the door of the school.

The headmistress threatened that if he ever returned to the school this way again, she would call the police on him. He retreated from the school but not very far. Instead, he stood for hours in front of one of the kiosks opposite the school, waiting for me to leave. He remained there until someone he knew passed by, and they went off together to the bus stop, where they disappeared. (I was watching him from the windows of my various classrooms.)

Some days later I presented my papers to the court, requesting a divorce, but did not receive it easily, because I did not have adequate evidence to justify a divorce and because my spouse contested the separation. If that was not enough, there was no documentation of his actual address. My husband and his acquaintances played other games as well to delay the judgment and prolong the length of the judicial procedure. The important point is that I did not receive the divorce until 2009, after hiring more than one attorney and spending exorbitant amounts of money.

After I rented a suitable furnished residence close to my sister's and bought new electric appliances for it, I transferred my daughters to schools near that house. I hired a driver to take me daily to the university and bring me back, when I was accepted as a student in the doctoral program, after successfully completing the admissions requirements and obtaining leave from work for two years to complete my PhD.

Our life proceeded peacefully until my former husband began to frequent my sister's house, claiming that he was eager to see his daughters. Every time my sister contacted me, asking me to bring the girls to her so their father could see them, I would ask her to come and fetch them from me while I stood at a location at some distance from my home.

My former husband found a way to ingratiate himself with his daughters. Each time they would return from a visit with him, they would treat me hostilely and angrily—as if I were the reason their happy life with their father had been ruined.

Chapter Fourteen

Toward the end of the year, I received a strange message from a fellow writer who had stopped attending the writers union after she married. She informed me that there had been numerous posts on many internet sites from an important Iraqi organization and that these posts contained the names of many writers, cultural figures, poets, and professors whom the organization said should be executed. My name was on that list.

I was amazed by this and went as soon as I could to an internet café in the central post office. When I established the truth of this report, I was terrified and tried to think of even one reason that my name would be included on such a list. I was not one of the writers who had composed panegyrics in honor of Saddam Hussein or who had supported him and his regime. I had also not expressed support for the current, wobbly government. So how could people be calling for my death?

I felt obliged to contact my brothers and sisters to tell them about this matter, but none of them had any solution to offer. The news seemed to have quickly found its way to my former husband, who sent me a message via one of my sisters. The gist of it was: "If you are considering leaving Najaf with my daughters, you will die."

I discussed the predicament with my daughters and explained how serious it was and how urgently we needed to travel somewhere far from Najaf and even Iraq. But they were not convinced by what I said.

One day when I returned from my university, I did not find my children in our house. My youngest daughter and her brother were at my sister's house. Then I discovered that the two older girls had contacted their father using their aunt's phone. He had come and taken them home with him. I wept bitterly, feeling that my hopes for my daughters had been dashed, along with my constant effort to safeguard them.

When that death list was published again by even more sites and in a local newspaper, I was obliged to leave Najaf and go into hiding. I summoned my brothers and sisters and distributed my furniture to them. At dawn I left for Baghdad to reflect on what I had to do.

I took with me only my two youngest children, my cell phone, laptop, and some cash. I got this idea from one of my fellow teachers who had left Najaf for the capital. With help from that friend, I rented a studio apartment, which was the only vacant flat in that friend's building.

I had lived there for approximately two months when I opened Facebook to learn news of my family and close friends. On Facebook I'd made the acquaintance of an Iraqi lady who was living with her family in Eskişehir, Turkey. Each time I went on Facebook, I would find that she had left me a message—encouraging me to leave Iraq and come to Turkey. She left me stunning photos of the beautiful apartment she lived in there and the view from it over the sea.

Even so, I did not take her suggestion seriously and ignored what she was saying, because I really didn't want to leave Iraq. But that changed as my fear increased, since I found myself threatened by my ex-husband's promise to kill me and that of the militias to exterminate me.

Because I was serious about reclaiming my other two daughters, I contacted my sister and asked her to find a way for me to speak with them. She agreed, and two days later I received a call from my sister's phone. The speaker was one of my two older daughters. She began by crying. Then she asked me to return to live with her father once more. When I rejected her request and told her she had to come to Baghdad and live with me, she hung up. I did not feel angry at her, because I knew how much pressure she was under.

In my new digs, I would go out shopping every three or four days. On one occasion I took both my children with me and went in the morning to the market. When I returned, I found that my apartment's door had been broken and my basic household items had been strewn about. The intruder had been looking for something of value.

At first, I felt frightened by comments written on the wall with charcoal. These predicted that all I had to look forward to was death. I thanked God many times when I found my laptop in the place where I had hidden it before leaving the flat.

When I asked my neighbor who shared that floor with me if she had witnessed or heard what had happened in my apartment, she replied that she had not been home all day and that such events were common here, especially after people learned that a woman was living alone without a husband. That was when I decided to leave Iraq. So I communicated with my friend on Facebook, thinking of her as my sole life preserver. She supplied me with all the details about what I would need to go to Turkey.

At five the next morning, I was waiting with my two children at the door of the travel agent for the bus that would take us to Erbil and then on to Turkey. Before leaving, I gave my neighbor all the furnishings from my apartment. For my new friend in Turkey, I purchased what she had requested: makeup and an Arabic keyboard.

We reached Erbil on the bus with a temporary visa. There we switched from the Iraqi bus to a new Turkish one. When I reached Istanbul, I contacted my friend and found that she, her husband, and their young children—who were the same ages as mine—were waiting for us.

We all boarded the flying train—this is what they call an express train—after she kissed me and introduced me to her small family. I was not surprised that the entire family had come to greet me and attributed this to her not having anyone she could have left her children with if she had come with only her husband to greet me. I was, however, surprised when her husband asked me to pay for all seven tickets. When I told him I did not have any Turkish liras, he did not immediately volunteer to pay for the tickets; instead, he took my Iraqi money from me and exchanged those bills for Turkish ones he took from his wallet.

Since I did not know the exchange rate for Iraqi dinars to Turkish liras, I kept my silence. When we reached the city of Eskişehir, the woman's husband asked if we were hungry, and we all said yes. Then he immediately entered a restaurant that sold meat pastries, and we followed him. Once he had eaten his fill, he left abruptly, and his wife and their children followed him, leaving me and my children behind. When the waiter came with the bill, I did not understand how much he wanted, because I did not know any Turkish. So I called the woman, who answered me brusquely and rudely, "Get your money changed by a money changer! Don't delay us!"

I quickly left that place, taking my children with me but leaving my suitcase in the restaurant as I searched for a money changer. I found one in that same area and gave him my Iraqi money, which he exchanged for Turkish liras. I returned to the waiter, who asked me to give him fifty liras (approximately fifty US dollars). Then I left, dragging my heavy suitcase behind me, trailing these people who were beginning to disclose their true nature to me. My two children were fascinated when an electric trolley passed down the middle of the street.

After leaving the main thoroughfare, we followed narrow streets till we entered a miserable apartment that did not resemble in any way the picture she had posted on Facebook. When I asked her about the picture she had sent me with the view of the sea, she initially laughed. Then she said sarcastically, "Enjoying the water of the fountains is better!"

That woman's mendacity struck me like a thunderbolt when I found that her wretched apartment was packed full of other Iraqis who had also been trapped in the snares of this woman and her husband.

When I entered the room reserved for me, my hostess came to receive the presents she had asked me to bring her. Then she informed me that she and her husband would accompany me the next day to a rental agency to transfer the lease to my name, on the understanding, as she informed me, that she would travel to Australia at the end of that week and leave me the apartment.

After I had handed her the presents and she had left, I heard a light knock on the door. I rose and opened it to find that one of the other Iraqi ladies was asking my permission to enter. I invited her into the room with some reserve and caution. Then she informed me that I had fallen into the family's trap of lies, that this family had been rejected by the UN agency, but that, even so, they claimed they were leaving Turkey for Australia in order to split the hiked rent with the other families.

She also informed me that there were more than ten people living in the three-room apartment—most of them men. She, for almost two months, had been searching with her husband and children for another city where they could go and live. I was so alarmed by what I heard that I barely slept that night after I went on tiptoe with my children to the bathroom.

The next morning, I left the apartment after refusing to go to their rental agency. When a young Iraqi man, who was sitting in a coffee-house that looked out on the apartment, saw me, he came quickly toward me. After greeting me, I informed him I was looking for a place to live.

He took me to a rental agency that leased me an excellent furnished apartment for just one month. Before the end of the month, I realized that this European-style city was very expensive and dominated by university students.

When, in a public garden, I saw that same woman who had told me she wanted to leave Eskişehir, I learned from her that her husband had located a place to live in a city called Afyonkarahisar. I then asked her to discuss with her husband whether I might accompany them there. By the end of that month, we were all waiting in the train station for a train that would take us to mountainous Afyon, where many Iraqis who had previously lived in Iraq, Syria, and Jordan had settled.

Houses and apartments were available there for a rather reasonable rent, although rates for electricity and water were very high, and this was a mountain town with harsh winters. By three in the afternoon, the temperature might descend below zero degrees centigrade. Then some of the vendors' fruits and vegetables—like tomatoes and cucumbers—would freeze in the markets and the vendors were forced to toss them out.

During the year and a half that I stayed in Turkey, I did not meet a single Turk who spoke English or Arabic. Fortunately an Iraqi child of Turkmen ancestry in Afyon spoke fluent Turkish, and we hired her for a modest fee to interpret for us whenever we went to a government bureau.

It was not easy to enroll my children in school. Several principals refused to admit them on the grounds that they did not know Turkish. Then I was forced to appeal to the superintendent of education there. When he asked why I wanted to send my children to school even though they could not speak Turkish, I replied, "To protect them from the cold!"

This was my sole reason for insisting my two children be admitted to school, where they would be warm—unlike our apartment, which was unbearably cold. In the neighborhood where we lived, residents used coal-fired space heaters. I bought one but was never able to get it to operate properly, even after repeated tries. Coal smoke would fill the entire apartment, and whenever I lit it, we almost suffocated. Enrolling my children in school was the only way I could protect them from the cold. At night, in our one large bed, we wore heavy clothes: a couple of pairs of wool socks, caps, and leggings, and occasionally mittens. Then we slept huddled together beneath four blankets.

Turkey is known for its open-air markets. These are held daily but in different locations. Where we lived, there were two. What was called the Friday market was held each Friday morning in the valley. The other market, held on Sunday, took place on the mountain. Most people who lived in this city walked to these markets.

To reach other markets, a person had to ride a bus, and the Turks did not like to ride buses in the winter. All the same, for me, shopping on Sunday was rather like mountain climbing. One day when I shopped while my children were in school, my foot slipped. Then I fell a long way down the slope. People gathered to help me and carried me home on a sturdy wooden stretcher they used in accidents like mine. I could not get about for two weeks. When my pain became a little more bearable, I sought treatment in a public clinic.

When I had healed some, I had little time to enjoy that because my son caught German measles from his classmates. I took him to a doctor, who wrote a prescription for him. The medication cost eighty Turkish liras (about eighty US dollars at the time). This was a horrific sum compared to the cost of food. Fresh fish, for example, might cost five liras. All the same, I had to purchase this medicine for my son, even though that meant I lived on bread and water for a time. What else could I do when I was unemployed?

After I purchased this medicine, an Iraqi neighbor woman told me there was a clinic to which people donated unused medicine, including bottles they had opened. The clinic distributed these to people who needed them. I did not go there for fear those medicines were past their expiration date or unfit for use for some other reason.

Fearful, anxious, and lonely, I realized that my psychological condition was deteriorating. I also began to suffer from chronic insomnia;

I had lost the ability to sleep at night. If I did fall asleep, I would wake a couple of hours later after having nightmares and terrifying dreams about men chasing me and trying to slay me or blow up where I was. Then I was terrified and bathed in sweat.

I asked the agency in charge of Iraqi refugees in my city whether there was a psychiatrist who would treat me. A month later, an employee contacted me to tell me a woman psychiatrist could see me the next Friday at the bureau. I went and found her waiting for me with an Iraqi woman, who translated for me. The Turkish physician asked me some general medical questions and why I had come to see her. I told her candidly about my daily travails. She simply advised me to mix with other people, read the Qur'an, and wear a blue headscarf!

What could I do but thank her and leave? I wondered, though, whether this woman was really a physician. This was the last time in Turkey, or America, that I thought of consulting a psychiatrist. I adjusted to the fact that I had terrifying nightmares and weird dreams.

I did follow the physician's suggestion to try to socialize more and started taking my children to a large public park called the Vali's Garden, where people from various neighborhoods congregated and chatted while their children played. Because Friday was a school and government holiday, I began to take my children to this park each Friday morning. Every time Turks sitting there caught sight of us, though, they would laugh, mocking me and my kids because our complexion was darker than theirs. I was forced to sit in a far corner of the park, away from the adults and near where the children played.

Our landlady had divided a large house into four small apartments. She lived in the best one, which had a sunny balcony, and sunshine flooded her apartment during the morning. The other units, which were cold and damp, were inhabited by three Iraqi families. This Turkish landlady was very domineering. She had even accused her husband of theft and sent him to prison. She lived there with only her teen-age daughter. She owned a huge dog that she fed meat and bones she purchased from the butcher. She kept this dog on a long chain by the main entrance to the building, and it would bark at residents entering or leaving.

She also traveled to Istanbul frequently, going there more than four times a month. Whenever she was out of town, she entrusted care of her dog to my Iraqi neighbor who lived on the ground floor with his wife. He fed the dog, made sure it had water, and cleaned up after it. In the absence of its mistress, however, this dog was vicious during the day and would not stop barking all night long. Its caretaker was frequently bitten, but whenever the dog's owner heard what her dog had done, she would laugh and boast about her beast's heroism.

Each month, just as soon as I paid her the rent, this landlady would ask me for more money—a loan she would never repay. When I refused, she would become angry and speak so loudly that I could not understand her. As if that weren't enough, she seized our lower water and electricity bills and left us *her* higher bills, because she felt certain the lower ones were intended for her.

We awoke one morning to the sound of heavy pickaxes. When I opened the door, I was surprised to see three workmen outside with the landlady. She had hired them to demolish the steps to the apartment I lived in. Infuriated, I contacted the police, who came and phoned the child interpreter and her father. Then I asked the girl to explain my plight to the policemen. They took no action against the woman, however, because she said she was remodeling the apartment for a visit from her mother during the Eid. She also claimed that the new steps would be completed by the next morning. They were not, and we were confined to our quarters for three days, unable to clamber out.

During those days I wrote out a shopping list for an Iraqi neighbor. I placed it with some money in a basket that I lowered to her with a rope. Then she bought whatever we needed and brought our provisions to us when she returned home that evening.

My dreadful, frightening experiences and my insomnia motivated me to try to write a novel. So I wrote a novella 152 pages long and called it *I Hate My City*. One day I was on Facebook, chatting with a friend, and told her about my manuscript. When I asked about the possibility of publishing it, in Iraq or elsewhere, she suggested I send her the file, offering to try to submit it to a publishing house in Erbil, in northern Iraq. So I did. Soon afterward my friend sent me an email to tell me that the publisher had agreed to publish and distribute the novel. As soon as it was edited, he would send it to the printer. Three months later I learned from my friend that the novel had been released and would be displayed at an international fair in Erbil. She also mailed five copies of the novel to me in Turkey.

I never felt comfortable in Turkey, because it was not a safe distance from Iraq. My ex-husband or one of his friends might easily come and take vengeance on me for disobeying him and taking my two children with me to Turkey when I fled. I never felt secure there and was haunted by fear and anxiety. Then I started asking fellow Iraqis in Turkey about the possibility of leaving for a distant country. They told me that I needed to register with the United Nations in Ankara.

I took my children by bus to Ankara, leaving at dawn. The trip took about three hours. When we reached the UN office, we found a lot of people waiting outside the door. After we waited a long time, we were finally admitted to a lobby crowded with many people from various parts of the globe. Everyone was asking for a place of refuge.

Once we had registered, staff members asked me why we were applying for humanitarian refugee status. Then I recounted the history of my calamities. After taking some photos, they requested my cell phone number. They said they would telephone us to conduct a second interview once they had verified my story. They did phone me, and that call was followed by a third one.

All the same, I waited for six months. One day I went to the UN office to ask what was happening about my request for refugee status.

Once I furnished my information to the young Iraqi man who was working there, he searched for me quickly on his computer. Then he informed me that my application had been accepted but that the country that would accept me had not been determined yet.

I waited a long time, for a year and a half, with repeated trips to Ankara for apparently futile meetings. I felt very tired and had almost lost hope of leaving this cold place and its haughty people.

One night I fell asleep to find myself in a place where the world had ended and been racked by devastation and destruction. My children and I were searching for a safe place to shelter. An American policeman approached and asked us to accompany him onto a helicopter that was waiting by the skeleton of a destroyed building. When we started to board, the propeller of that helicopter began to rotate. The loud roar of its motor mingled with the ring of my phone, which had already rung several times. I woke up immediately and responded to an unfamiliar number. An Iraqi man told me his name and then greeted me enthusiastically: "Congratulations, Mrs. Faleeha! Your application for you and your children has been accepted by the United States of America!"

An interview was arranged with a representative of the US Refugee Admissions Program. The Americans arranged a three-day workshop for us, and during it we had physical exams to check that we had no contagious or chronic diseases. Because I had no family or relatives in America, a representative of a Roman Catholic charity in New Jersey contacted me and told me that my children and I would be received by them in New Jersey. One rainy day in August, we reached America. At the Philadelphia Airport, we found two Americans from the charity and an Iraqi translator waiting for us. They took us to the charity's headquarters in Camden, where Mrs. Cathy, the head of the organization, welcomed us. She had rented an apartment for us, paying the rent in advance for three months. They also provided us with food vouchers.

Some of our new neighbors, though, did not like having Arab Muslims near them, and a woman living there started harassing us.

She would turn up the volume of her TV till it was extremely loud and leave it like that all night long. At six in the morning, she would play the childish prank of ringing our doorbell. She would drop some metal weights her husband used for physical training very hard on the floor, making our whole apartment shake. After I discovered her taking photos of my children with her mobile phone, I became so frightened and furious that I complained to the manager of the apartment complex. She wasn't able to stop the woman's harassment, and I contacted the police. My tormentor told the officer that her husband had been deployed to fight in Iraq and that, since we were Iraqis, we should be killed. The policeman merely smiled and did not write her up. So I was obliged to move to another apartment, fleeing yet again from the endless war that has shadowed me for most of my life.

Now I live somewhere pleasant, but even so, it isn't easy being a Muslim woman who wears a headscarf in America. Many people, knowing nothing about me, assume that I'm a terrorist. The limit of their knowledge about Islam is the distorted picture that some media outlets continue to broadcast every day. My one request is for people not to hate other individuals because they differ in appearance, complexion, race, or creed. We all share a common humanity. That's what is important.

This is just a suggestion, but the next time you meet a woman wearing a headscarf, you might say "Salam," or "Good day." She may be an Iraqi poet who would like to tell you how great her children are doing in their school.

AUTHOR'S NOTE

I have used the actual names of people and cities except for these: Nur, Hashim, and Umm Najah. I have not mentioned my former husband's name in my memoir, because he shares this name with one of my brothers and I wished to avoid any confusion between the two of them.

Faleeha Hassan
February 2, 2022
New Jersey

ABOUT THE AUTHOR

Faleeha Hassan is a poet, playwright, writer, teacher, and editor who earned her master's degree in Arabic literature and has published twenty-five books. A nominee for both the Pulitzer and Pushcart Prizes, she is the first woman to write poetry for children in Iraq. Her poems have been translated into twenty-one languages, and she has received numerous awards throughout the Middle East. Hassan is a member of the Iraq Literary Women's Association, the Sinonu Association in Denmark, the Society of Poets Beyond Limits, and Poets of the World Community. Born in Iraq, she now resides in the United States.

ABOUT THE TRANSLATOR

William Maynard Hutchins has translated many works of Arabic literature into English, including (for Amazon Crossing) Mortada Gzar's memoir, *I'm in Seattle, Where Are You?*, which was long-listed for the PEN Translation Prize for 2022. Hutchins holds degrees from Yale University and the University of Chicago and has taught in numerous institutions, starting in Sidon, Lebanon. He is now a professor emeritus at Appalachian State University in North Carolina.